Eros as the Educational
Principle of Democracy

Studies in the
Postmodern Theory of Education

Joe L. Kincheloe and Shirley R. Steinberg
General Editors

Vol. 114

PETER LANG
New York • Washington, D.C./Baltimore • Boston • Bern
Frankfurt am Main • Berlin • Brussels • Vienna • Oxford

Kerry T. Burch

Eros as the Educational
Principle of Democracy

PETER LANG
New York • Washington, D.C./Baltimore • Boston • Bern
Frankfurt am Main • Berlin • Brussels • Vienna • Oxford

Library of Congress Cataloging-in-Publication Data

Burch, Kerry T.
Eros as the educational principle of democracy / Kerry T. Burch.
p. cm. – (Counterpoints; vol. 114)
Includes bibliographical references (p.) and index.
1. Critical pedagogy. 2. Democracy–Study and teaching. 3. Love. 4. Feminism
and education. I. Title. II. Series: Counterpoints (New York, N.Y.); vol. 114.
LC196.B75   370.11'5–dc21   99-20592
ISBN 0-8204-4481-2
ISSN 1058-1634

Die Deutsche Bibliothek-CIP-Einheitsaufnahme

Burch, Kerry T.:
Eros as the educational principle of democracy / Kerry T. Burch.
–New York; Washington, D.C./Baltimore; Boston; Bern;
Frankfurt am Main; Berlin; Brussels; Vienna; Oxford: Lang.
(Counterpoints; Vol. 114)
ISBN 0-8204-4481-2

Cover design by Lisa Dillon

Cover art *Untitled*, 1922, by Vasily Kandinsky. Watercolor, wash,
india ink and pencil on paper. Solomon R. Guggenheim Museum,
New York. The Hilla von Rebay Foundation. Photograph by David Heald
© The Solomon R. Guggenheim Foundation, New York. (FN 1970.48)

© 2000 Peter Lang Publishing, Inc., New York

Printed in the United States of America

For the daring young

who resist and create

Eros once again limb-loosener whirls me sweetbitter, impossible to fight off, creature stealing up.

—Sappho

Eros is a verb.

—Anne Carson

Plato's Eros inspires us through our sense of beauty, but Eros is a trickster and must be treated critically.

—Iris Murdoch

Civilization is a process in the service of Eros, whose purpose is to combine single individuals, and after that families, then races, peoples and nations, into one great unity, the unity of mankind. Why this has to happen we do not know; the works of Eros are precisely this. But man's natural aggressive instinct, the hostility of each against all and all against each, opposes this programme of civilization. And it is in this battle of the giants that our nurse-maids try to appease with their lullaby about Heaven.

—Sigmund Freud

Spiritual procreation is just as much the work of Eros as is corporeal procreation, and the right and true order of the Polis is just as much an erotic one as is the right and true order of love.

—Herbert Marcuse

The dichotomy between the spiritual and the political is false, resulting from an incomplete attention to our erotic knowledge. For the bridge which connects them—the sensual—those physical, emotional, and psychic expressions of what is deepest and strongest and richest within each of us, being shared: the passions of love, in its deepest meanings.

—Audre Lorde

Wisdom is one of the most beautiful of things, and Eros is the love of beautiful, so it follows that Eros is necessarily one who engages in a search for wisdom, and as a seeker of wisdom is in between being wise and being ignorant.

—Diotima

We become what we love. Our destiny is in our desires, yet what we seek to possess soon comes to possess us in thought, feeling, and action. That is why the ancient Greeks made the education of eros, or passionate desire, the supreme aim of education.

—Jim Garrison

Table of Contents

Acknowledgments

I want to express my thanks to the many people who contributed to the completion of this book. Without their support, guidance, and in some cases, provocation, the project could not have begun, nor could it have developed in the direction that it did. Some of these influences occurred well before the formal inception of the book. Although it would be impossible to name all of my debts, intellectual and otherwise, I am especially grateful

—to Rhody McCoy, for introducing me to Paulo Freire's *Pedagogy of the Oppressed* while I was an undergraduate at the University of San Francisco, a chance event that launched my teaching career;

—to Vernon Ruland, S.J., of the University of San Francisco, for introducing me to the works of Jung and Freud, and for offering strong criticism of my interpretation of Augustine;

—to Maxine Greene, for transforming my preconception about what it means to teach during my enrollment at Columbia University Teachers College;

—to Professors Abdul Aziz Said, Adrienne Kaufmann, and Dudley Weeks for leading a superb graduate institute in global citizenship at The American University in the summer of 1990, an experience that led me to reconsider peace studies as a curriculum to change not only external structures, but *internal structures* as well, a redirection of focus which finds expression in this book;

—to Kathy Ferguson of the Department of Political Science at the University of Hawai'i-Manoa, for chairing my dissertation committee and helping to make it a great experience, and for stimulating me to think anew about issues of gender and power, and intellectual work as a political act and commitment;

—to Manfred Henningsen of the Department of Political Science at the University of Hawai'i-Manoa, for his sublime talent in exposing my ignorance, and for persuading me that ancient political thought can aid in the progressive reconstruction of American democracy;

—to Cheryl Hall of the Department of Government at the University of South Florida-Tampa, whose dissertation provoked me to think about eros in ways that I had never considered before;

—to my friends in Honolulu, Kailua, Kualapu'u, and to everybody at the Friends of Buddhism, *aloha!*

—to my father, Thomas L. Burch, whose generosity fueled my education and whose friendship I dearly miss, especially our lively political discussions;

—to my mother, Marjorie A. Burch, whose support, unselfishness, and friendship over the years remain a constant source of inspiration;

—to my sister, Shelley Bagri, for her radical enthusiasm and support of my academic career;

—to Richard Brosio, for his encouragement of my academic work;

—to my editors at Peter Lang, Shirley Steinberg and Joe Kinchloe, for believing in the project;

—to Jan Vander Meer of Northern Illinois University for her considerable proofreading and formatting skills;

—to an anonymous reviewer at *Studies in Philosophy and Education* for offering constructive criticism of an earlier draft of chapter 5;

—finally, to *Studies in Philosophy and Education* for granting me permission to reprint "Eros as the Educational Principle of Democracy."

Introduction

Teachers as Lovers or Managers?

Somehow, if we are to remake the democratic culture and if we are to awaken an ethical consciousness, we have to discover how to arouse passion again, the passion that accompanies the belief that things can be otherwise, that everything has not been done.

—Maxine Greene (1990)

The purpose of this book is to provoke the next generation of teachers to think about their vocation in radical new terms. What it means to be a teacher today is all too often defined within the logic of an educational paradigm that is increasingly bereft of civic vitality. Judged on the basis of democratic criterion, the reigning paradigm bears all the earmarks of obsolescence despite its evident institutional strength. For example, this dominant framework has no theory or category to capture the meaning and value of eros, or, for that matter, no concept or appreciation of what might be called *soul*. These categorical omissions remind us that the sanctification of test scores and other instrumental forms of knowledge are now functioning to deteriorate genuinely person-centered forms of knowledge from playing any role in the education of teachers. I maintain the crucial problem with this hegemonic form of common sense is its devaluation of eros, defined broadly as passion and connection. This emotional devaluation undermines democratic culture, but it does so in ways that are not immediately visible. One of the prime tasks of this book is to describe how this prejudice against eros, which is tantamount to an epistemological prejudice against the *feminine*, impedes democratic forms of culture.[1] As an educational principle, eros can provide the vocabulary and symbolic value system that critical pedagogy needs to rejuvenate both the vocational identity of teachers and the hope of democratic renewal in America. Since eros, as a discourse, perfectly reflects the vernacular language of liberation, teachers interested in the transformational potential of education ought to be familiar with this outlawed form of knowledge.

Eros is one of the ancient Greek words for love, that creative power which propels the knowledge quest and gives full resonance to the search for meaning. As Rollo May writes, "eros is a state of being," an ardent desire which provides the condition of possibility for an individual to be "magnetized" toward the vision of an imagined good, however interminable or incomplete that process turns out to be.[2] Few would deny that the *experience* of eros enables education to occur: in a sense, eros is the *radical* of the educational moment, the square root of its power. If we can acknowledge that the experience of eros defines the transformative quality of education, why not take the next step and elevate eros to its proper status as an organizing principle of education? Wouldn't the privileging of eros as an organizing principle encourage students and teachers alike to better grasp non-economistic meaning narratives? For this step to be taken, however, one would have to first identify, understand, and ultimately jettison certain common sense assumptions of the liberal/modernist paradigm.[3] This book is intended to provide insight into why, exactly, the concept of eros is devalued within the dominant liberal epistemology and why it should be revalued in light of intensifying social contradictions within the American classroom. In making this case, I want to contribute to the emerging scholarship on eros and help lay the groundwork for advancing eros not only as an important educational principle but as *the* educational principle of democracy.

Adopting a genealogical analysis, I explore representations of eros during four pivotal moments in Western history, from ancient to contemporary times. In each of these moments, the qualities ascribed to eros have direct and profound implications for critical pedagogy and the democratic project. The life-enhancing energies of eros have long been recognized as vital to the process of self-knowledge and to the development of community. I submit that the categorical denial and discursive forgetting of eros leads to its experiential erosion in individual lives, a phenomenon which effectively defines a root cause underlying the multidimensional crisis we face today. This crisis may accurately be referred to as paradigmatic in nature since it embraces so many dimensions of society. Consider, for example, rising levels of student apathy and privatism, the atrophy of democracy and citizenship, the ecological devastation, the cannibalizing tendencies within the American negotiation of identity, and increasingly technocratic forms of teacher education. Each of these predicaments, while separate, are still connected in that they reflect what Hannah Arendt described as the real crisis in education: a diminishing sense of a viable public, the loss of a "common world."[4] Taken together, these patterns suggest the broad outlines of the current political and educational crisis.

I maintain that these multiple crises can neither be understood nor transformed in isolation from one another, but ought to be understood in connection, paradigmatically, at the level of deep-structure. In other words, we need to perceive the common denominators which exist among seemingly disparate social phenomena, and then ask ourselves from the standpoint of this wider perspective what the essential features of our collective predicament are. If, as Paulo Freire says, we dare see differently, we may realize how indispensable the concept of eros is for the project of transcending the various crises that confront us. What the five crises discussed below have in common is that they are all defined by an *absence of eros*.

Example: Student Apathy. The etymology of *apathy* tells us that the word means "without passion." Studies published over the last decade demonstrate that the passion for public affairs on college campuses has steadily declined. Such an apolitical environment has given rise to the production of what could accurately be called a civicless self.[5] This research generally uses the 1960s as an Archimedian point for measuring variations in campus attitudes. Mark Edmundson discusses how the growing privatization of identity he finds in his University of Virginia students reflects characteristics that run counter to the public qualities of mind democratic culture needs in order to be democratic.[6] Increasingly, the education of youth identity is being administered by powerful commercial forces whose interests lie in the further corporatization of identity. Today, sophisticated pedagogies of advertising entice youth desire in ways that eclipse the relatively meager effect that schools exercise on the construction of identity.[7] The erosion of a public self is functionally related to conditions of boredom and apathy on university campuses. Far from representing an ideologically "neutral" development, these trends are a telling political index of what happens when the logic of the market spills over into the previously uncommodified spaces of civil society.

Example: The Eclipse of the Citizen. Citizenship education will never be genuinely democratic so long as public education remains anchored in the inherently unequal soil of local property tax. The class basis of "public" education in present day America means that the eros of affluent citizens continues to be cultivated, while the eros of citizens residing in poor school districts is subjected to a systematic regime of discipline and neglect by omission. One class of citizens is thus educated *to govern*, while another class of citizens—generally people of color—are schooled *to be governed*.[8] The perpetuation of such a system with so little public indignation exposes the conceit of American self-conception as a democratic society. Furthermore, since many educators operate unselfconsciously within a liberal paradigm, the overwhelming majority of teachers emphasize the state-centric and procedural aspects of democracy as if these dimensions define the heart of democracy. By defining democracy preeminently by its institutionality, students are miseducated to reduce democracy to an episodic voting performance.

This hegemonic form of common sense amounts to a kind of blissful ignorance which prevents a deeper understanding of democracy from being enacted. Indeed, it provides students with the comfortable illusion that "we live in a democracy," an assumption which tends to preempt the questioning of where present day social power actively resides and who is "in" on the decision-making process regarding the allocation of local and national wealth, arguably the very inquiries which should define citizenship education in any historical context. As C. Douglas Lummis, Sheldon Wolin, John Dewey, and others have written, the nucleus of the democratic moment has nothing to do with the state, but is rather an individual and collective *state of being.*[9] As a moral ideal, democracy refers mainly to a set of cultural dispositions. Renewed emphasis on the "associational" qualities which sustain democracy, such as questioning and trust and passion for public affairs (to mention a few of democracy's learned virtues), further suggests the importance of eros as the educational principle of democracy.

The striking conceptual affinities between eros and democracy, as two intimately connected *states of being,* represent a correspondence which has been virtually erased from mainstream discourses of citizenship education. Few conceptual affinities, however, could be more important for educators to grasp. Horkheimer and Adorno describe the eros/democracy connection with great eloquence: "If fear and destructiveness are the major emotional sources of fascism, eros belongs mainly to democracy."[10]

Example: Ecological Alienation. The awesome power of the Enlightenment project to extend human mastery and domination of nature has exacted a heavy price. We pride ourselves on our ability to control and exploit the earth's resources, a capacity which has provided levels of material affluence that would have been unthinkable in past centuries. Yet, on the other hand, if everyone on the planet consumed at the same level as the average American, the earth and its inhabitants would surely be thrown into apocalyptic conditions from a combination of resource wars and environmental catastrophes, situations that would intensify the severity of global crisis. Juliet Schor refers to the "new consumerism" as the latest symptom of America's cultural malaise, persuasively arguing that "the ecological devastation created by the national lifestyle has become unacceptable."[11] The perpetual upscaling of consumer desire logically implies the existence of ecological disconnection. The works of Gregory Bateson, Fritjof Capra, Carolyn Merchant, Susan Griffin, and Juliet Schor, to name a few, cogently identify the human consequences wrought by this loss of connection.[12]

In their formulations the ecological crisis cannot be solved by technological advances, but only at a more profound level by transforming the dominant paradigm of identity in relation to earth and cosmos. Because eros is a principle which *means* connection and which has historically been represented as an energy which "binds things together," it can serve as a useful heuristic device to help lessen the distance between humans and their environment.

Example: National Identity and Multiculturalism. "American" national identity has always been defined by crisis because no objective and fixed identity has ever existed. Of course, there have been continual attempts by those who wield institutional power to represent national identity in such a way that it appeared to be objective and fixed. But representations of national identity and ideas about what it means to be an American are symbolic and imagined constructions largely dependent on the ever-shifting ground of power relations. This is not a bad thing, for at least it implies "America" is a site of intense and unremitting contestation. Arguably this is a good thing, even sublime, for it demonstrates that national identity is a constant negotiation subject to continuous reconceptualization, hopefully along democratic lines.

As many scholars have demonstrated, the dominant construction of American national identity was and continues to be predicated on hierarchy, on a vertical model of defining the self/other relation.[13] The ethos of multiculturalism is controversial and deemed dangerous in some quarters because its main structural feature is predicated on a horizontal model for defining the self/other relation. The significance of this shift in perceiving identity cannot be overestimated. Historically, the vertical model of identity embodied an ethical hierarchy so that those with power were positioned to declare themselves more American than those identities without power, who were subsequently represented as "outside" or "below" the privileged norm. The horizontal model for conceptualizing identity/difference demolishes the perception of an inside/outside, superior/inferior, and hence reconfigures the structural imperative that would render difference in hierarchical terms. The "culture wars" reflect the tensions generated from these two paradigms of conceptualizing and knowing difference. Eros is an educational principle consistent with the tenets of critical multiculturalism not only because it has historically been coded as that which defies hierarchical distinctions, but also because the qualities of eros, such as passion and connection, are uniquely endowed to disrupt the historic nexus between war and national identity. This is the case because if eros is privileged as an epistemological principle, its associational qualities would make it difficult to dehumanize the other and use the radical rejection of otherness as a fulcrum for the construction of one's own "superior" identity.[14]

Example: Technocratic Teacher Education. Many aspiring teachers enrolled in schools of education today are in the process of having their *artistic vocation* reduced to little more than a hyper-disciplinary, technocratic function. When the mantras of *performance-based outcomes*, *accountability*, and *standardized testing* are allowed to dominate teacher education, we no longer educate teachers as lovers of learning so much as train obedient and passive managers of information. The distinction is crucial. These opposing curricular purposes represent competing visions of what schooling and democracy ought to mean. In a scathing indictment of this trend, William Ayers refers to the "standards movement" as nothing less than a "fraud," a "deceptive crusade in the service of the status quo."[15] Lest education deteriorate into mere schooling, teacher preparation must honor rather than marginalize the critical tradition. This tradition rejects the positivist assumption that only knowledge which is quantifiable is valuable, and thus seeks to widen the conversation about what it means to educate democratic citizens.[16] The main assumption being enforced in teacher education today seems to be that if you can't measure or quantify something, such as wisdom, soul, or the development of critical thinking and a sense of irony, it is by definition irrelevant to teacher education. When we encounter young teachers whose received knowledge informs them that the concepts noted above are "irrelevant," serious doubts are raised about how a teacher with such a prejudice can be expected to actually practice the civic responsibilities that are entailed in teaching, to say nothing about the prospects of encouraging others to do so.

Because the dominant values of teacher education render invisible qualities like soul, passion, imagination, wonder, and the "unrationalizable" essence of teaching, such narratives are incapable of deepening and extending the democratic project. Eros is the antidote to the dominant regime of knowing, since it coheres a broad set of epistemological qualities that challenge the central assumptions of the liberal/modernist paradigm.

This broad-brush overview suggests that eros and the qualities it represents are conspicuously absent from each of the crisis situations discussed above. How should this absence be read? Arguably, the suppression and subsequent absence of eros qualities constitute an underlying feature of our historical epoch. We need to value eros not only in an experiential sense, but at the level of an organizing principle, on par with the categories of Reason, Justice, and Equality. While such an understanding would represent the revaluation of a love concept, this revaluation would not carry any institutional religious freight despite the obvious spiritual capacities of eros. Citizen educators should acknowledge that for democracy to be revived, a secularized theory of love is required to lend coherence and direction to the highest aspirations of democratic culture. By familiarizing ourselves with the educational meanings of the eros concept, teachers can look upon their artistic vocation with renewed purpose as they obtain critical distance from their former roles as obedient managers of neutral information.

Fortunately, scholars from a variety of disciplines are beginning to draw attention to the significant educational qualities of eros. Recently, we have seen many superb efforts to recover the value of eros: James W. Garrison's *Dewey and Eros: Wisdom and Desire in the Art of Teaching* (1997), Robin May Schott's *Cognition and Eros* (1989), Susan Griffin's *The Eros of Everyday Life* (1996), Haunani-Kay Trask's *Eros and Power: The Promise of Feminist Theory* (1986), bell hooks's *Teaching to Transgress* (1994), and Ursula Kelly's *Schooling Desire* (1997) are a few works which attempt to rethematize the eros concept along more positive lines.

My genealogical approach, however, differs from these works in that I explore representations of eros found in key texts throughout Western intellectual history, providing a much needed historical orientation to the eros concept. I am attentive not only to dimensions of eros important to critical pedagogy and democracy but also to the unique capacity of eros, as an educational principle, to cohere alternative ways of understanding what it means to be and to create a self in an indivisibly social world. Because genealogy emphasizes the historicity of all identity formations, it defamiliarizes the varied practices and forms of common sense that we tend to take for granted as *natural* in the process of constituting our own identities. From this perspective, the absence of an eros discourse within the contemporary paradigm of education begins to look very strange indeed. Genealogy thus reveals that the lack of an eros discourse and the subsequent absence of erotic desire is also a social construct.[17]

Severe difficulties are entailed in this project. For instance, in defining eros as an educational principle there is a danger that it could become a convenient signifier for everything good, true, and beautiful: from feeling, connection, questioning, and wonder, to democracy and the examined life. While this positive coding of eros is not without merit, it is also true that we do not always desire or love the right things or have clarity about knowing good desires from destructive ones, a fact which underscores the importance of the pedagogical motif of *educating the desires*. Since eros signifies a specific form of desire, I argue that the education of eros should become a defining feature of critical pedagogy.

In this regard, the book is more an invitation to engage the predicaments of transformative education than it is an attempt to resolve the complexities that arise from such ambitious purposes. Further, since I construct eros as an overarching principle, some level of generalization is necessary. On the other hand, if eros is defined too broadly its boundaries may become uncomfortably diffuse, transforming the concept into a kind of theoretical sponge capable of absorbing all things wholesome.

Rather, I focus on the (inter)textuality of eros, which means that when eros is invoked in the pages ahead, I try to identify its versatility as a symbol, discourse, experience, relation, critical unit of analysis, and as an educational principle. This approach must also consider the politics of eros, the idea that, however eros is or is not represented, it occupies a contested symbolic terrain which has been designated outlaw territory by those whose representational power permits them to establish and institutionalize such boundaries. The book is thus part of a political struggle to liberate the principle of eros from the patriarchal narratives that have historically distorted and devalued its meaning.

Another problem in discussing eros is the popular yet false idea that it is synonymous with sexuality. If this assumption goes unchallenged, a convenient basis is laid upon which to dismiss the legitimate educational claims of eros. Although eros can be seen to include sexual desire, to define it exclusively in this way, to use an analogy, is like saying there is only one shade of the color blue. Out of the infinite variety of shades of blue, no one can isolate one particular shade and argue that, objectively, this is what blue is. My definition of eros is similarly nonreductionistic. Yet, at another level of analysis, the color analogy is inadequate because it tends to overlook the power relations that determine how the concept is defined. For example, the excessive sexualization of eros is coterminus with its despiritualization, a correspondence which is profoundly instructive when viewed from the standpoint of gendered power relations. This reductionist maneuver effectively precludes eros from having any educational and spiritual meanings whatsoever. In this book, I try to bring these forgotten meanings of eros into conceptual relief.

Given the frequent feminine associations of eros, its revaluation would also be tantamount to the revaluation of the feminine, a paradigmatic transition of meaning which would have far-reaching consequences for democratic culture. Teachers as cultural workers should find eros, as a principle and unit of analysis, conducive to their projects of working toward gender balance in the schools. In the following pages, I hope to show that when only disembodied forms of knowledge are privileged within institutional settings, it instantiates a character formation at odds with the education of dispositions essential to democratic culture. In underlining the importance of eros to psychic well-being, bell hooks writes, "understanding that eros is a force that enhances our overall effort to be self-actualizing, that it can provide an epistemological grounding informing how we know what we know, enables both professors and students to use such energy in a classroom setting in ways that invigorate discussion and excite the critical imagination."[18]

The book is organized in five chapters. The first chapter establishes the distinction between pre-philosophic and philosophic eros, a distinction which reflects a crucial benchmark in the history of eros as an idea. To express Plato's view of a now-educationalized eros, I examine the *Symposium*, selected parts of *Phaedrus,* and the *Republic* (the Parable of the Cave). I highlight the metaphoric inventory of Platonic pedagogy and demonstrate that Plato's aim was to eroticize conventional understandings of reason. In giving the Parable of the Cave a contemporary update, I show how this perennial text can be read critically to illuminate the ways in which the power of eros is prevented from occupying space within the *American* cave.

The second chapter moves from an ancient representation of eros to a Christian one, exemplified by Augustine's interpretation of the Garden of Eden story. I explore the proposition that the fourth century represents a sharp discontinuity in the discursive career of eros because at this time Augustine codified original sin, a move which henceforth created a profound anti-erotic bias within Western culture. In addition, I identify the ways in which this anti-erotic prejudice has become ensconced in our educational and political culture. I contend that the educational ideology of Horace Mann was deeply marked by Augustine's Edenic narrative and that Mann's ghost remains very much with us today.

Chapter 3 examines Jean-Jacques Rousseau's *Emile* as a modern representation of eros. This chapter focuses on the representational difficulties which occur when interpreting "eros" in different languages and different historical contexts. For example, educational theorist Joel Spring emphasizes Rousseau's use of eros. Yet Rousseau never used the term; he referred rather to *amour de soi* and *amour propre*. This chapter tries to disentangle Spring's conflation of these two concepts with eros. Finally, I critique Rousseau's gendered love discourse, which is absolutely central to Emile's education but is completely invisible in Sophie's education.

Chapter 4 focuses on contemporary accounts of eros, particularly those found within the corpus of feminist theory. Many of the fascinating conceptual questions in interpreting eros stem from its gendered associations. Is eros peculiarly feminine as some writers believe? To what extent are the qualities of receptivity, connectedness, empathy, and so on, linked to eros? This chapter attempts to come to grips with these patterns of signification. In addition, I deploy eros as a critical unit of analysis to illuminate both the Nazi devaluation of the feminine as well as the recent violent episode at Columbine High School in Littleton, Colorado. I go on to argue that feminist and Socratic pedagogy share some rather striking structural features that are seldom treated in the literature. I want to suggest to authors in critical and feminist pedagogy that Socrates is best understood as a moral ironist and demophile, and not as a political conservative, as many would have it.

In the concluding chapter, I propose a conceptual framework for thinking about the pedagogical relationship between eros and democracy. Based on insights derived from preceding chapters, I draw out the conceptual affinities between eros and democracy and explore the implications these affinities have for the development of a new philosophy of democratic pedagogy.

The motivation for writing this book stems in large part from my experience teaching about the institution of war and its role in shaping images of external and internal "evil others" within the American negotiation of identity. As a high school history teacher, I sought to apply Freire's *conscientization* to representations of war expressed in American history textbooks. With more exposure to the textbook system, it became increasingly evident to me the ways in which national security narratives sequestered in textbooks function to write cultural identity on school bodies: certainly they provide the deep-script for masculinity, defining what it means to be a hero; that is, a compliant citizen-warrior. The more we observe how the war discourse in these texts is deeply gendered, the more we see how the emotions of *love* and *anger*, to name two significant examples, are emotional conditions socially orchestrated within the public space of the classroom. I believe that love's allegiance to the nation state, on the one hand, and the anger or fear channeled toward officially designated evil others on the other, represent learned "emotional rules of conduct"[19] that must be disrupted if critically reflective democratic citizens are to be educated. Yet we should not forget that anger or indignation at the perception of social injustice can also spring from the emotion of love. Many of the speeches of Martin Luther King, Jr., for example, reflect emotions that are more closely alloyed to eros than to agape or philia. In any case, the relational dynamic between love and "educated" anger is a rich conceptual terrain that invites further analysis.

Another key predicament in reconstructing American civic identity is the recognition that wars have historically provided an awesome means for feeling intense, transcendent purpose. There is a sense in which the memory of wars functions as the symbolic oxygen of the nation-state: in United States history, wars have been instrumental in rendering an intrinsically fragile national identity secure. But how to construct a public bond outside the dominant war discourse? How to construct alternative, gender-balanced mythologies of cultural heroism? My interest in an ancient Greek concept of love is grounded in the premise that a fatal intimacy has evolved between violence and American national identity: eros represents an educational principle well-suited to the pedagogical task of disrupting this nexus and transforming American self-conception.

As someone inspired by America's civic "religion of possibility,"[20] I believe that new formations of hero-citizens can be educated if the construction of civic identity were to revolve around an alternative but critically informed conceptual axis. In this regard, eros matters. But why eros? Why not concentrate on two other Greek valences of love, such as *philia* or *agape*? As I try to show in the following pages, as valuable as *philia* and *agape* may be in some respects, eros is the most educational concept of love in the Western tradition.

Notes

1. A useful starting point for identifying the feminine and masculine dimensions of eros is by acknowledging that (a) eros cannot be reduced to either side of the binary, and (b) feminine does not mean female and masculine does not mean male, since these characteristics are human potentialities that are not inherently rooted in sex difference. Fritjof Capra argues that the Chinese motif of yin/yang reflects a clear feminine/masculine interplay. Within this theoretical scaffolding, the yin or feminine qualities include *contractive, conservative, responsive, cooperative, intuitive, synthesizing*. The yang or masculine qualities include *expansive, demanding, aggressive, competitive, rational, analytic*. I maintain that the associational characteristics of strong democracy require "feminine" qualities like responsiveness, cooperation, intuition, and synthesizing (as the ability to think holistically and make connections). See Fritjof Capra, *The Turning Point: Science, Society, and the Rising Culture* (New York: Simon and Schuster, 1982), 38.

2. Rollo May, *Love and Will* (New York: Norton, 1969), 72–89.

3. The principle deep-structure assumptions of the liberal/modernist paradigm grow largely out of the writings of Immanuel Kant and Rene Descartes. For analysis, see Robin May Schott, *Cognition and Eros: A Critique of the Kantian Paradigm* (Boston: Beacon Press, 1989) and Susan Bordo, "The Cartesian Masculinization of Thought," *Signs* 11 (Spring 1986): 439–56. Interestingly, one of the central claims in what is widely regarded as the finest biography of John Dewey, is that Dewey's concept of democracy is *at odds* with the main tenets of liberalism. See Robert Westbrook, *John Dewey and American Democracy* (Ithaca: Cornell University Press, 1992).

4. Hannah Arendt, "The Crisis in Education" in *Between Past and Future* (New York: Viking Press, 1968), 173–96. For the purposes of this inquiry, it is significant that Arendt argues the crisis in education will only be resolved when we decide to "love the world" sufficiently enough so as to prepare students for the task of "renewing a common world" (196).

5. See Christopher Shea, "Disengaged Freshman," *Chronicle of Higher Education*, January 13, 1995, A29; Paul Rogat Loeb, "You Make Your Own Chances," *Generation at the Crossroads: Apathy and Action on the American Campus* (New Brunswick: Rutgers University Press, 1994), 11–26.

6. Mark Edmundson, "On the Uses of a Liberal Education, 1: As Lite Entertainment for Bored College Students," *Harpers Magazine* (September 1997): 39–49.

7. Henry Giroux, *Disturbing Pleasures: Learning Popular Culture* (New York: Routledge, 1994); *The Mouse That Roared: Disney and the End of Innocence* (Lanham, Md.: Rowman and Littlefield, 1999).

8. San Antonio Independent School District v. Rodriguez, U.S. 71–133Z (1973). In this pivotal case, the U.S. Supreme Court held in a 5–4 decision that funding public schools on the basis of property tax was not unconstitutional. Just as the *Plessey* decision (1896) denied civic equality on the basis of race, this decision denies civic equality on the basis of class; that is, on the capricious standard of property tax. Revealingly, the majority opinion conceded that the Texas system of funding public education was "chaotic and unjust" (59), yet their adherence to the principle of judicial restraint prohibited them from favoring a constitutional remedy. In the dissenting opinion, Justice Marshall and others argue that the perpetuation of unequal public educational structures deny certain citizens an equal opportunity, as citizens, to develop and exercise their First Amendment rights, which, to a significant degree, depends on the ability to effectively read, write, and think critically. At stake in this decision are two entirely different conceptions of *American civic identity* and two entirely different *interpretations of law*. Clearly, these two realms are dialectically related. The difference between the majority opinion (rooted in an abstract, procedural principle) and the dissenting opinion (rooted in a substantive, relational principle) corresponds to the competing theories of moral development associated with Lawrence Kohlberg and Carol Gilligan. In America's quest to enact a more democratic version of itself, the Marshall/Gilligan understanding of law and morality provides the best framework for revisioning civic identity.

9. See C. Douglas Lummis, *Radical Democracy* (Ithaca: Cornell University Press, 1996), 159–63; Sheldon Wolin, "Norm and Form: The Constitutionalizing of Democracy," in *Athenian Political Thought and the Reconstruction of American Democracy* (Ithaca: Cornell University Press, 1994), 29–58; and John Dewey, *The Public and Its Problems* (New York: Free Press, 1931), 255.

10. Theodor Adorno and Max Horkheimer. *The Authoritarian Personality* (New York: Norton, 1950), 976.

11. Juliet Schor, *The Overspent American* (New York: HarperCollins, 1998), xiii.

12. Gregory Bateson, *Steps to an Ecology of Mind* (New York: Ballantine, 1972); Fritjof Capra (see note #1); Carolyn Merchant, *Radical Ecology: The Search for a Livable World* (New York: Routledge, 1992); and Susan Griffin, *The Eros of Everyday Life: Essays on Ecology, Gender and Society* (New York: Doubleday, 1995).

13. See Michael Shapiro, *Cartographies of War* (Minneapolis: University of Minnesota Press, 1997); David Campbell, *Writing Security: United States Foreign Policy and the Politics of Identity* (Minneapolis: University of Minnesota Press, 1993); and Lawrence W. Levine, *The Opening of the American Mind* (Boston: Beacon Press, 1996).

14. The capacity of eros to "lessen the threat of difference" is described in Audre Lorde's essay, "Uses of the Erotic: The Erotic as Power," in *Sister/Outsider* (Freedom, CA: The Crossing Press Feminist Series, 1984), 53–59.

15. William Ayers, "The Standards Fraud," *Boston Review* vol. 24, no. 6 (December 1999): 16. Ayers' is one of several articles appearing in this journal under the title, "Educating a Democracy: Standards and the Future of Public Education," edited by Deborah Meier.

16. Of course, thousands of educators actively oppose these dominant trends, and their valuable work shows it, but two works which encapsulate my specific argument here can be found in *The Educational Conversation: Closing the Gap*, ed. James W. Garrison and Anthony J. Rud (Albany: SUNY Press, 1995); and Bruce Wilshire, *The Moral Collapse of the University: Professionalism, Purity, and Alienation* (Albany: SUNY Press, 1990).

17. Michel Foucault, "Nietzsche, Genealogy, History" in *The Foucault Reader*, ed. Paul Rabinow (New York: Pantheon Books, 1984), 76–100. A uniquely American model of genealogical analysis can be found in Cornel West's *The American Evasion of Philosophy: A Genealogy of Pragmatism* (Madison: University of Wisconsin Press, 1989).

18. bell hooks, "Eros, Eroticism, and the Pedagogical Process," in *Teaching to Transgress: Education as the Practice of Freedom* (New York: Routledge, 1994), 191–99.

19. Megan Boler, *Feeling Power: Emotions and Education* (New York: Routledge, 1998), xx, 32.

20. Roberto Mangabeira Unger and Cornel West, "The American Religion of Possibility," in *The Future of American Progressivism* (Boston: Beacon Press, 1998), 6–13.

1

Platonic Eros and the Emergence of Pedagogy

These are the activities of eros, Socrates, into which you could probably be initiated. I don't know whether you are the sort of person for the final rites and mysteries, for which these former things are the preparation, *if one can let go in the right way.*

—Diotima

The safest general characterization of the European philosophical tradition is that it consists of a series of footnotes to Plato.

—Alfred North Whitehead

Contrasting Prephilosophical and Philosophical Eros

Centuries before Plato reinterpreted and effectively transformed the meaning of eros, the prephilosophical cosmogonies which existed in ancient Greece had already established its divine and mythopoetic status.[1] According to early Greek mythology, eros was the oldest of the gods, the creative power which injected life into previously vacant forms. The noted scholar of Greek mythology, Robert Graves, tells us that eros was believed to be "hatched from the world-egg," the "first of the gods," a force so elemental that it enabled further deities to come into being. At this prephilosophical stage of representation, one of the defining features of "eros" is its plural, ambiguous parentage:

Others hold that he was Aphrodite's son by Hermes, or by Ares, or by her father, Zeus, or the son of Iris by the West Wind. He was a wild boy, who showed no respect for age or station but flew about on golden wings, shooting barbed arrows at random or wantonly setting hearts on fire with his dreadful torches.[2]

Several instructive images of eros are expressed here. These and similar prephilosophic representations invariably show eros as a force happening to an individual *randomly* or *wantonly*, as an abrupt intervention from a source located entirely outside oneself. Such representations express a deified eros, a force wholly external to the individual and impervious to human intention and action. We shall see in the following pages how Plato rejects this interpretation of eros and instead proposes the radical notion that human beings can and should understand eros as amenable to human intention and action. Thus, while Plato brings eros "down to earth," so to speak, and humanizes the concept, he simultaneously inaugurates the idea of pedagogy. The two concepts are in fact inseparable, since pedagogy in its Platonic conception is the educational form required to channel the powers of eros toward the good. Without the art of pedagogy to help corral and direct the life-affirming energies of eros, the concept would remain essentially *pre*philosophic, containing no person-centered educational quality.

The gendered associations which attach to eros are striking regardless of historical context. For example, the personification of eros frequently assumes an androgynous form, as is shown in the fifth-century B.C. statue entitled *Eros* located today in the British Museum. This exquisite representation reflects eros as a figure located between two terms: embodied as mortal flesh, yet endowed with divine wings, possessing both male and female sexual characteristics. Joseph Campbell writes that this "in between" status characteristic of eros applies to age as well: significantly, eros tends to elude binary oppositions of all types, including old/young, male/female, mortal/immortal.[3]

If one were to consider three of the four gods named as original in Greek mythology, Gaia, Chaos, and Tartarus, we would observe a metaphoric representation describing places; Eros alone is represented as a *dynamic movement*. Hesiod, in *Theogony,* describes eros as a love which overwhelms all other forms of intelligence.[4] Kirk and Raven, writing in *The Pre Socratic Philosophers*, observe that Hesiod employed the metaphors of "rain" and "semen" alternately to denote how eros joined the separation between sky and earth, man and woman. In both instances a fecund imagery is used to convey the "holding together" of a pair of opposites, a defining feature of eros not only during its prephilosophic phase, but throughout its discursive history. In Aristophanes' *Birds*, eros becomes the movement binding the universe together, from which is born a race of immortal gods.[5]

Given the rich inventory of images and associations surrounding the eros concept, it should not be surprising that the revolution in education which Plato introduced would have eros at the center of a new paideia: an educational framework grounded in the assumption that human beings are defined by inquiry, by a search for a wider identity. Since this search is interminable, one is confronted by a perception, sometimes an intense feeling, of lacking in self-knowledge. If this absence is experienced as intolerable, eros, as the desire to know, is elicited, and this elicitation transforms how subjectivities view their own ignorance; that is, their own relation to unconsciousness. In this way, Plato gives eros a vital moral and epistemological dimension, a theoretical advance which constitutes a radical departure from prephilosophic understandings of the concept.

Plato rethematized eros in an educational sense for the purpose of transforming the individual and the political community. If ever there was a paradigm shift in the history of educational ideas, it occurred when Plato, inspired by Socrates, integrated the realms of philosophy, education, and politics into a person-centered blueprint for the art of conversion, or *periagoge*.[6] Plato's rethematization of eros is the basis of his educational theory, for without the clarifying principle of eros his educational insights become disconnected and incoherent. He inherited a mythological or supernatural conception of eros and transformed it into a powerful educational principle. This transition marks a crucial benchmark in the history of eros as an idea.

Plato tries to demonstrate that, unlike prephilosophic eros, desire and passion can be complementary to reason, not destructive to it. Absent the influence of passion, Plato argues, reason cannot fulfilled. Of course, one of the good things about Plato is that his writings are more a series of open-ended dialogues beginning and ending in questions than they are systematic expositions of an absolute knowledge. On my reading of Plato, the reason/passion binary is intentionally disrupted by his novel understanding of eros, a concept he marks deeply with gender. The main aim of this chapter therefore is to illuminate the educational and gendered dimensions of eros and to explicate the conceptual relationship which exists between Platonic eros and the concept of pedagogy.

Two of Plato's dialogues, the *Symposium* and the *Phaedrus*, serve as the principal texts for examining eros in this phase of its genealogy. In the first section, an analysis of the *Symposium* provides an understanding of Platonic eros and the emergence of pedagogy. In section 2, selected parts of the *Phaedrus* will be examined to demonstrate how Plato sought to disrupt conventional ideas about the reason/passion dichotomy. To help clarify the conceptual linkages between eros and the political nature of pedagogy, section 3 provides a critical analysis of the Parable of the Cave. In relying on this parable as a valuable heuristic device for the purposes of advancing critical multiculturalism, I want to explore how the symbolic presence of eros is insinuated in what I call the "politics of the cave." This exploration suggests that while Plato constructed pedagogy so that "teaching" became coded as a spiritual ascent, a poetic art of conversion, and a political commitment to the cause of human freedom, it can also be read as a text pregnant with questions regarding the ethical predicaments which arise when educational and liberatory projects are implemented. What is liberation? Who decides?

Platonic Eros and the Emergence of Pedagogy

The *Symposium* consists of a series of seven speeches in praise of eros given at a fictional party in fourth-century B.C., Athens. As is well known, the work has generated endless volumes of commentary. My analysis is intended primarily to map the diverse metaphors these speakers ascribe to eros more than it is to enter into debates as to the relative merits of Plato's conceptual framework. While judgments about Plato's educational theories may be unavoidable, to an extent, readers should bear in mind that this inquiry is concerned foremost with examining the discursive codings which surround the eros concept. Only when a sound understanding of the ways in which eros has been represented in diverse historical texts is obtained, will it be plausible to make the argument that eros is the educational principle of democracy.

The speech which has received by far the most scholarly attention is the second to last, given by Socrates, a remarkable account of his tutelage under a Manitean priestess named Diotima. One may well ask why a woman's voice is deployed to capture the finest expression of love Plato ever provides! What is Plato attempting to say when he introduces this woman as the teacher of Socrates on the subject of eros? I foreground Diotima's discourse in order to explore the cluster of associations she attributes to eros and to further describe the functional relationship between eros and the transformation of consciousness.

The meaning of the concluding speech has always been a site of intense controversy as well, not so much as an intellectual construction of eros, but as an agonizing speech about Socrates' *erotic effect* on the speaker, Alcibiades, and to what extent, if any, he contradicts Socrates' conclusions regarding eros. Because these final two speeches display some of Plato's most poignant and enduring insights into the connection between love, education, and selfhood, they have tended to overshadow the value of the previous interpretations. While this emphasis is understandable, it should be borne in mind that all of the speeches in praise of eros should be viewed as comprising distinct yet related interpretive strands. In the *Symposium*'s seven speeches, Plato constructs a "terracing" of eros. Although all of the interpretive modes are valid, there is a sense in which each one is superseded by the next, as Plato charts the transition from prephilosophic to philosophic eros. A symbolic hierarchy or "ladder" of eros is posited within the structure of the *Symposium*, but the highly nuanced portrait of eros Plato provides can only be understood in the context of the interconnected whole. In other words, eros defies reduction to any one representation.

The first speech is given by Phaedrus, who immediately quotes Hesiod to support the conventional view that eros emerged from Chaos and is "first among the gods." By conflating eros with God, a standard prephilosophic assumption, Phaedrus is moved to the conclusion that eros is "the cause of our greatest blessing."[7] According to his view, eros is that mysterious power which summons us beyond ourselves, enabling cities and communities to come into existence.

Certainly an interesting if controversial aspect of this speech is the claim by Phaedrus that the pederastic homosexual relationship is the prime space within which the highest levels of love are attained (*Sym.*, 179a). This speech seems to foreclose the possibility that heterosexual relationships are as exalted as homosexual ones in terms of generating love. No one can deny, of course, that the pederastic homosexual relation was valorized in ancient Greece. Many of Plato's dialogues are punctuated with such references, although Plato and most of his contemporaries did not view pederasty unproblematically. As Nussbaum and Halperin make clear in their respective analyses, the ancient paradigm of consciousness did not contain any binary opposition which would revolve one's identity around a strict either/or, heterosexual/homosexual conceptual axis.[8] Thus, one of the pedagogical values of the speech is its capacity to reveal the arbitrary and non-universal qualities of the social construction of self, thus rendering visible one facet of the "invisible paradigm" of the liberal/modernist hegemony. Engagement with these paradigmatic conundrums exercise the mind and pry open new space for imagining meaning narratives outside the reigning orthodoxy. To hasten the return of eros from the strange academic and discursive exile which has been imposed upon it, we need to expand opportunities for students to exercise a kind of epistemic mobility that is not only interdisciplinary but critically situated, attentive to the historicity of all identity formations.

Pausanias, the second speaker, begins his encomium by sharply rebuking Phaedrus for making the assumption that all love is good. Pausanias argues that people frequently love and desire the wrong things and thus make choices which grow out of an apparent failure to act upon one's true or best desires. He draws a sharp distinction between vulgar or common love, on the one hand, and heavenly love on the other. Having established the existence of two polar kinds of love, Pausanias then further develops what Phaedrus had earlier introduced, namely a defense of the pederastic homosexual relationship. Pausanias gives a brief sketch of the laws and customs regarding pederasty in other Greek cities. We learn that in Ionia, for example, sexual relations among men and boys are forbidden by law. For Pausanias, such prohibitions are characteristic of an inferior culture (*Sym.*, 182b). In places like Elis and Boetia, he says, they have no prohibitions about these matters at all, yet, according to Pausanias, these cultures are not praiseworthy either. Thus we have a speech which articulates a discriminating kind of pederasty, one that is sensitive to the intrinsic asymmetrical power relation involved and to the negative effects the experience of submission might have on a young male's future capacity as a citizen.

Clearly this speech is intended to defend pederasty against its detractors. In my view this does not mean that Plato endorses a sexually based definition of eros, but that he wanted to describe what was then a standard, if contested, attitude toward this particular cultural practice. There is a sense in which Plato invokes these prior speeches to illuminate how his own insights into the eros concept are different, and how something significant would be lost if eros were reduced to sexuality, as was frequently the case in its prephilosophic stage of representation. As many have observed, the speech by Pausanias is abruptly interrupted by Aristophanes when he experiences a violent episode of hiccups. The introduction of this device by Plato could be read on several levels. At the very least, we are told that it functions to change the order of the speeches. While Aristophanes is recovering his composure, it is decided that Eryximachus will speak in his place. Since the hiccup does usher in a new arrangement of speakers, the new arrangement could possibly mark an epistemological divide between Plato's prephilosophic and philosophic boundaries of eros. This interpretation gains credence when we examine the contrasting descriptions of eros provided by Eryximachus and Aristophanes.

When Eryximachus states that eros is located "in everything there is," including "bodies of all animals and even plants that grow in the ground" (*Sym.*, 186b), he exemplifies a naturalistic interpretation of the concept, an essential feature of prephilosphic eros. He would agree, in other words, that an acorn is moved "erotically" to become an oak.

However, Plato's specific epistemic emphasis concerning eros reminds us that, unlike the acorn, human beings become human beings not automatically or naturalistically but through a myriad of social and political factors, including the ethical orientation one adopts to the *aporias* in one's identity. That is to say, how one relates to the vast sea of ignorance which attaches to the human condition, something which could also be described—inadequately and metaphorically—as the unconsciousness which shadows all consciousness. Socrates moves this slippery and unquantifiable, yet utterly compelling relation, onto the terrain of ethics and pedagogy. This space becomes the fecund psychic terrain, the internal wilderness, from which Plato attempts to educationalize the powers of eros. In this philosophical representation, there is an intimate nexus between eros, ignorance, pedagogy, and irony.

Continuing to speak, Eryximachus, the medical doctor, contends that medical science was founded on the principle of restoring harmony in a body beset by "hostile oppositions." For Eryximachus, eros becomes the "governing god of medicine," that which mediates and harmonizes the clash of opposites (*Sym.*, 187a). To further clarify this dimension of eros, he points out that music is a realm which is fundamentally enabled by the vast expanse of eros. "Rhythm, for example, results from bringing the fast and the slow, which are first in opposition, into agreement. As with medicine earlier, here it is that music is a knowledge of the activities of love with regard to harmony and rhythm" (*Sym.*, 187c).

According to Plato, the prephilosophic view of eros is not so much inaccurate as incomplete. By understanding eros only in its prephilosophical form, for example, the ethical and educational dimensions of eros go unrecognized. In such formulations, eros is located epistemologically "everywhere," attaining a cosmic, gravity-like quality, but whose creative powers still do not possess the quality of being susceptible to human intention and action. Plato's educational theory is an attempt to render the energy of eros visible and available to individuals, an elicitation which occurs as a consequence of the quality of one's conscious intent upon ignorance, perhaps the most vital ethical relation in Plato's educational theory. For this reason it was imperative for Plato to construct a qualitatively different representation of eros, one that would tap into the sublime powers elicited when one actually does philosophy. That is, to critically reflect and question what one does or does not know is itself a tacit acknowledgment of unknowing which can mobilize an intense desire to know, if one is troubled enough by the perceived lack! In this way, Plato's great educational accomplishment was to connect the ethical component of human agency to a now-humanized realm of eros. Perhaps we could say that Plato built a wobbly theoretical scaffolding around the pedagogical insights he gleaned from observing the richly ironic Socrates as eros personified.[9]

A macabre account of eros issues from the next speaker, Aristophanes. Yet, beneath its bizarre surface, it not only contains a trenchant analysis of the human predicament, but importantly, explicitly joins human intentionality to the realm of eros. Because of this emphasis, it may be plausible to assume that the incremental shift from prephilosophic to philosophic eros begins with the speech by Aristophanes. Using mythological imagery, Aristophanes tells us that originally human beings sought to rival the gods, and for having such unbridled levels of hubris they were cut in two, leaving them a mere fragment of their original selves. His description of these creatures seems to wed tragedy with comedy, perhaps the true parents of irony (*Sym.*, 189e). Forever denied the possibility of returning to experience the (mythic) unity of their prior condition, humans live in a permanent state of desire and longing for an unattainable sense of wholeness, a transcendent meaning. The functional relation between eros and the emptiness of "ontological incompletion" (to use Freire's terminology) is summarized by Aristophanes:

> It is from this situation, then, that love for another developed in human beings. Eros collects the halves of our original nature, and tries to make a single thing out of two parts so as to restore our original condition. Thus, each of us is the matching half of a human being, since we have been severed like a flatfish, two coming from one, and each part is always seeking its other half. (*Sym.*, 191d)

Eros is coded as a psychological wellspring whose movement flows toward an inchoate sense of completeness, a seeming magnetic pull which leads us toward some vision of good, however differently one's definition of the good may be. The movement toward the good in this particular myth is synonymous with the movement toward the other. In continuing his story, Aristophanes suggests our happiness hinges on whether or not we chance across another soul whose presence mysteriously evokes love. Adding to the confusion, the bodies we inhabit are seldom if ever identical with our imagining selves, thus magnifying the separation between the fact of death on the one hand and our symbolic power to imagine transcendence on the other. Classicist Werner Jaeger links the educational dimensions of eros to the predicament Aristophanes describes:

> Aristophanes is considering love as part of the process by which the self attains perfection. It can only do so through its relation to another, to a beloved, who will complement the powers in it which need completion, help them to take their place in the original whole, and thereby at last enable them to be properly effective. This symbolism draws eros right into the process of educating and building up the personality.[10]

Here eros is linked to education and psychological growth. For the purpose of clarifying an important quality of eros, however, there is a crucial distinction to be made between a desire for a sense of wholeness, on the one hand, and the interminability of the quest on the other. His final remark, "so the name eros is given to the *desire* for wholeness" (*Sym.*, 193a), should not be confused with the idea that self-knowledge can be reached and the learning terminated. Indeed, as we shall see in chapter 2, Augustine rejects eros in favor of *agape* precisely because the character of eros could offer him no enduring peace, no permanent sense of completion. Eros knows no completion, yet relies curiously on the *idea* and *feeling* of completion as one of its defining, ironic features.

This is the first speech in the *Symposium* which expresses the idea that the human being is constituted by a search whose trajectory is pushed by eros; or would it be more accurate to use another metaphor and say "pulled" by eros? Can one be both pushed and pulled by eros? Rollo May, as one astute interpreter, criticizes the reduction of eros to an "instinctual push" and instead emphasizes the capacity of eros to entice and lead us toward a vision of the good.[11] What do these opposite representations imply about the source(s) of erotic power? Should this curious force be regarded as something that emerges from a space "internal" or "external" to the individual, or should eros be regarded as "potentially emergent" from either side of the binary? In any case, it is difficult to avoid the conclusion that if one remains incarcerated within dichotomous patterns of thought, a full perception and understanding of eros is foreclosed. Many of these epistemological, ontological, and teleological questions about the boundary-crossing nature of eros will recur in one form or another in every chapter of the book.

In opposition to standard interpretations of the Aristophanic myth, Jonathan Lear argues that "eros functions as a resistance to ascent" by limiting us to the realm of human relations in seeking fulfillment: "this absorption in the purely human realm serves as a distraction from the transcendent."[12] Indeed, the interpretive tension which Lear alludes to is informed by a dichotomy between the human and transcendent, mundane and sublime. Lear maintains that Plato, through the speech of Aristophanes, deliberately locates eros in the human realm to contradict Socrates' apparent emphasis on the transcendent. This earth/heaven binary opposition is the subject of an incredibly rich scholarly dispute between Gregory Vlastos and Martha Nussbaum over the ultimate meaning and characterization of eros in the *Symposium*. Although this tension will be discussed in some depth in the following pages, it bears mentioning that what is chiefly at stake in this study is to explore how diverse and (deliberately) contradictory representations of eros might help us to develop a better grasp of the concept. For this reason, I think it is far more important to reflect upon the various tensions, ambiguities, and ironies Plato constructs within the structure of the *Symposium* than it is to pit one speech in praise of eros against another, as if the full meaning of eros could be determined in isolation, cut off from the larger context.

The next symposiast is the recent winner of the dramatic competition, the young Agathon. In contrast to Aristophanes, Agathon elaborates a highly optimistic picture of eros and its relation to human experience. He waxes poetic: eros is young, not old; soft and gentle, not coarse and difficult (*Sym.*, 195e). Agathon further declares that eros is the ultimate cause of all things good and beautiful, whose character is poetic-creative, representing the best in everything, including wisdom, things which simply cannot be comprehended without a knowledge of eros, the greatest of the gods (*Sym.*, 197c). In this short yet robust speech, Agathon clearly makes the argument that eros *is* god, *is* wisdom, *is* beautiful, *is* the good. The other speakers are swept away by his oratory. Each of these assumptions about the nature of eros, however, is soon dismantled by Socrates.

Socrates begins in his characteristic way by asking the assembled guests if he might pose a few questions to Agathon about his encomium to eros. The others agree, a discontinuity from the established pattern insofar as it marks the first time a speaker actually questions a prior speaker about the meaning of his words. Could this symbolic move, in itself, be intended to enhance our understanding of eros, in addition to the many speeches describing it? Can the act and process of questioning, for example, be separated, conceptually, from the powers of eros? No! As we shall see, eros has consistently been represented as that which constitutes the process of questioning. This characteristic of eros parallels arguments by contemporary scholars who assert that democracy is defined centrally by the value and practice of questioning. The qualities which eros and democracy appear to share, as two related *states of being*, are striking indeed. (The affinities linking eros to democracy will be developed in chapter 5.)

Returning to the *Symposium*, Socrates says he once envisioned eros just as Agathon did, but was then educated out of this view by an account of eros presented to him by a woman named Diotima, a cultural healer from Manitea. But before Socrates tells us what Diotima told him directly, he first questions Agathon in an attempt to demonstrate what eros is not. He tries to accomplish this through the elenctic or dialectic method, a logical interrogation of the unexamined assumptions upon which Agathon's idealized version of eros rests.[13] Clearly this method forms part of the basis of what we call critical pedagogy today. But what is generally misunderstood by contemporary theorists of critical pedagogy is that Plato's conception of pedagogy was never intended to be defined by the elenctic method alone. As we shall see, the project of defining what eros is requires another epistemic and pedagogical shift, a shift that transcends the logocentrism at the center of the elenctic method.[14]

Though Agathon spoke eloquently about eros being synonomous with the beautiful, under Socrates' critical gaze he is forced to admit that love loves what it does not have. Love of something, logically, implies its lack. But what if one loves what one already has? Socrates:

> When someone says, "While I am healthy, I also want to be healthy, or while I am wealthy, I want to be wealthy, or I desire those very things I have, we will say to him...My good fellow, while you possess wealth, health, and strength, what you also want is to possess them in the future as well...So, is this what love is of in such a case: what is not in hand and what one does not have, the preservation of these things as one's possessions in the future." (*Sym.*, 200d-e)

With this, Agathon is compelled to recognize that if eros desires the beautiful, it must at the same time lack the properties of the beauty sought. This line of questioning induces Agathon to see that eros is not beautiful if it desires the beauty it lacks: "It seems likely, Socrates, that I didn't know what I was talking about earlier" (*Sym.*, 201b). Socrates then proceeds to "deconstruct" Agathon's other key assumption; namely, that eros is the good:

> "Doesn't it seem to you that what is good is also beautiful?"
> "It does to me."
> "Then, if love lacks what is beautiful and what is good is beautiful, he would also lack what is good?"
> "I myself cannot refute you, Socrates. Let it be as you say."
> "No Agathon, my friend, it's the truth you're unable to refute, since it's not difficult to refute Socrates." (*Sym.*, 201c)

In this exchange, we see that Plato has Socrates employ the dialectic to reveal the unexamined assumptions which informed Agathon's view of eros. Prior to this dialogic interrogation, Agathon was ignorant of his own ignorance. By the end of their dialogue, however, Agathon has become reflectively aware of his ignorance concerning eros. This qualitatively different *reflexive ignorance* is perhaps the most fertile teachable moment imaginable, for it provides the necessary precondition for igniting the desire to know, the *sine qua non* of learning itself.

It is also quite significant that Plato has Socrates abandon this form of pedagogy once a certain stage of cognitive understanding is reached. Although Plato is often accused of laying the historical foundation for a masculinist logocentrism (and thus the conventional wisdom that Plato is synonomous with conservative politics), the very structure and content of the *Symposium* strongly refutes such an interpretation. A critical reading of the *Symposium* indicates that while the dialectic or elenctic method does include elements of "masculine logic," what is frequently overlooked in such formulations is that Plato clearly seeks to illuminate its *limitations* insofar as comprehending truth is concerned. Once Agathon's epistemic crisis has resulted in his reflective ignorance, and once the concept of eros has been disentangled from the categories of the beautiful and the good, Plato introduces a revolutionary new pedagogical strategy. This new approach is aimed at subverting, or at least decentering, the masculine discourse which underpins Athenian society. The importance of this strategic displacement should not be dismissed. At precisely this moment, the priestess Diotima emerges to provide Socrates with an alternative education, a crucial step which brings us to a new level of appreciation for the conceptual mutuality between eros and pedagogy.

None of the preceding speeches are remotely similar to the account of eros which Diotima gives. Diotima, after all, was "absent" from the dinner party, yet considering her power to influence Socrates, she is also very much "present." This interpretive tension has given rise to an intriguing debate within the corpus of feminist theory.[15] In terms of structure, substance, and the types of metaphors used to describe eros, a vast distance separates Diotima's discourse from the other speeches. After the brief interrogation of Agathon is concluded, Socrates introduces the figure of Diotima to the other symposiasts:

> I once heard an account of eros from a Mantinean woman named Diotima who was wise and skillful in this and many other things. At one time, by having the Athenians offer sacrifices before the plague occurred, she produced a ten-year postponement of the disease for them, and she instructed me in the activities of love. I'll try as well as I can to repeat her account for you on my own, using as a basis what was agreed to by Agathon and myself…I think the easiest thing would be for me to proceed as the foreign woman did, describing how she questioned me at the time. I was saying to her more or less the sorts of things Agathon just now said to me: How eros is a great god and is beautiful. And she made the assertions to me that I made just now: How according to my account eros could be neither beautiful or good. (*Sym.*, 201e)

Here we observe an image of a woman who not only renders a pedagogical service to Socrates but who also assumes the role of cultural healer, two apparently separate vocations which are merged in this passage. The blurring of Diotima's vocational identity becomes the first instance among many where dualistic conceptions are shown to preclude a holistic understanding of the world. The cornerstone of Diotima's pedagogy, significantly, consists in breaking down many of the dichotomies which structure one's vision. For example, Socrates describes how astonished he was to be told by Diotima that eros was neither good nor beautiful. Still beholden to dichotomous views regarding eros, Socrates asks: "What are you saying Diotima, is eros then ugly and bad?" (*Sym.*, 202a). In response, she refers to the "opposites" of wisdom and ignorance and inquires whether or not a person must be one or the other. In foregrounding the apparently separable space between wisdom and ignorance, Diotima then joins them conceptually:

> Don't you know about having correct opinions without being able to give an account of them? That isn't having knowledge, for how could what lacks an account be knowledge? Nor is it ignorance, for how could what happens to be accurate be ignorance? Correct opinion is just this sort of thing, something that is between understanding and ignorance. Don't say that what isn't beautiful is necessarily ugly, or that what isn't good is necessarily bad. When you agree that eros is neither good nor beautiful, don't then assume that he must be ugly. On the contrary, he is *between* these two. (*Sym.*, 202b, emphasis added)

The linguistic bridge which serves to connect these categories, rather than to separate them, is the Greek term *metaxu*, which means in-between.[16] This metaphor is a recurring motif in Diotima's pedagogy and is intimately connected to philosophic representations of eros.

At the next tier of Diotima's pedagogy, Socrates *unlearns* the final mythological truth: the popular conception that eros is a god, exemplified by the early speakers in the *Symposium*. During this exchange, Diotima persuades Socrates that no god would ever lack goodness or beauty and would therefore not desire anything. The importance of this principle is conveyed in the following dialogue between Socrates and Diotima:

> "Do you say, then, that the happy are those who possess good and beautiful things?"
> "By all means."
> "Yet, you have agreed that eros, because he lacks good and beautiful things, desires those very things he lacks."
> "I have agreed to that."
> "So, how could one who has no share in good or beautiful things be a god?"
> "He couldn't in any way it seems."
> "Then do you see, that even you believe that eros is not a god?"
> "Then, what is eros? I replied, a mortal?"
> "That least of all."
> "But what, then?"
> "Just as in earlier cases, he's in between mortal and immortal."
> "What is he then, Diotima?"
> "A great *daimon*, Socrates. Everything that is daimonic is between god and mortal." (202e)

Diotima names eros as an intermediary, a third term which holds two opposing terms together in dynamic tension. Eros thus becomes a connective *metaxu*, a channel connecting the realm of becoming to the realm of being. To digress briefly, it should be recalled that in the opening passages of the *Symposium*, reference is made to why Socrates arrived late to the dinner party. We learn this delay was due to the fact that Socrates was standing outside on the porch "transfixed" in thought, focusing with great intensity on his daimon (*Sym.*, 175b). As the scribe of the dialogue,

Plato skillfully associates Socrates' daimonic meditation with a quest for wisdom. Once Socrates had decided to come in, Agathon declares:

> Socrates, recline here beside me so that by touching you I may gain the benefit of the wisdom that came to you on the porch. You obviously found it and are holding onto it, for otherwise you wouldn't have come in. (*Sym.*, 175d)

Considering that the Greek word for happiness is *eudaimonia*, meaning to have a good daimon, it follows that happiness is linked to being awake to and connected with the powers of eros.[17] One plausible interpretation of this early episode in the *Symposium* suggests that the performative act of questioning which propels the knowledge quest is vital to the cultivation of a good daimon. Socrates historicized this ideal. He responds to Agathon's request:

> I'd be happy, Agathon, if wisdom were the kind of thing that would flow from one of us with more of it to the one with less when we touch each other, the way water flows through a piece of yarn from the fuller cup to the emptier. My own is surely as worthless and ambiguous as a dream, but yours is bright and has great promise. (*Sym.*, 175e)

The fact that Socrates would define his wisdom as worthless and ambiguous as a dream ironizes the interminable nature of the search. Like philosophy, wisdom is never something one possesses, but refers to a process, to the quality of one's orientation to the search itself. Socrates' wisdom is non-existent because it's anchored in a process of radical questioning, a practice which eludes quantification and termination.

For the moment, let us bear in mind that eros is defined as a kind of daimon, a "transitional space" which enables us to exist as spiritual beings.[18] According to Diotima, the daimonic quality of eros functions to create a channel of communication between human beings and the gods: "It interprets and conveys things to the gods from human beings and to human beings from the gods" (*Sym.*, 203a). Once again we find eros in the position of the great *metaxu*, a third term binding the whole together: "Since it is in the middle it fills in between the two so that the whole is bound together by it" (*Sym.*, 203a). To reinforce an earlier point, we could say that prephilosophic eros presents the notion of an unbridgeable gulf between the human and the divine, whereas Plato's conceptual framework presents the notion that eros is a kind of bridge connecting the human to the divine.

However, as Diotima tries to convey the mysterious nature of eros to Socrates, she nevertheless *begins* by describing its parentage in mythological or prephilosophic terms. It is true there is a tension in Plato's representation of eros, a tension between different modes of knowing what eros is or isn't, and where its boundaries should be drawn. On my reading of Plato, however, there is no problem in using a prephilosophical framework to describe eros, provided its novel educational dimensions are ultimately understood. Plato does not fully abandon the explanatory features of prephilosophic eros; on the contrary, he makes ample use of its representational schemes, but also considers this framework profoundly limited by itself. The point to remember is that Plato was the first to lend coherence to the educational qualities of eros. To the extent that aspiring teachers are unaware of eros as an organizing principle, the insurgent potential of their pedagogy will remain theoretically underdeveloped.

Despite the non-educational core of prephilosophic eros, insight into other aspects of the concept can still be obtained from stories about its mythological origins. We learn how eros is the son of Resource and Poverty, whose conception occurred when Poverty (represented as female) seduced Resource (male) in Zeus's garden. This wondrous event happened on Aphrodite's birthday, so eros became a follower and servant of the personification of beauty (*Sym.*, 203c). Once more we see eros straddling a set of opposites, emptiness/fullness, female/male. The capacity of eros to partake of both sides of such binaries, and hence its unique capacity to disturb dichotomous patterns of thought, reflects part of this concept's insurgent educational character. In this regard, many of the values which characterize eros are consistent with every significant tenet of multiculturalism, from its capacity to break down stale dichotomies to revisioning the self/other relation. For this reason, the principle of eros holds great promise as a heuristic device (this theme will be further developed in chapter 6).

In an instructive counterpoise to Agathon's flowery speech, Diotima deploys a series of images which have the effect, metaphorically, of bringing eros back down to earth. In the amazing passage below, notice how the metaphors used to name eros directly repudiate prephilosophic representations of the concept:

> In the first place, he is always poor and far from being gentle and beautiful, as most people believe. On the contrary, he's tough, wrinkled, barefooted, and homeless. He always lies on the ground, since he doesn't have a bed, he sleeps in doorways and alongside the road in the open air. (*Sym.*, 203d)

This passage repudiates every tenet of prephilosophic eros. Moreover, by locating eros "on the ground," as "barefoot" and "homeless," near "doorways" and "roads," the symbolism clearly invokes earthbound journeys of transition and movement. Of course, this description of eros bears all the earmarks of Socrates himself, a figure who was poor and barefoot and always in passageways.

Diotima continues her dialogue with Socrates by developing the idea that eros holds together the tension between wisdom and ignorance, appearance and reality (*Sym.*, 204a). The wisdom/ignorance dynamic is a particularly important opposition to grasp, since it exemplifies the educational qualities of Plato's reconfigured eros. Here eros is not presented as a naturalistic force against which the individual is powerless to contend. Rather, the suggestion is that the energies of eros can be "recruited" for human purposes if, first of all, one *feels one's ignorance* and if this recognition proceeds to be oriented on a certain philosophical-ethical plane. In exploring the links between pedagogy and psychoanalysis, Shoshona Felman argues that "ignorance" should be understood foremost as a performative act, a passion to ignore, not as a mere absence of some quantifiable knowledge.[19] It's the attitude toward not knowing that counts.

The ethical dimension of eros resides in this crucial relationship. For the elicitation of eros to occur, one must not only feel deficient in terms of self-knowledge, but experience this deficiency to the marrow, reflectively; that is, ethically: to impute meaning to the non-existence of knowledge and to take action to transcend the condition of absence.

Socrates now queries Diotima: "So who are those who engage in the search for wisdom, if they are neither wise nor ignorant?":

> It should be clear by now that it's those who are between these two conditions...For wisdom is a very beautiful thing, and love is a love of the beautiful. Thus, love is necessarily one who engages in the search for wisdom, and a seeker of wisdom is in between being wise and being ignorant. (*Sym.*, 204b)

The concept of being in-between, once again, invites examination. Plato would be the first to say that the discursive formation of "in-between" is a theoretical scaffolding, not to be confused with the condition of in-betweenness itself.[20] We are engaged in an inquiry of eros on several levels: as a discourse, educational principle, experience, event, relation, and as a cluster of symbolic associations. What it means to be "in-between" at the individual level will be developed in the pages ahead, but, to digress briefly, it's worth noting that, in terms of "symbolic associations," democracy could also be described as an in-between type of condition. For one thing, democracy is defined by its questioning, perpetually unfinished character. These qualities are in-between, mobile. Eros and democracy are alike in a remarkable number of ways: they are both questioning, forever incomplete, and ethically laden states of being somehow propelled by visions of the good.

Diotima now asks Socrates why some people are able to participate more with or in eros, while others seem to participate less (*Sym.*, 205a). Socrates, however, is vexed by her questions. He is too confused at this point to even formulate a question. By pointing out that people experience different levels of eros, Diotima intends to highlight elements of eros which are subject, at least in part, to human agency. In other words, the relative presence or absence of eros in an individual's life was seen to hinge on the kinds of choices human beings made when confronted with the spectre of their own ignorance.

Without securing an account from Socrates on her earlier question, Diotima then poses yet another question: "What is the function of love, can you say?" (*Sym.*, 206b). Socrates is uncharacteristically speechless. Diotima, however, continues: "Then I'll tell you," she said. "*It is giving birth to beauty both in body and soul...All human beings are pregnant,* Socrates, *both in body and soul* (*Sym.*, 206d, emphasis added). This passage signals another crucial shift in Diotima's metaphoric and pedagogical strategy. By joining *soul* to *pregnancy* in a single image for describing eros, Diotima subverts the conventional ways of knowing sequestered within the dominant male discourse. The representations of *pregnant soul* and *giving birth to beauty* are indebted to female experience, a strategic move that Plato thought necessary to break the hold of the predominant truth regime. As we now begin to see uniquely philosophic representations of eros displayed in the *Symposium*, Diotima's metaphors evoke female experience as an epistemic basis for developing a new understanding of eros.[21]

Elaborating on this theme, Diotima tells Socrates that "love is not of the beautiful" but, rather, "of procreation and giving birth to beauty" (*Sym.*, 206e). For if love was merely *of* the beautiful, it would remain static in the mode of passive perception. By making the distinction between the perception (or aesthetic appreciation) of beauty on the one hand, and *giving birth to beauty* on the other, Diotima links eros to creativity and to the desire for immortality:

> You know that creation is a broad notion. For when anything whatever passes from non-existence into existence, the whole cause is creation, so that even the works made by the crafts are acts of creation and all the makers of these are poets. (*Sym.*, 205c)

The Greek term for creation is *poiesis*, from which "poetry" is derived.[22] Here the boundaries of what typically constitutes poetry are expanded, so that all creative projects qualify as poetic in form, a move which enables men to symbolically "give birth" to beauty as well. In this way, Diotima universalizes the capacity to be pregnant in soul and to give birth. Susan Hawthorne develops this point:

> Although the birth metaphor is extended to all people, it comes from a view of the world that takes the female principle as its starting point, and by analogy and metaphor extends it to the male population. Diotima speaks from her experience of the body, as a woman, and it is from this experience that her perceptions, and her metaphors derive."[23]

Such gendered imagery is often deployed by Socrates, for example, when he describes his vocation as a "midwife" in *Theaetetus* (149a–151d). If we were to think about pedagogy as a vocation, a unique calling, metaphors of creation, birth, and connectivity would be central to any humane conceptualization. In this way we could accurately speak about the *poetics of pedagogy*: teaching as a performative act of creation. But what to create, and how to create it? Questions like these should occupy the center of the teacher-education curriculum. One measure of the ethical and democratic component of teaching would therefore be revealed in the process of deciding, critically and reflectively, what, exactly, one wishes to create within the space of the classroom, and how. Yet, sadly, since most teacher-education programs today increasingly emphasize principles of scientific management, technocratic efficiency, and "legislated learning," the autonomous space within which teachers might freely create "novel ends" is being systematically eroded.[24]

By reading the *Symposium* as a text about the purpose, structure, and metaphoric inventory of Platonic pedagogy, the conceptual inseparability of eros and pedagogy becomes increasingly evident. And even if we agree that the eros/pedagogy conceptual affinity is important for aspiring teachers to be familiar with, existing power relations still function to privilege one definition of the pedagogical project over other definitions, so that today the *vocationality* of pedagogy is being suppressed in favor of a de-skilled, corporatized model of teaching. The continued domination of this type of educational purpose and value represents the political and institutional repression of eros.

Diotima proceeds to explain the superiority of producing symbolic offspring as opposed to the mere physical reproduction of children. She recognizes that both endeavors represent the quest for immortality; not surprisingly, however, philosophic creativity is valorized. At this stage of her teaching she decides to repeat her provocative metaphor: "Those who are pregnant in soul…are pregnant with and give birth to what is appropriate for the soul" (*Sym.*, 209a). The image evoked is worth pausing over: *soul pregnancy*. Again, we observe how eros is described as a symbolic bridge linking the material to the spiritual, human to the divine, something which is very much *in process*.

Using this provocative symbol, Diotima reveals the existence of another pedagogical step in the ascending staircase of love. She expresses doubt, however, about Socrates' ability to take this apparently larger step. Her expression of doubt about *how* Socrates knows raises a significant question: What, exactly, prevents Socrates from understanding what she calls the "final rites" and "mysteries" of eros?

> These are the activities of eros Socrates, into which you could probably be initiated. I don't know whether you are the sort of person for the final rites and mysteries, for which these former things are the preparation, *if one can let go in the right way*. (*Sym.*, 210a, emphasis added)

Evidently, for Socrates to be properly "turned around," for him to grasp the full meaning of Diotima's eros, he must somehow "let go" of the conventional way of knowing. Since Socrates is a champion of the dialectical method, it is not inaccurate to identify him, at least to some degree, with a logical, hyperrationalized, disembodied, masculinist way of knowing. Yet, we should also remember that the intrinsic limitations of this method are being explicitly exposed here and forcefully criticized by Plato. This is no small criticism to declare that the dialectic cannot be the final avenue for ascertaining the deeper meanings of eros! Diotima suggests that such an epistemology, taken by itself, is an encumbrance: thus, for Socrates to let go in the right way, he must unlearn this masculinist over-determination. Diotima's adroit use of feminine symbolism, therefore, is intended to disrupt key assumptions of Socrates' gendered paradigm of knowledge. Similarly, in the *Gorgias*, Callicles criticizes Socrates as an "effeminate philosopher" with unusual hostility, a gendered rebuke which Plato orchestrates to expose the masculine/feminine heirarchy of knowledge and its relation to the truth quest (484d–485d).

As Diotima's conversation with Socrates draws to a close, she proceeds to map the ascendance of eros from its lower to higher forms. Starting out by observing beautiful things in their particularity, such as bodies or objects, Diotima keeps moving Socrates to the realization that beauty inheres to a multiplicity of forms. Further, according to this view, behind all these separate instances of beauty lies the faint yet enduring glimmer of beauty itself. Diotima tells Socrates that to approach these matters correctly one must be able to love the beauty of souls more than the beauty of bodies. Since souls, in essence, are immortal they are drawn like a magnet to that which is also immortal, what Diotima refers to as the "sea of beauty." Indeed, the idea that "all learning is remembering" (*Meno.,* 70–71a, 82a) grows out of the recognition of an unnoticed dimension within that is suddenly perceived to have been there as an unceasing presence. Thus, the ultimate anchor of knowledge, virtue, and the good is to be found as a consequence of a radically re-situated perception of one's psyche or soul. Since this notion constitutes an important part of Plato's philosophical and educational scaffolding, the concept of soul and its relation to eros and reason will be further clarified in section 2.

By likening the form of beauty to a vast sea, Diotima implies that all specific instances of beauty are but mere drops of water whose particularity dissolves once they are placed in the context of the infinite sea. Those who remain fixated to the beauty of the body or to any other particular are described as slaves to the world of appearances. Diotima traces this evolution:

> And looking towards the great extent of the beautiful, he will no longer, like some servant, loving the beauty of a particular boy or one set of customs, and being a slave of this, remain contemptible and of no account. But turned towards the wide sea of the beautiful and contemplating, he gives birth to many beautiful and grand speeches and reasonings in his abundant love of wisdom. (*Sym.*, 210c)

The ascent of consciousness toward greater levels of intelligibility and meaning is a structural feature of Diotima's pedagogy. Human beings, in this view, are defined by their capacity for transcendence, for their capacity to be creators of meaning. In Plato's metaphysics of education the concepts of eros, pedagogy, and soul constitute different parts of a larger conceptual scheme. The "advancing stages" metaphor of consciousness accurately describes the pattern found in Diotima's speech. The person who is at the final stage of exploring the activities of eros, she declares, "will suddenly see something astonishing that is beautiful in its nature" (*Sym.,* 210e). As Werner Jaeger notes in his translation, Plato defined pedagogy as a *spiritual ascent.*[25] In this incremental process, one's line of sight, by degrees, "turns round": what may have been a faint glimmer of the idea of beauty can gradually be recognized as a brilliant glow acting to pull the soul upward in its ascent from the shadows of non-reflexive ignorance. Diotima maps the ascent:

> In the activities of love, this is what it is to proceed correctly, or be led by another: Beginning from beautiful things to move ever onwards for the sake of beauty, as though using ascending steps, from one body to two to all beautiful bodies, from beautiful bodies to beautiful practical endeavors to beautful examples of understanding, and from beautiful examples of understanding to finally come to that understanding which is none other than the understanding of beauty itself, so that in the end he knows what beauty itself is. Here is the life that a human being should live, studying the beautiful itself. (*Sym.*, 211c)

This passage raises several pertinent questions: Is this ascent to be understood as a movement away from human attachment? Does this speech repudiate the Aristophanic myth which holds that fulfillment is to be found in the human realm? These questions are central to assessing the meaning of eros within the *Symposium*; they will figure prominently in the pages ahead as we examine the conflict between Diotima's and Alcibiades' accounts of eros.

At another level of analysis, what does Diotima mean when she declares that the proper end of the activities of eros is the study of beauty itself? Readers who are unfamiliar with Plato or who may interpret these lines without reference to other dialogues, may easily conclude that such educational ends are irrelevant to their practical teaching experience. If one is committed to educating for radical democracy, for example, and angry about the continued existence of the caste system of public education in the United States, Plato's talk of "beauty itself" may appear to represent the groundwork for an elitist view of education. When the "idealized end" of the pedagogical process is interpreted within a wider context, however, as one of *several* important educational values, Plato's political radicalism becomes readily apparent. As I argue in section 3, the Parable of the Cave ought to modify the meaning one attaches to the ideal of studying beauty, for it draws our attention directly to externally imposed, institutional constraints which systematically diminish the human capacity to search and transcend. In other words, the perception and study of beauty cannot be understood apart from the political context within which it occurs, or is *prevented from occurring*. For this reason, the "politics of eros" should become a central unit of analysis within critical pedagogy. The systematic denial of eros-oriented qualities within public schools to a certain class of students, based on the capricious standard of local property tax, not only compromises the capacity of these nascent citizens to exercise their First Amendment rights, it also denies them an opportunity to educate the erotic, philosophical dimensions of their being.

In this connection, it is also important to note that in an earlier explanation of what should be born from a pregnant soul, Diotima asserts that some of the most beautiful creations are political ideas about the regulation of cities and households. She claims that what is most important for the soul to bring forth are the conditions of possibility that would promote the creation of just political communities (*Sym.*, 209a). In her final words to Socrates, Diotima argues that all virtue is anchored in a form of beauty, a form which is alleged to exist independent of human discourse:

> What do we think it would be like if someone should happen to see the beautiful itself, pure, clear, unmixed, and not contaminated with human flesh and color and a lot of other mortal silliness, but rather if he were to look upon the divine, uniform beautiful itself? Do you think it would be a worthless life for a human being to look at that, to study it in the required way, and be together with it? Aren't you aware that only there with it, when a person sees the beautiful in the only way it can be seen, will he ever be able to give birth, not to imitations of virtue, since he would be reaching out toward an imitation, but to true virtue, because he would be taking hold of what is true? By giving birth to true virtue and nourishing it, he would be able to become a friend of the gods, and if any human being could become immortal, he would. (*Sym.*, 211e–212a)

Notice the clear line of demarcation sketched between appearance and reality, the unreal and the real, becoming and being. Here is the conceptual scaffolding Plato builds around his understanding of reality. Again, it bears mentioning that the main purpose of this study is not so much to evaluate Plato's educational edifice, but to grasp the ways in which eros fits into his conceptual scheme. Eros is not mentioned explicitly in this intellectual construction, but its daimonic presence is implicit throughout, as a third term, the tension between appearance and reality, becoming and being, the human and divine. According to Jacob Needleman, only when these separate realms are brought into relationship through the mediating influence of eros can an individual experience one's spiritual being, an expansion of vision, awareness, and identity.[26] Socrates now signals that the report of his conversation with Diotima has come to an end. He tells us that he has been "persuaded" by her account of eros and tries to persuade others "that one could not find a better collaborator with human nature for acquiring [immortality] than eros" (*Sym.*, 212c).

But if Socrates is indeed persuaded of the ultimate truth of Diotima's teaching, why doesn't Plato stop the action there? Why does he choose instead to conclude the *Symposium* with the raucous and drunken entrance of Alcibiades, who alone claims to tell the truth about eros? "I shall tell the truth. Will you allow that?" Only as Alcibiades stumbles into the party does he learn that the evening has been devoted to praising eros. Perhaps the most significant debates about the meaning of eros in the *Symposium* turn on the question of how to interpret Alcibiades' incredible speech. For example, the contradictions between different interpretations of eros are openly displayed when Alcibiades declares: "Were you persuaded by any of the things Socrates was just saying? Do you realize that everything is just the opposite from what he said?" (*Sym.*, 214d).

The speech is not so much an intellectual construction of eros as it is a speech about Socrates *as* eros, and about the visceral effect his personality has upon Alcibiades. These facets of eros which Alcibiades introduces, including the strong doubts he expresses about the truth value of what Socrates says, may be interpreted as compensatory, inasmuch as they highlight features of eros left unattended by the previous speakers. While the previous speeches sought to frame eros in terms of *intellectual* descriptions, Alcibiades' speech consists of an agonizing *experiential* description. From this perspective, the intensity with which Alcibiades is simultaneously attracted to and repelled by Socrates reveals an ambivalence instructive to our inquiry.

Alcibiades begins his speech by comparing Socrates to two types of objects that were commonplace in Athens. First, he claims that Socrates resembles a particular kind of statue widely available in the agora. Hidden inside these statues (called the Sileni) was a small inner compartment which contained miniature statues of many gods. The analogy is not difficult to grasp. Like the statues, there is within Socrates a divine, internal self that is impervious to external circumstances. The image of invulnerability to external forces is reinforced four times in Alcibiades' speech: Socrates' resistance to sexual seduction (*Sym.*, 219c), his fearlessness in combat (221a), his immunity to drink (220a–223d), and his barefoot meditation in the snow for an entire day, conversing with his daimon (220c). Each of these instances demonstrates how Socrates' steadfast allegiance to an inner source of power transposes his identity beyond the regime of sensation.

Alcibiades provides a second analogy in which he compares Socrates to a flute player. The flute players were known to enchant and possess people with their beautiful music, and played a key role in Athenian religious practice. According to Alcibiades, Socrates is like the flute players, except that instead of music he uses words and ideas to touch and move the soul. The range of *erotic effects* which Socrates exercises on Alcibiades deserves to be quoted at length:

> I myself, at any rate, gentlemen, if I wouldn't seem to be totally drunk, would tell you under oath how much I have been influenced by this man's words and even now I am still affected by them. For, when I hear them, my heart pounds and the tears flow—even more than among the Corybantes—from the effect of this man's words. And I see a good many others who are affected the same way. I believe that Pericles and other good orators I have heard spoke well, but I was not affected like this. My soul didn't clamor or get angry about my servile state. However, I have been put in that position many times by this Marsyas here, with the effect that it seemed to me that I ought not to live the way I have. And even now, I know in my heart that if I would open my ears, I wouldn't be able to resist, but would be affected the same way. He forces me to agree that though I have many faults I neglect my own needs and busy myself with the affairs of the Athenians. So, I forcibly stop up my ears and run away, as from the Sirens, so that I won't grow old just sitting there beside him. Socrates is the only human being in front of whom I have experienced what no one would believe possible for me—a sense of shame in front of someone—though I only feel shame in front of him. I know in my own heart that I cannot refute him and so I ought to do what this man commands, but then I go away, a slave to the honor given by the masses. So, I desert him and escape, and whenever I see him, I am ashamed because of what we had agreed on. Many times I would gladly have seen the end of his existence among human beings, but if that ever came to pass, I well know that I would be even more distressed, so that I don't know how to deal with this man. (*Sym.*, 215e–216e)

Alcibiades portrays himself as a divided soul: part of him recognizes the possibility of attaining a higher level of identity, yet he is unable to translate this recognition into an enduring value informing his life. Similar to one of the characteristics of eros itself, Alcibiades is *in-between*, oscillating from one shifting identity to another, unable to reconcile contradictory visions of himself. Alcibiades is unwilling to surrender the egotistical benefits he reaps from his enormous popularity, even as he feels shame for doing so (at least temporarily, in front of Socrates). Without the presence of Socrates to evoke an alternative vision of the good, little to no internal tension would exist within Alcibiades: the negotiation of his identity is rendered complex and conflictual only when the tensions of eros are introduced. Alcibiades explains the erotic effect: "Now, I have been bitten by something more painful than a snake and in the most painful place one can be bitten, in the heart or soul or whatever it should be called. I have been struck by the arguments in his philosophy, which take hold more savagely than a viper" (*Sym.*, 218a). Alcibiades' anxiety magnifies as his awareness of *incompletion* intensifies the closer he gets to Socrates. Jacob Needleman insightfully describes the yearning feeling, the delicious ache, which is elicited when one's incompletion is magnified by an erotic vision of completion:

> The impact of Socrates is to produce...a specific sort of suffering that involves seeing oneself against a very high criterion of what man should be. But this seeing of oneself is not a moralistic effort to persuade oneself to do better. On the contrary, its effect is to kindle eros, a longing for being.[27]

Alcibiades' predicament is similar to the Aristophanic myth which posits the notion that human beings, as incomplete beings aware of their incompletion, seek ultimate fulfillment in locating their "other half." In the speech of Aristophanes, for example, the "other half" is represented as a flesh and blood human being, which metaphorically grounds eros to earth, away from transcendence. In Alcibiades' speech, the symbolic "other half" is sought through sexual conquest, but Socrates' sharp rejection of

Alcibiades' sexual imperialism codes eros as a desire toward a good which transcends finite persons. Socrates thus represents a paradox: he is the personification of eros at the same time that he repudiates the idea that one can actualize its highest forms through another person. Alcibiades, on the other hand, arguably represents another paradox: he is the experiential embodiment of eros, defined as intense yearning and desire, yet his speech seems to demonstrate that eros cannot be reduced to its sexual or physical manifestations.

Given Alcibiades' overdeveloped hubris, it should not be surprising that he seeks to resolve his inner contradictions by seducing the person most responsible for bringing them to the fore. A drunk Alciabiades proceeds to tell the assembled guests a story about his elaborate scheme to seduce Socrates. Socrates, however, is shown to be oblivious to Alcibiades' sexual designs. After many indirect attempts fail, Alcibiades bluntly states what he's after. To this, Socrates responds:

> Alcibiades, my dear friend, you may not in fact be so stupid, if what you claim about me turns out to be true and there is some power in me by means of which you could become better. You must see in me a beauty that is extraordinary, and quite different from your own good looks. If, having detected this, you're trying to partake of it with me and to offer beauty for beauty, you shouldn't think you can obtain more for me in return for less. You're attempting to acquire true beauty in exchange for apparent beauty, 'gold for bronze.' Well, you blessed fellow, look closer lest you fail to notice I am not what you think. (*Sym.*, 218e–219a)

Alciabiades divulges how Socrates "disdainfully laughed at my youthful good looks, in a quite outrageous manner" (*Sym.*, 219e). For Alcibiades, this brutal rejection was a blow to his well-preened ego. He concludes this astonishing tale by saying that he slept next to Socrates that night "in a way that had no more significance than sleeping with a father or an older brother." Although Alcibiades was confident that he would be able to use his alleged sexual power over Socrates and somehow find relief from the various tensions within himself, in the end, it was his own powerlessness that was revealed: "So I was destitute, enslaved by this man as no one has been by anyone else" (*Sym.*, 219e). The question is raised: which of these two figures, Socrates or Alcibiades, best represents the nature of eros? Needleman puts the dilemma quite well:

> In the entire corpus of Platonic writings the figure of Alcibiades stands out as the man in between. All the other interlocutors are generally unequivocally for or against Socrates; Alcibiades alone feels what is true but sees that he cannot move toward it. Alcibiades alone is a man who is himself in question and, in that respect, although he is portrayed as running away from Socrates, he may be the most authentic pupil of Socrates in the Platonic dialogues.[28]

The historical fate of the mercurial Alcibiades, accused of treason and later assassinated, is perhaps some indication that he failed to give full birth to a higher self which he had glimpsed but could not actualize. Alciabiades is an interesting figure because he apparently ignores his own best interests and refuses to learn from Socrates, thus raising some doubt about the value of his mentors' pedagogy. Offering an incisive interpretation of Alcibiades, Martha Nussbaum observes:

> His story is, in the end, a story of waste and loss, of the failure of practical reason to shape a life. Both the extraordinary man and the stages of his careening course were legendary at Athens; they cried out for interpretation, and for healing. The *Symposium* situates itself in the midst of this and confronts the questions it raises for our thought about love and reason.[29]

Taking a cue from Nussbaum, we might see Alcibiades' speech as a heuristic device deployed by Plato which invites us to grapple with the tricky relationship between love and reason (the primary focus of section 2). She poses the question of whether the passion of Alcibiades can be reconciled with the deliberative qualities of practical reason exemplified by Diotima/Socrates. Can the truth claimed by Diotima be reconciled with the truth claimed by Alcibiades? Why this interpretive tension at the conclusion of the book?

It may be useful to recall a previous discussion regarding the earlier speech by Aristophanes. An interpretive dilemma was identified concerning whether the Aristophanic solution of finding fulfillment only through the medium of another person, represented the denial or fulfillment of eros's transcendent function. In Jonathan Lear's psychoanalytical interpretation, eros functions as a *resistant* to ascent precisely because it culminates or fulfills itself only in another person. Recall that in the Aristophanic myth, the gods punish humans for desiring to be like them: to prevent this "ascent" from happening again, they "limit" eros to the human realm. Clearly, then, Diotima's speech stands in opposition to this representation, since for her, the end of eros is located beyond the human realm, residing in the contemplation of beauty itself. It appears that a tension is set up between eros as earth and person bound, and eros as that which transcends human finitude. Alcibiades' speech thickens this conundrum. His attempted seduction of Socrates symbolizes the effort to realize the good through another person, and its failure to succeed, as well as Socrates' stinging rebuke about not wanting to trade "bronze for gold," indicates that eros transcends the sexual and human realms. Lear provides further insight into the clash between Diotima's and Alcibiades' accounts of eros:

> In the meeting of Socrates and Alcibiades, divine and human manifestations of the erotic intersect; and it is their failure to communicate which casts doubt on the idea that anything like Diotima's path of ascent from the mundane to the transcendent could be possible. Though intrigued, fascinated, and captivated by Socrates, Alcibiades can neither learn from him nor grow in response to him. As any contemporary reader of the *Symposium* would have known, Alcibiades will go on to betray his polis with tragic consequences for Athenian civilization.[30]

Should Alcibiades' "historical failure" to educate his desire along more positive lines stand as an indictment of Socratic education? Further, does Alcibiades' inability to learn from Socrates cast doubt on Diotima's concept of eros as constituting a transcendent ascent? Lear notes that it is not Alcibiades alone, but "*their* failure to communicate" which is the problem, an attribution which suggests the failure was mutual. To better understand the conceptual issues at stake in interpreting eros at this juncture, let us turn to the Vlastos and Nussbaum debate, since these two respected Plato scholars respond to the interpretive dilemmas posed by eros in totally opposite ways.

Gregory Vlastos develops a criticism which strikes at the core of Diotima's eros of ascent. He argues that the "cardinal flaw" of Diotima's speech is that whole individuals are not loved, but only those specific qualities of a person that are somehow valorized, or turned into "abstract versions" of something else beyond the merely human. According to Vlastos, instead of loving the totality of a person, our love is restricted to that facet of a person we deem good and beautiful. Vlastos is suspicious of the "other worldly" dimensions of eros expressed through Diotima:

> We are to love persons so far, and only insofar, as they are good and beautiful. Now since all too few human beings are masterworks of excellence, and not even the best of those we have a chance to love are wholly free of streaks of the ugly, the mean, the commonplace, the ridiculous, if our love for them is to be only for their virtue and beauty, the individual, in the uniqueness and integrity of his or her individuality, will never be the object of our love. This seems to me to be the cardinal flaw in Plato's theory. The high climactic moments of fulfillment—the peak achievement for which all lesser loves are to be "used as steps"—is the one furthest removed from affection from concrete human beings.[31]

In this formulation, Vlastos would seem to agree more with the speeches by Aristophanes and Alcibiades with their emphasis on an earth-bound eros. Martha Nussbaum argues that Vlastos is mistaken to interpret Diotima's speech in isolation. Clearly, when Vlastos identifies the "cardinal flaw" in Plato's theory, in effect he isolates Diotima's account of eros from all the others, thereby dismissing a contextualized interpretation of eros. In Nussbaum's view, important accounts of eros both precede and follow Diotima's speech. Contexuality, she holds, must be part of one's hermeneutic tool kit when interpreting an elusive signifier like eros. In her response to Vlastos, Nussbaum develops a nuanced reading about the meaning of eros within the structure of the *Symposium*:

> If a writer describes a certain theory of love and then follows that description with a counterexample to the theory, a story of intense passion for a unique individual

as eloquent as any in literature—a story that says the theory omits something, is blind to something—then we might hesitate before calling the *author* blind. We might want to read the whole of what he has written, and find his meaning emerging from the arrangement of all its parts. I sense that a deep understanding of the Symposium will be one that regards it not as a work that ignores the prephilosophical understanding of eros, but as one that is all about that understanding, and also about why it must be purged and transcended, why Diotima has come once again to save Athens from a plague.[32]

Nussbaum's interpretive framework is less conclusive than the one Vlastos provides, since she projects an indefinite meaning onto the "arrangement of the parts," whereas he projects a singular meaning onto one decontextualized speech. The open-endedness of Nussbaum's theory of eros is also nonreductionistic. The rich tensions and ironies Plato orchestrates within the structure of the *Symposium* ought to be seen as part of the meaning of eros, too, even if no conclusive definitions of the concept are reached. On my reading, Nussbaum's interpretation of the *Symposium* is preferable since it leaves open the possibility that Plato may have been trying to convey something important about eros in highlighting its boundary crossing capacities.

Instead of debating whose account of eros is the best, or if eros is properly of earth or heaven, why not step back with some critical distance and consider the tensions which exist between and among all of the interpretations? While this approach may not provide any single "answer" about the nature of eros, it may illuminate some fruitful questions. Arguably, if we were to interpret Diotima's and Alcibiades' accounts of eros from the standpoint of a larger, structural context, we might see how an agonistic relationship is created in the *Symposium* between eros and reason, that is, between the figures of Alcibiades and Diotima/Socrates. Perhaps Plato intended to "arrange the parts" in such a way that readers would be encouraged to critically interrogate the assumption that eros was exclusively "of the body" and reason was exclusively "of the mind." Within the structure of the *Symposium*, there is a sense in which this conceptual tension is presented to us in a remarkable way: Is eros complementary to reason, or, like the conflicting representations of eros found in the speeches of Alcibiades and Diotima/Socrates, shall these two realms forever fail to communicate with each other? The tension between eros and reason will be the main focus as we turn now to section 2.

Eros, Reason, and the Soul

In the introduction I asserted that Plato reconfigured eros in a way which broke sharply from the prephilosophic conception. The principal discontinuity was that eros was now to be understood as an educational concept, an innovation as bold as it was unprecedented. Explicit in this reconfiguration was the idea that eros should no longer be seen as a blind, irrational force. In effect Plato humanized eros as a philosophical concept, so that henceforth it was to be seen as an energy and power which could be recruited to enable and fulfill reason itself. This section will explain how Platonic eros was intended to be seen as a constitutive element of reason not in spite of, but because of its passionate dimensions. The analysis includes aspects of the *Pheadrus* which touch upon a conception of "soul" as well. Unlike the previous interpretation of the *Symposium*, which embraced every speaker in the dialogue, the following analysis of the *Phaedrus* will be limited only to that text which illustrates these points explicitly.

The *Phaedrus* is set outside the boundaries of the city, along a tree-shaded riverbank. Phaedrus has led Socrates away from his usual haunts in the city to relate a particularly impressive speech he has heard given by a local speechwriter named Lysias. The speech forcefully argues the commonsense position, still prevalent today, that "love is blind."[33] Based on this premise, we are told that Lysias claims it is better for one to love a non-lover than a lover. The assumption is that the "madness" of love leads inexorably to calamity for all concerned, and should thus be avoided if one wants to retain one's rationality. In the early phase of the dialogue, Phaedrus supports this claim by Lysias about the dichotomy between eros and reason. Phaedrus recounts for Socrates this speech which defines eros as an "affliction" and as something which makes people take leave of their senses (*Phaedrus*, 231d). Phaedrus is deeply moved by this account and declares that because of the illusory features of eros the advantages which accrue to non-lovers are far superior to the obvious disadvantages which plague lovers. The view that reason must necessarily be devoid of passion or emotion is the kind of thinking that Plato wants to de-center. For if Plato were to accept this premise entirely, the power and value of eros as an educational concept would necessarily be de-legitimated. We see, however, that Socrates challenges the idea that the madness of the lover is wholly negative:

> That speech is not true which says that when a lover is at hand one ought instead to gratify someone who does not love, on the grounds that the former is mad and the other is in command of his senses. If it were a simple fact that madness were evil, that would be good advice, but as it is, the greatest goods come to us through the madness that is given as a divine gift. (*Phaedrus*, 244a)

Interestingly, Socrates' next reference is to the prophetess at Delphi and the priestesses at Dodona, who do "admirable things" for Athens when they are "mad," but contribute little to nothing of value while in possession of their senses (*Phaedrus*, 244b). The image of women as spiritual teachers operating on a higher epistemic plane recalls the *Symposium*, where Diotima questions if Socrates can "let go in the right way" so as to perceive the final mysteries of eros (*Sym.*, 210a). Such a clear connection between these two dialogues implies that what ought to be *let go of*, then, is the absolute distrust of passionate, embodied knowledge. The implication appears to be that only eros has the requisite power to "turn the soul around" and to thus fundamentally transform one's self-conception. In his attempt to disabuse Phaedrus of privileging an arid form of rationality, Socrates submits that a passionate friend should be preferred to a judicious one. He makes the provocative claim that the so-called madness of eros, far from something that should be avoided, as Lysias argues, is actually "given by the gods for the greatest possible good fortune," and adds that this proposition "will not be believed by the clever, but it will be believed by the wise" (*Phaedrus*, 245c).

The distinction Socrates makes between the clever and the wise echoes the distinction Diotima makes when she wonders if Socrates is capable of letting go of his previous way of knowing, an obvious signal revealing the limits of the dialectical/logical mode of intelligence. Passages such as these fairly demolish the idea that Plato is an uncritical exponent of disembodied knowledge. Just as in the *Symposium* the logic of the dialectic is employed to make certain preliminary points but is eventually "let go of," so too, in the *Phaedrus*, the dialectical mode is initially used but then abandoned at a later stage in favor of a more erotic orientation to knowing. What this pattern indicates is *not* that Plato embraces a purely arid or masculinist form of rationalism, but that he points to its limitations and challenges its epistemic supremacy. Plato stakes out a position which engages the reader in the dynamic tension between the two orientations. Such a stance should not be dichotomized into either a masculinist or feminist way of knowing! In his continuing effort to demonstrate how the madness of eros can represent "the greatest possible good," Socrates declares that an inquiry into the soul (psyche) will be necessary.

Socrates argues that every soul is immortal because that which is continually changing is immortal. He launches into a series of logocentric proofs which attempt to show that the soul is an unceasing movement whose only constant is that of change. He asserts that the soul is originless:

> Everything that comes into being necessarily comes into being from an origin, but the latter does not itself come from an origin. For if an origin came into being from something, it would not come into being from an origin. Since it does not come into being, it also necessarily does not perish. (*Phaedrus*, 245d)

In this elaboration of the soul, we are asked to accept the proposition that change "has no origin." Socrates then proceeds to connect this particular principle to an essential feature of the soul, a rather abstract and ambitious argument which seeks to build a theoretical scaffolding around a concept which eludes representation in the first place. Although contemporary readers may be skeptical of any "soul discourse" whatsoever, I would argue on educational grounds that it is preferable for students to focus on this signifier rather than not to focus on it, even if no tidy definitions are forthcoming. Thus, Socrates forges ahead and seeks to define the undefinable:

> Therefore the origin of change must be what changes itself, and it is not possible for this to be destroyed or come into being. Otherwise, the entire universe and everything that comes into being would collapse into a static condition and that which is changed would never come into being. Now, since what is changed by itself has been shown to be immortal, one is not ashamed to say that this very characteristic constitutes the essence and definition of the soul. (*Phaedrus*, 246a)

This representation of the soul as a principle of movement is touched upon in less abstract terms in the *Symposium* as well. By briefly examining it now we may obtain a clearer picture of what Socrates means when he refers to this principle of the soul. Diotima explains to Socrates that an individual person may appear to be a stable and fixed entity, but this appearance is deceptive. She alludes, for example, to the constant flux of bodily change in one's hair, flesh, bones, and blood:

> This is so not only with regards to one's body, but also with regard to one's soul. One's habits, characteristics, opinions, desires, pleasures, pains, fears, none of these ever stays the same in anybody; some are coming into being while others are passing away. (*Sym.*, 207e)

Despite this constant changing, the person is still regarded not as a congeries of different identities over a period of years but as a singularly enduring identity, enabled by the function of memory. Having thus established this principle, Socrates then introduces a second principle which enables an identity to sustain an enduring coherence: the principle of perception. For without this element of intelligibility functioning as the "pilot" of the soul, one could never speak of being reflectively aware: aware of consciousness as consciousness *of* consciousness. When both of these principles are taken together, the logic that "all learning is recollection" can be more easily understood. The kind of knowledge which is re-cognized and re-collected is that which is unceasingly accessible but forgotten, owing to new physical embodiments as well as to one's perception being "turned away from" the source or ground of one's changing changelessness. Indeed, the deepest Platonic insights are always couched in terms of "complex irony" and paradox.[34] Readers who may be turned off by the vague or inadequate character of such formulations should bear in mind that in the *Seventh Letter* and in the *Phaedrus*, Plato explicitly refers to the inadequacy of language to capture things in themselves. Yet, acknowledging the impossibility of defining the soul with precision, for example, does not mean that our efforts to approximate what it is have no value. Throughout many of Plato's dialogues, once a certain conceptual basis is laid, he lets go of the logic of the dialectic method in favor of an allegorical mode of representation.

Returning to the *Phaedrus*, Socrates now discusses what he calls the form of the soul. Socrates tells Phaedrus that it is impossible to describe exactly what the soul *is*, but that he can suggest what it might be *like* (246a). He refers to a winged charioteer and two winged horses, one of which is noble in stock and character, the other of an opposite stock and character (246b). The driving is "difficult and troublesome" since the horses tend to pull the chariot in opposite directions. The charioteer represents the principle of perception, the idea that the reason/intellect constitutes the "pilot" of the soul while the horses represent the tension created by unreflective appetitive desires. However, the pilot cannot simply leave the unruly horse behind but must come to grips with these unruly tendencies and somehow lead it in the right direction. Without the combined power of both horses the pilot cannot move toward the pursuit of wisdom. The wings are symbolic of eros, seen here as the transcendent potential of human being:

> The natural function of a wing is to carry what is heavy upward and raise it to the region where the race of gods dwell. In a way, they have more in common with the divine than any other bodily part, and since the divine is noble, wise, good, and everything else of that sort, such things are nourishing to the wings of the soul and make them grow, while shame, evil, and other things of the opposite sort are detrimental and can even destroy them completely. (*Phaedrus*, 246e)

The just, good, and happy individual is the one who is able to negotiate the interminable tension between these components of the soul. As is well known, Plato's understanding of the just, good, and therefore happy society, depends entirely on how individuals negotiate this tension and to what extent they undergo the *periagoge* experience.[35] Such an experience is defined as the "turning around" of the soul, a metaphor of transformation which shares the same structural features as Freire's *conscientization*.

As Socrates continues to try and persuade Phaedrus that genuine reason should not be conceived of as separable from eros, we observe dimensions of the eros concept which are by now quite familiar. In the passage above, notice that the "wings of eros" once more are coded as halfway between the human and divine, expressing its daimonic character. At this juncture, Socrates describes the enthusiasm one feels in the process of giving birth to a new idea:

> At this point the entire soul is throbbing with excitement. It is like the experience of cutting teeth and the itching and irritation which occur around the gums when the teeth are just coming through. The soul of the one who is beginning to sprout feathers itches and is irritated and excited as it grows its wings. (*Phaedrus*, 251d)

Another aspect of eros's symbolic inventory important to consider in this context, is its intimate connection to the word *enthusiasm*. The etymology is crucial, for *enthousiazon* means literally, "having a god inside."[36] If we recall that eros is a daimon which, as an intermediary, connects the human to the divine, we see clearly that the quality of enthusiasm is a first cousin of eros, so to speak. As the passage above suggests, the educational moment is one in which the individual, filled with enthusiasm, is no longer the same staid self, but is transported out of a prior regime of identity. It is precisely this dynamic transportation of identity which is associated with the madness of love, giving rise to the popular notion that love is blind. Socrates explains why it appears that the lover is blind:

> Since he stands apart from the busy antics of humankind and draws close to the divine, he is rebuked by most people for being out of his wits. They do not realize he is possessed...Whenever someone sees beauty in this world he is reminded of true beauty and his wing-feathers grow. Of all kinds of possession this is the best and is from the best source, both for the one who has it and for the one who shares in it, and it is because of his participating in this kind of madness that the one who loves the beautiful is called a lover. (*Phaedrus*, 249d-e)

For Plato, the madness of love, far from being something negative, becomes instead the precondition for breaking away from the "commonsense" world of appearance and convention. Rather than repeating the conventional wisdom that "love is blind," Plato insists that blindness is the conseqence of the absence of love. Thus, any form of rationality minus eros is, by definition, unfulfilled. This radical reformulation of love is teeming with political and educational significance, which perhaps goes a long distance toward explaining its omission from the American curricular structure. Aspiring teachers should begin to see this curricular omission as something quite strange, and ask themselves: On whose authority is it accepted that the theme of love cannot be educationally considered? As Sam Keen observes, "central though love is to all visions of human fulfillment, it is given no place in the curriculum."[37]

Wendy Brown beautifully captures the political and educational significance of Plato's educational theory:

> Our mental universe is shaped by logic, causal relations, and immediate necessity but also by imagination, dream, and desire. And for all of Plato's railing against the appetitive or desirous, the fanciful or poetic, he does not and cannot jettison these parts of our being. Socrates and Plato must awaken and inspire precisely these dimensions of us because they are involved in a political struggle to loosen

our engagement with the immediate realm of necessity and move our minds into a radically different, imaginative domain. They must break the conservative hold on the present and incite us to envision an order of existence and values utterly unlike our own yet identifiably human and livable. This cannot be accomplished merely by reasoning with us; rather, the sensuous, longing, appetitive elements of our being must be touched and drawn into the project.[38]

One can hardly imagine a finer expression of how indispensable the emotion of love in the form of eros is to the educational project. This passage not only illustrates the kind of epistemology which must be valued if Platonic reason is to be fulfilled, but at another level, it also testifies to the overlap between Platonic and feminist pedagogy, a theme which will be pursued in chapter four. We now turn to consider the ways in which the eros concept is implicated in Plato's pedagogical narrative of conversion expressed in Book VII of the *Republic.*

Eros and the Politics of Conversion:
Mapping the American Cave

As a narrative of liberation, the Parable of the Cave is a seedbed of interpretive opportunity. Its symbolic field contains provocative images of personal liberation as well as political oppression, images which can illuminate the spiritual vacancy of today's dominant educational paradigm. Conventional narratives of education, whether ancient or contemporary, "sophist" or "banking" by label, embody a view of students preeminently as means to a greater end, in that the educational development of a student's soul is subordinated to an overriding concern with molding them to fit a set of heteronomously prescribed roles. As a heuristic device, the Parable of the Cave can bring these contemporary biases and prejudices into conceptual relief and encourage critical distance from the reigning liberal hegemony.

For the purposes of this section there is no need to revisit every aspect of the Parable, since I assume readers are familiar with its main outlines. Rather, the intention is to mine specific aspects of the story which throw light on the theme of eros even though it's not mentioned explicitly in the allegory. Despite its discursive absence, the symbolic trappings of eros are embedded in the structure of this ancient yet remarkably contemporary parable. An ancillary aim of this section is to demonstrate the ways in which adherents of critical pedagogy depend a great deal, perhaps unconsciously, on the Socratic/Platonic thematic universe to give shape and purpose to their narratives of liberation.

In Socrates' discussion with Glaucon, he sketches an image of an underground cave in which several prisoners are chained down; their field of vision is both narrow and stationary. A fire burns behind the prisoners. An invisible power parades puppet figures by this fire, and these puppets are projected on the wall in front of the prisoners who then take these projected silhouettes to be representations of the real. The existence of these shackles, holding their bodies and vision in place, symbolizes an imposed constraint on their eros, preventing them from ascending outside the cave. Glaucon remarks to Socrates that this is a strange image with strange prisoners; Socrates replies, "they are like ourselves."[39] This close identification with the prisoners is pedagogically significant: it prevents Socrates from distancing himself, in any permanent sense, from the world of ignorance and illusion which define conditions in the cave.

One of the prisoners, mysteriously, struggles successfully to loosen the grip of the shackles and rises buoyantly yet painfully to the space above and beyond the illusions of the cave. Once outside the cave, the individual is no longer captive to the dominant system of knowledge and experiences this "turning around" to be a true and good thing. The "prisoner" is now a "human" insofar as she is able to create self-authored novel meanings. As comfortable a life as this new world of meaning is, Socrates insists that the newly freed ought to return to the cave and pedagogically "loosen the shackles" that bind their fellow prisoners to the realm of ignorance and illusion. As our unnamed protagonist heroically returns to the cave, we learn that the prisoners are so emotionally invested in the award system (or meritocracy) that has been established around watching and judging the shadows that they have come to like their oppression, and resent the effort to change their one and only meaning project. Socrates tells Glaucon that the prisoners will not easily accept the truth about their oppressed condition and speculates they will eventually conspire to murder the messenger in order to preserve their "happiness."

Plato choreographs the dynamic tension between a realm of knowledge outside the cave and a realm of ignorance inside the cave to introduce the appearance/reality motif. The appearance/reality distinction is a controversial trope, especially when one considers the question of power: Who gets to decide what is considered real knowledge as distinct from false knowledge, what is authentic and what is not? This conceptual predicament has led some to abandon the appearance/reality distinction altogether, dismissing it as inherently masculinist or imperialistic. Certainly the capacity to "impose" and "enforce" such distinctions has been the source of much oppression, but imposing and enforcing such rigid distinctions is not an activity intrinsic to the concept itself. In a sense, this binary opposition provides the "symbolic oxygen" necessary to all critical theory, for without the capacity to make distinctions at the moral and epistemological level (by whatever name or label), the transformative edge of critical pedagogy instantly evaporates.

Already we glimpse the extent to which the educational projects of Paulo Freire and the critical pedagogy movement are indebted to the Socratic/Platonic thematic universe. Additionally, the ontological distinction Freire makes between the banking and problem-posing pedagogies (a clear, "life versus death" binary) grows out of a prior capacity to distinguish between authentic and non-authentic forms of knowledge; that is, between "appearance" and "reality." The ability to make such distinctions and to place this conceptual framework in the service of certain educational and political aims was introduced by Socrates and Plato, and most transformative intellectuals today reside within this narrative structure, even as they may struggle against the putative "European" or "androcentric" character of its "origins."

Within this narrative, pedagogy becomes an art of conversion, an educational purpose focused on how best to ignite a transformation in consciousness, identity, and meaning. One of the chief obstacles to this conversion experience, both then and now, is the dominant form of education itself. Socrates declares:

> But then, if I am right, certain professors of education must be wrong when they say they can put knowledge into the soul which was not there before, like sight into blind eyes. (*Rep.*, 518a)

The critical disposition toward conventional forms of education evidenced here finds its present day equivalent in Freire's critique of the banking model of education. The unspoken assumption behind such an approach is that the purpose of education is not liberation, not to release a buoyant consciousness from the yoke of convention, but to discipline, to reproduce a prescribed narrative of identity. To the extent that students are habituated into a receiving mode, treated as passive retainers of "objective" knowledge, they are denied the opportunity to enact their own subjectivity, to become self-critical authors and subjects of their own history. In this vitiated form of education, the inquiring and imaginative potential of human being is atrophied, and the self and world increasingly become what official others prescribe them to be. Freire denounced the banking approach in the strongest possible way, borrowing Erich Fromm's term "necrophilia," love of death, to describe how this educational approach destroys the inquiring and creative capacities of human being.[40] The aim of both Freire and Socrates was to ignite an internal process of reflective questioning, not to implant textual information into one's inventory of knowledge:

> But our present argument shows that there resides in each man's soul this faculty
> and the instrument wherewith he learns, and that is just as if the eye could not turn
> from darkness to light unless the whole body turned with it; so this faculty and the
> instrument must be wheeled round together with the whole soul away from that
> which is becoming, until it is able to look upon and to endure being and the
> brightest blaze of being; and that we declare to be good. (*Rep.*, 518b)

Plato's distinction between appearance and reality is homologous to the realms of becoming and being. Similar to Freire's problem-posing approach, the aim of Socratic pedagogy is to recover in the learner an ethical orientation toward the act and process of knowing itself, a quality of mind which includes the development of a new relation to one's ignorance, defined here as that which is unconscious. Freire's pedagogy employs the identical strategy except that the binary opposition he utilizes for the appearance/reality distinction is labelled "doxa" versus "logos," that is, opinion versus knowledge.[41] Therefore, both thinkers rely on the trope of appearance/reality to give their aims intelligibility. These respective aims are nothing if not ambitious, since they seek to provoke a fundamental transformation in personal and collective identity. Given the radical intervention which Socratic and Freirean pedagogy calls for, the question arises how the appearance/reality distinction can be deployed in a non-dominative way.

Jacob Needleman offers an incisive interpretation of the becoming/being, appearance/reality polarity. Without a better understanding of this binary opposition in Plato's thought, one cannot appreciate how eros is directly implicated within the structure of the text. Needleman recognizes that noble ideas like truth, beauty, and the good, or principles like justice and equality which embroider Western history, are abstractions which generally do not inform the lives of individual people or the actions of nation-states. He offers the twentieth century as a measure of how little power these noble Western ideals seem to have had in preventing events such as Auschwitz, Hiroshima, Nagasaki, or in preventing countless individual cases of personal alienation and unhappiness. He asks: Why do these noble ideas tend not to be a powerful force in our individual and collective lives?

Needleman contends these abstractions remain mere abstractions if they have not been brought into relation with the deeper, unconscious layers of the mind. This "blockage" between the conscious mind (becoming) and the unconcious (being) is the principal cause of the absence of lived virtue. According to Needleman's interpretation, the purpose of Socratic self-interrogation is to establish a conscious channel between these two realms, becoming and being; in this way, the act of questioning mediates the tension between appearance and reality:

> The Socratic interrogation is not simply a project of asking questions about an issue; the interrogation itself is a material, chemical process by which the transformation begins to take place in onself. He questioned, but not as we question. His questioning created a channel within human nature for the reconciliation of mind and body, a channel of virtue or power.[42]

Eros enters the picture here as the *metaxu*, the in-between, a third term holding binaries in tension. Understood in this way, the invocation of appearance/reality speaks to the conscious/unconscious interrelation, and how individuals understand and negotiate this fluid condition. Of course, any radical questioning functions simultaneously as a great destroyer/creator, capable of unraveling one's self-conception, yet also paving the way for the construction of a new, presumably wider, identity. What happens, empirically, in the wake of such questioning? Needleman responds: "Nothing—except a new quality of mind that stands for a moment in actual relationship to the unconscious parts of human nature."[43] From this new quality of mind, issues the precondition for lived virtue. For Socrates, then, pedagogy is an art of changing one's inner listening:

> Education, then, will be an art of doing this, an art of conversion, and will consider in what manner the soul will be turned around most easily and effectively. Its aim will not be to implant vision in the instrument of sight. It will be to regard it as already possessing that, but as being turned in the wrong

direction, and not looking where it ought, and it will try to set this right. (*Rep.*, 518c)

The prisoners, in other words, do not lack knowledge so much as they are "not looking where they ought." Thus, the periagoge experience represents a revolution in the direction of our attention/intention: an extroverted attention to the passing image (becoming) moves round to an introverted intention to re-cognize the unconscious fount of mind, the fecund terrain of ignorance (being). In this connection, the writings of Shoshona Felman and Jonathan Lear show how Socratic pedagogy is effectively understood in conjunction with psychoanalytic theory, as an attempt to render the unconscious, conscious.[44] If, indeed, "ignorance" is coded as a state of "unconsciousness," as it should be, we must perceive that Socratic pedagogy seeks to interrogate and alter the relationship between conscious and unconscious. Creating this channel of communication between the two realms is precisely what the Socratic, Freirean, and psychoanalytic interpretive frameworks seek to establish as a first step toward widening one's identity. (Although these approaches share much in common, neither Lear nor Felman conflate psychoanalysis with radical pedagogy.)

The role of eros in the transformation of perception and identity can be identified in two ways. First, as previously mentioned, eros is the connective agent, as questioning, as the desire to know, that which holds together the tension between conscious and unconscious, appearance and reality. Secondly, the power and movement of eros is evidenced in the allegory when Socrates makes reference to the "natural destiny" of human life as one of ascendance, an overcoming of "limit-situations." Needless to say, the "symbolic shackles" represented in the allegory can be interpreted from multiple standpoints, but for the purpose of this inquiry, I see them as artificial instruments of oppression which function to suppress the buoyancy of a person-centered eros. In the final pages of the chapter, I want to use the Parable of the Cave as an interpretive device to explore the *historical form* these shackles of oppression may be seen to assume within the educational and political landscape of contemporary America.

The association of eros with beauty and philosophy should not be taken to mean that the eros concept contains no political dimension. For example, Jonathan Kozol's *Savage Inequalities* describes personal narratives which chronicle the powerful influence *public neglect* exerts on identity formation.[45] The students Kozol interviewed in East Saint Louis, Illinois, for example, were clear on one thing: the appearance of America as a symbol of hope was starkly different from the reality of America they were living. The level of injury is not only psychological, as in the perception of being forgotten, discarded, or in being denied a right to equal public education. The injury extends to the physical, since the school itself exists amid recognized toxic waste dumps. Compare that image to the rich public schools Kozol visited, overwhelmingly white, radiating with every educational opportunity, including well-attended philosophy classes. This curricular option symbolizes the highest form of democratic educational purpose since it affirms the students' identity as searchers and inquirers, gifted authors of their own destiny. But in the public school caste-system of America, no philosophy for poor folk!

The designated cave dwellers are given an education Freire accurately calls necrophilic. America's religion of possibility, of equal public opportunity upon which the future of democracy largely rests, is chained down by class structure. In 1968, Martin Luther King, Jr., declared that America needed to transform its "economic architecture" if peace and justice were to be historically realized.[46] Certainly the class basis of public schooling in America betrays a tragic compromise of the nation's alleged "commitment" to democracy. The savage inequalities visited upon those souls who happen to exist at the bottom of the Cave represent the "symbolic shackles" which function to suppress one's eros, a denial that is clearly a structural feature of American public education. In this way, the Parable of the Cave can be used as a heuristic device to expose the considerable hypocrisy in America's "democratic" self-conception.

In exploring the role of eros in the conversion experience it should also be acknowledged that Plato and Freire's pedagogical narratives are not confined to individual remedies, but are collective in nature, aimed at transforming society itself. How might the *periagoge* experience, as an individual "turning round," be understood when applied to transformations of collective identity? What theoretical frameworks exist which illuminate social, or collective, processes of conversion? Cornel West, for one, surveys the disease in American political culture and contends that any progressive social theory, educational or otherwise, requires a concept of "conversion" rooted in a "love ethic" in order to mobilize new forms of collective identity.[47]

For example, West argues that the nihilism within African-American communities can only be transcended by a "politics of conversion." In a sense, nihilism represents the disease of democracy, the dissolution of meaningful social bonds. Although West's analysis focuses on the nihilism evident in many African-American communities, it is plausible to assume that this disease seeps across boundaries of race and class. Based on West's insights, an argument can be made that any educational theory of citizenship, absent a critically theorized love ethic, is by definition limited and inadequate:

> If one begins with the threat of concrete nihilism, then one must talk about some kind of politics of conversion. Like alcoholism and drug addition, nihilism is a disease of the soul. Any disease of the soul must be conquered by a turning of one's soul. This turning is done through an affirmation of one's worth—an affirmation fueled by concern for others. A love ethic must be at the center of a politics of conversion. A love ethic has nothing to do with sentimental feelings or tribal connections. Rather it is a last attempt at generating a sense of agency among a downtrodden people.[48]

In this formulation, West associates a transformative love ethic with the promotion of a sense of personal agency. This representation is in full accord with the symbolic patterns of eros which have been identified thus far in the inquiry. The profile of eros which emerges is a complex one, since it occurs in many forms and at many levels. We have seen eros as a discourse, as a cluster of affective associations, as a builder of cities, as a sexual desire, as a perception of beauty, as a vision of the good, as an agent of connection, and as that which constitutes the essence of questioning. All of these patterns of signification demonstrate how central the concept of eros must be to any truly democratic conception of pedagogy. Based on these patterns we are led to the proposition that eros deserves to be recognized as a valuable educational principle and placed at the center of a new paradigm for pedagogy.

In chapter 2 we examine how and why Platonic eros was displaced in the first centuries of the common era by the ascendant Christian narrative of *agape*. We shall examine what effects this transition in the representation of love exercised on the social construction of self and other. In addition, we will explore the ways in which this fourth century anti-erotic legacy still *in*forms narratives of "common sense" dominant in educational institutions today. These inquiries will lead us to investigate the writings of the powerful Bishop of Hippo, Saint Augustine.

Notes

1. Jane Ellen Harrison, *Prolegomena to the Study of Greek Religion* (New York: Meridan Books, 1955). See chapter 12, 624–58, "Orphic Cosmogeny," for an account of prephilosophic eros as interpreted from a range of Greek religious practice.

2. Robert Graves, *The Greek Myths* (Mt. Kisco, N.Y.: Moyer Bell, 1960), 30–31.

3. Joseph Campbell, *Myths to Live By* (New York: Basic Books, 1973), 152–73.

4. Hesiod, *Theogeny* (New York: Penguin Books, 1973), 116–46.

5. Aristophanes, *Birds*, ed. Nan Dunbar (New York: Clarendon Press, 1995), 693–95.

6. Eric Voegelin, *Plato* (Baton Rouge: Louisiana State University Press, 1966), 115. Sam Keen, in his *Faces of the Enemy: Reflections of the Hostile Imagination* (San Francisco: Harper and Row, 1991), frequently uses the term "metanoia" to describe the revolution in consciousness which Plato refers to as "periagoge." Keen writes: "This is the way of metanoia, changing our minds, reversing our perspectives, making conscious the projections of our shadows onto the enemy" (92). Or: "In theory, metanoia is simple, in practice, agonizing. The method of conciliation, the method of compassion, leads through the heart of darkness: begin with the projection, the image of the enemy, and return to the self. Reverse the direction of the current. Introjection rather than projection" (98). Although periagoge and metanoia seem alike in that they both refer to a "turning around" of one's identity, the Christian appropriation of metanoia (a Greek word) has given the term a religious connotation. However, upon close examination, it is not clear that periagoge, as a philosophical turning about, is appreciably distinct from metanoia. *The Oxford English Dictionary*, for example, reports: "Of metanoia, as Jesus used the word, the lamenting of one's sins was a small part; the main part was something more active and fruitful, the setting up an immense new inward movement for obtaining the rule of life" (see *The Oxford English Dictionary*, 2d ed., s.v. "metanoia"). If educators take seriously the theme of transformation and further acknowledge that such transformations can be interpreted differently, it seems reasonable to assert that these two categories ought to be recovered from their present obscurity.

7. William S. Cobb, ed., *The Symposium and The Phaedrus: Plato's Erotic Dialogues*, (Albany: SUNY Press, 1993), 178b. Subsequent references for this book in the text are cited with the abbreviation *Sym.*

8. See Martha Nussbaum, *Cultivating Humanity: A Classical Defense of Reform in Liberal Education* (Cambridge: Harvard University Press, 1997), 226–38; and David M. Halperin, "Homosexuality: A Cultural Construct," in *One Hundred Years of Homosexuality* (New York: Routledge Books, 1990), 41–53.

9. David L. Hall, *Eros and Irony* (Albany: SUNY Press, 1982), 56–58.

10. Werner Jaeger, *Paideia: The Ideals of Greek Culture* (New York: Oxford University Press, 1943), 2:184.

11. Rollo May, *Love and Will* (New York: Norton, 1969), 72–98.

12. Jonathan Lear, *Open Minded: Working Out the Logic of the Soul* (Cambridge: Harvard University Press, 1998), 131–33.

13. Gregory Vlastos, *Socrates, Ironist and Moral Philosopher* (Ithaca: Cornell University Press, 1991), 107–31. Chapter 4 gives a more complete account of the *elenchus*, or elenctic method. Briefly, this mode of questioning and interrogation can be defined as a logical, proof-oriented system of analysis, used to provoke an epistemic crisis in the learner, an approach often equated with the dialectic method.

14. Wendy Brown, "Supposing Truth Were a Woman: Plato's Subversion of Masculine Discourse," in *Feminist Interpretations of Plato* (University Park: Pennsylvania State University Press, 1994), 157–80.

15. For two opposing interpretations, see Susan Hawthorne, "Diotima Speaks Through the Body," in *Engendering Origins: Critical Feminist Readings in Plato and Aristotle* (Albany: SUNY Press, 1994), 85–89; and Luce Irigaray, "Sorcerer Love: A Reading of Plato's *Symposium*, in Diotima's Speech" in *Feminist Interpretations of Plato* (University Park: Pennsylvania State University), 181–95.

16. Hawthorne, 85.

17. F. E. Peters, ed., *Greek Philosophical Terms: A Historical Lexicon* (New York: New York University Press, 1967), 66.

18. Lear, 133.

19. Shoshona Felman, "Psychoanalysis and Education: Teaching Terminable and Interminable," in *Jacques Lacan and the Adventure of Insight* (Cambridge: Harvard University Press, 1987), 79.

20. Plato, *Phaedrus and Letters VII and VIII* (London: Penguin Books, 1962), 342–45. Plato expresses his belief about the limitation of language and every theoretical invention to capture the truth of things in themselves, a critical disposition that reminds us to be suspicious about attaching truth claims to mere "conceptualizations."

21. Brown, 157–64; Hawthorne, 83–91.

22. See William S. Cobb, *The Symposium and The Phaedrus: Plato's Erotic Dialogues* (Albany: SUNY Press, 1993). In his note 40, Cobb translates "poiesis" as "creativity."

23. Hawthorne, 86.

24. James W. Garrison, "Style and the Art of Teaching," in *The Educational Conversation: Closing the Gap* (Albany: SUNY Press, 1995), 60.

25. Jaeger, 192.

26. Jacob Needleman, "Socrates and the Myth of Responsibility," *The Heart of Philosophy* (San Francisco: HarperCollins, 1982), 35.

27. Needleman, 38.

28. Needleman, 40.

29. Martha Nussbaum, "The Speech of Alcibiades: A Reading of Plato's Symposium," *Philosophy and Literature* (Spring 1986): 132.

30. Lear, 152.

31. Gregory Vlastos, "The Individual as an Object of Love in Plato," in *Platonic Studies* (Princeton: Princeton University Press, 1983), 31.

32. Nussbaum, 135.

33. See note #7; subsequent references to this book in the text are cited with the abbreviation *Phaedrus*.

34. Gregory Vlastos, "Is the 'Socratic Fallacy' Socratic?", in *Socratic Studies* (London: Cambridge University Press, 1994), 67–86; see also Hall, *Eros and Irony*, 213–15.

Both of these scholars foreground the role irony plays in the Socratic conception of knowledge.

35. Voegelin, 115–16.

36. Cobb, 153.

37. Sam Keen, *To a Dancing God: Notes of a Spiritual Traveler* (New York: HarperCollins, 1990), 57.

38. Brown, 156–57.

39. Plato, *The Republic*, trans. by Benjamin Jowett (New York: Vintage, 1962), 515a.

40. Freire, *Pedagogy of the Oppressed* (New York: Seabury, 1992), 58.

41. Freire, 62.

42. Needleman, 25.

43. Needleman, 39.

44. For an interesting breakdown of the pedagogy/psychoanalysis overlap, see Lear, 162–66, and Felman, 69–80.

45. Jonathan Kozol, *Savage Inequalities: Children in America's Schools* (New York: HarperCollins, 1991), 1–39.

46. *Eyes on the Prize: "1968: The Promised Land,"* prod. Henry Hampton, Blackside, 1986. Videocassette.

47. Cornel West, *Race Matters* (New York: Vintage Books, 1994), 28.

48. West, 28–31.

2

Eros Denied: The Garden of Eden Myth as a Pedagogical Metaphor

> What is the difference whether it is in a wife or mother, it is still Eve
> (the temptress) that we must beware of in any woman.
> —St. Augustine (Ep. 243)

> Whereas the orthodox often blamed Eve for the fall and pointed to
> women's submission as appropriate punishment, gnostics often depicted
> Eve—or the feminine spiritual power she represented—as the source of
> spiritual awakening.
> —Elaine Pagels (1988)

This inquiry highlights significant shifts in historical representations of eros. Such a reconstruction confronts severe methodological hazards, starting with the recognition that in the discursive arena, all representations are simulacra: representations not traceable to a fixed origin to serve as an anchor for meaning.[1] Thus, the exact meaning of a complex symbol like "eros" is not pre-given, but fluid, dynamic, and contested. When this condition of interpretive "open-endedness" is taken into account, representational struggles over who, exactly, shape the meaning of discursive eros within any given historical period must emerge as a vital category of analysis. Such a *political* analysis will be particularly revealing, since eros as an educational principle refers to a set of epistemological qualities which inform the deepest wellsprings of identity formation. The representational power to name eros positively or negatively, or to permit it to go unnamed and undiscussed is surely an exercise of immense power, containing profound implications for how identity is imagined and learned. In this chapter, among other questions, we shall consider the educational and political implications of representing one definition and valuation of eros over alternative definitions and valuations. The main site of analysis for assessing these interpretive conflicts over the meaning of eros will be the Garden of Eden myth in the pivotal fourth century C.E., when the positive value of eros was institutionally denied.[2]

Within the Western intellectual tradition, the fourth century C.E. represents a sharp discontinuity in the discursive career of eros. During this time a shift occurred which transformed eros from a concept with positive associations to a concept with purely negative ones. As a result of Augustine's powerful influence, the symbolic currency of eros was actively disappeared and driven into the realm of the *unnamed*, while at the same time, many of its associated qualities were severely distanced and objectified as both evil and feminine. Augustine was successful in dividing concepts of love into separable categories: eros (as bad) was sharply distinguished from agape (as good). In this way, the Bishop of Hippo played a crucial role in institutionalizing an ethical hierarchy of love.[3] At the basis of Augustine's hierarchy is the assumption that eros and agape are in fact separable, and that in evaluating these two valences of love, eros is assumed to be inferior owing to its association with the body and its connection to the condition of permanent questioning. Here eros is coded as a dangerous power, signaling the *absence* of ontological closure, while agape offers a divinely-inspired release from the tensions wrought by eros, the interminably incomplete. To permit Eve to go unpunished for her "defiant transgression" of seizing the apple, Augustine reasoned, would be to privilege eros and all the "appetitive" and earthbound qualities it stood for. As the original sinner (bracketing Lilith, for the moment), Eve would have to learn not to enquire into things she was instructed not to enquire into.

Eros's discursive devaluation and marginalization is readily observed in Augustine's interpretation of the Garden of Eden myth. This story was to become the rich symbolic terrain out of which the bishop successfully institutionalized the notion of "original sin," a doctrinal move that was to carry vast consequences for Western understandings of what it means to be a "woman" and a "man" as well as a "citizen" in a "state." In appraising the devaluation of eros from the standpoint of political analysis it is worth noting that eros was devalued precisely at a time when an unprecedented church/state alliance had emerged in 313 C.E. This institutional convergence gradually resulted in the exercise of greater levels of disciplinary social power, powers which would expand Augustine's ability to map (and enforce) the boundaries of a new type of ascetic, "confessing" self.[4]

I argue that the mutually reinforcing systems of patriarchy (as the "rule of the fathers") and the "banking" system of education are symbolically anchored in Augustine's interpretation of the Garden of Eden. By re-examining the Garden of Eden myth, we can illuminate the ways in which the pedagogical meanings of this symbolic landscape are "written into" our present-day educational and political culture. I want to render these accepted pedagogical meanings problematic and show how different interpretations of this educational landscape may result in radically different attitudes toward specific civic qualities, such as obedience, rebellion, and whether or not it is a good thing to question authority.

Specifically, I explore the ways in which different interpretations of the Garden of Eden myth throw valuable light on contested images of eros and how these contradictory interpretations, each in their own way, offer insight into the construction of individual and collective identity. Owing to the work of Elaine Pagels, who has translated various Gnostic texts from the first three centuries of the common era, we can glimpse alternative interpretations of the Garden of Eden. The recently unearthed "Nag Hammadi" texts offer contemporary readers an opportunity to imagine completely different interpretations of this foundational myth. Reading these remarkable Gnostic interpretations, one is compelled to ask: Why *isn't* Eve interpreted as a symbol of *spiritual awakening*? Why all the sinister associations with woman? Since most Gnostics praised and revered Eve, it is particularly instructive that these same Gnostics would eventually be violently suppressed by the ascendant Christian orthodoxy. In revisiting these long-forgotten Gnostic texts, I do not intend to signal unqualified support for their interpretations, but rather, I believe that these alternative accounts of Eve in the Garden of Eden serve to loosen the hold that the Augustinian interpretation still maintains on the western social imaginary. By loosening this hold, we pry open space for imagining alternative views of eros.

I submit that the dominant, Augustinian interpretation of the Garden of Eden myth can be usefully read as a pedagogical metaphor, as a "reigning paradigm" which shapes and informs contemporary educational and political thought and practice far more than we may realize. However, because this mythic structure refers to the deep past, it is difficult to identify its active presence and influence within our educational and political culture. Despite these difficulties, the effort to identify and understand the ways in which various Edenic narratives are installed in contemporary educational and political thought is necessary if we hope to transcend today's hegemonic conception of eros. I argue that alternative forms of civic identity based on a posthegemonic conception of American identity need to be consciously and explicitly de-linked from the logic of this foundational myth. In his *Augustinian Imperative*, William Connolly describes the Garden of Eden myth as a symbolic field rich in hermeneutic value:

> If the core myths help both to consolidate the cultural unconscious and to hold it up as a mirror in which we observe ourselves, the biblical story of Genesis, as a story of the very first "founding," may remain the most important story to read, reread, and work on in the West.[5]

The following analysis is an effort to "read, reread, and work on" how selected aspects of this myth encode present understandings of eros and education, and how these understandings could be radically different. In mapping the ascendance of agape and the simultaneous decline of eros, special attention is focused on Augustine's conversion experience as expressed in his *Confessions*, and on his interpretation of the Garden of Eden in *The City of God.*

Interpretations of the Garden of Eden myth before the fourth century were multivalent, and thus, no single meaning was imposed. But this open interpretive climate, once characterized by a toleration of ambiguity, was suddenly transformed into a one-dimensional anti-erotic posture after the fourth century. The symbolic shift is illustrated most decisively by the practical end to the debates about the meaning of the Genesis account of the Garden of Eden. Augustine's successful effort to institutionalize the concept of original sin and vanquish oppositional voices represents a shift of tectonic proportions insofar as "setting" the boundaries of Western identity is concerned. Such a doctrinal move was part of a larger project to corral or destroy the diverse sects which comprised early Christianity.

In the period after 313 C.E., the Roman emperor Constantine gave state sanction to various religious sects identifying themselves as Christian. The ascendant "Church Fathers" saw the need to establish new levels of theological and political unity. Soon the diversity which characterized early Christian social reality came to be seen as anathema to the very existence of the Church. The social cohesion these leaders sought could only be accomplished by drawing new boundaries between orthodox and heretic, Christian and pagan. The Gnostics, for example, posed a grave threat to Church stability on the grounds that they were too experiential and anti-institutional in their spirituality to care about the bureaucratization of truth. As Elaine Pagels shows in her translation and commentary on the Gnostic texts, many Gnostic Christians interpreted the Garden of Eden myth and the value of Eve in ways which directly challenged the rising social power of the church/state alliance. By recovering the intensity of conflict, ambiguity, and contestation which defines this foundational myth of origins, Pagels helps to reopen the debate about the codification of the New Testament canon of texts.

Pagels discusses the implications that the Nag Hammadi recovery holds for us today, something which promises to inspire new ways of thinking about, identifying, and evaluating the core myths underpinning contemporary culture:

> Had they been discovered 1,000 years earlier, the gnostic texts almost certainly would have been burned for their heresy. But they remained hidden until the twentieth century, when our own cultural experience gave us a new perspective on the issues they raise. Today we read them with different eyes, not merely as "madness and blasphemy" but as Christians in the first centuries experienced them—a powerful alternative to what we know as orthodox Christian tradition. Only now are we beginning to consider the questions with which they confront us.[6]

The Garden of Eden Revisited: Surveying the Anti-Erotic Interpretation

Obviously, the Genesis account in the Old Testament contains a great number of symbolic motifs which could be interpreted from many viewpoints. The scope of my analysis, however, is limited to only a few motifs displayed within the Garden of Eden story. Within this limited purview, "Eve" is the central focus, since for Augustine, she personifies the power of eros. The dominant but not hegemonic interpretations during the first centuries tended to emphasize the idea that the book of Genesis in general, and the Garden of Eden in particular, signified moral freedom and responsibility. During this time a diversity of interpretations of the Garden of Eden flourished. The idea that Eve was a sinister figure had not yet gained wide acceptance. By the fourth century, however, the seizure of the apple was suddenly coded pejoratively, providing demonstrated evidence of humanity's "original sin."

How to account for these dramatic shifts in interpretation? Pagels outlines these interpretive tensions and links them to underlying socio-political factors:

> From these explorations I came to see that for nearly the first four hundred years of our era, Christians regarded *freedom* as the primary message of Genesis: freedom in its many forms, including free will. Freedom from demonic powers, freedom from social and sexual obligations, freedom from tyrannical government and from fate; and self-mastery as the source of such freedom. With Augustine this message changed...In a world in which Christians not only were free to follow their faith but were officially encouraged to do so, Augustine came to read the story of Adam and Eve very differently than had the majority of his Jewish and Christian predecessors. What they had read for centuries as a story of human freedom became, in his hands, a story of human bondage. (*Adam*, xxvi)

This passage flags attention once more to the Augustinian shift, a shift that was to have enormous consequences for the discursive value of eros, for the value of the feminine, and for the West's emerging political culture.

Under his official aegis, Bishop of Hippo, Augustine thus transformed a multidimensional story of human freedom into a one-dimensional site for discipline and control. If one accepts the basis of Augustine's view that human beings are inherently sinful (that they cannot not sin), it becomes less difficult, indeed welcome and necessary, to accommodate oneself to an external authority, to the judgment of a power outside oneself. The effects of this new code of externalizing authority would eventually become internalized as a set of personality traits entrenched in what Connolly refers to as the "cultural unconscious." These personality traits are manifest today as a chronic absence of curiosity, as a readiness to locate the source of knowledge outside oneself, and as a devaluation of the body and of feminine qualities generally. These general characteristics, I believe, grow in large measure out of the Augustinian interpretation of the Garden of Eden. The King James version of Genesis reads:

> Now the serpent was more subtle than any other wild creature that the Lord God had made. He said to the woman, Did God say, "You shall not eat of any tree of

the Garden?" And the woman said to the serpent, "We may eat of the fruit of the trees of the Garden; but God said, 'You shall not eat of the fruit of the tree which is in the midst of the garden, neither shall you touch it, lest you die.'" But the serpent said to the woman, "You shall not die. For God knows that when you eat of it your eyes will be opened, and you will be like God, knowing good and evil." So when the woman saw that the tree was good for food, and that it was a delight to the eyes, and the tree was to be desired to make one wise, she took of its fruit and ate; and she also gave some to her husband, and he ate. Then the eyes of both were opened, and they knew they were naked; and they sewed fig leaves together and made aprons. (3:1–8 KJV)

For Augustine, the "disobedience" Eve displays becomes the act which expels humanity from "Paradise." From that point on, according to Augustine's literal reading, humanity was forever infected with original sin, transferred generation after generation through the vehicle of semen. As is well known, Augustine regularly expressed contempt for embodied existence (*contemptus mundus*): "I was the prisoner of this disease of the flesh...In this way my soul's disease was fed and kept alive."[7] The rigid separation he constructed between "the world" and "God" compelled Augustine to despise his body and the world. Karl Jaspers refers to the "radical contradiction" in Augustine's world-view, a view which ardently loves God but hates the world.[8] Since eros represents, among other things, embodied desire, we can already detect how Augustine's theology of the fall is predicated on an anti-erotic, if not misogynist, ideology. Pagels describes the tremendous political advantage the doctrine of the fall would have for both Church and State:

> The declarations of the African synods, engineered primarily by Augustine and his associates, signaled a major turning point in the history of Western Christianity. They offered to the bishop of Rome and to his imperial patrons a clear demonstration of the political efficacy of Augustine's doctrine of the fall. By insisting that humanity, ravaged by sin, now lies helplessly in need of outside intervention, Augustine's theory could not only validate secular power but justify as well the imposition of church authority—by force, if necessary—as essential for human salvation. (*Adam*, 125)

Once the assumption was made that human beings were inherently depraved, a corresponding imperative was invented to develop systems of control to check "unauthorized" modes of behavior and to begin shaping a new kind of man, the confessing, ascetic self. If my thesis is correct, namely, that Edenic narratives are sequestered within the contemporary educational culture, it is reasonable to expect that these influences would reproduce codes, norms, and other cultural dispositions designed to "save people from themselves" via well-rationalized and sacrosanct ideologies of obedience. To explore this question further, let us briefly examine the origins of both civic identity and public education in the United States to determine if such social characteristics and values were indeed present at the creation, so to speak.

Civic Identity, Critical Pedagogy, and the Edenic Narrative

If one were to fast-forward chronologically from the fourth to the eighteenth centuries for the purpose of examining the dominant assumptions the founders of the American state made about the nature of human nature, democracy, and the capacity of ordinary people to be educated, it is clear the dominating voices of the elite class who functioned as architects of civic identity were speaking within an Edenic, Augustinian paradigm. The framers of the 1791 Constitution were explicit about their fears of losing control and their distrust of the common man and the haunting spectre of democracy. The "common man" and "democracy" were collapsed into one as representing the same basic threat. Indeed, these interconnected fears, far more than other contributing factors, are what propelled the second constitution into existence, providing the major impetus to restructure the organization of power and sovereignty to check and divide the "unruly" democratic processes emergent in the wake of 1776.[9]

James Madison, in Federalist Paper 10, employs a nature discourse to suggest that the universal human being he has in mind is not fundamentally good or educable, but rather has an inherent, quasi-evil humanity which does not permit anything but a Hobbesian condition of brutish, unremitting conflict. Madison writes: "the latent causes of faction are sown in the nature of man."[10] This view explains the human problem of social conflict as something caused or brought about by "nature," an explanation which conveniently removes class conflict from the domain of politics and history. Rather than seeing the causes of faction rooted in a vertical, anti-democratic structure of power maintained by force, as was obviously the case in his context, Madison prefers to locate the cause in the "incurable" nature of man. In doing so, he provides vested institutional interests with the necessary justification for strong authoritarian government. This is the case because the human being becomes defined by its powerlessness to change; hence its need to be controlled and managed by external authorities. Since the corrupted nature of ordinary people cannot be altered and is impervious to human intervention and reconceptualization, it represents a profoundly anti-democratic definition of human potential. Within this view, human beings have no capacity to learn or to transcend limits.

Such assumptions about human nature, although presented as universally valid, were not universally shared, even among the elites. Thomas Jefferson, for example, in an oft-repeated passage, responded to this dominant assumption by declaring: "I know of no safe repository of the ultimate powers of society but the people themselves, and if we think them not enlightened enough to exercise their control with a wholesome discretion, the remedy is not to take it from them but to *inform their discretion*" (emphasis added).[11] The historical production of American civic identity is thus a pedagogical site of intense contestation in which elite and radical democratic conceptions of citizenship vie for primacy. The point here is that "informing one's discretion" is the essential project of democratic education, and since the dominant republican model of civic identity rejects the idea that such an education can happen in the first place, educators need to expose its anti-democratic underpinnings.

As Richard Hofstadter and other noted historians have shown, the Constitutional framers explicitly, repeatedly, and passionately denounced democracy and democratic conceptions of citizenship.[12] What they favored was a starkly different republican model of citizenship, one in which the citizen was envisioned as a *"loyal subject,"* in the words of Sheldon Wolin.[13] Because the republican model of citizenship prevailed over the democratic model (represented by the moral and democratic ideals of the Declaration of Independence), democratic civic identity in the United States was bound to atrophy within the new and heavily centralized structure of governance which emerged from the Constitution. Wolin further argues that the presidential form adopted by the framers represented a kind of *"monarchy above politics,"* a *"father figure"* that would serve as an accessible symbol of unity. In his critique of American civic identity, Wolin contends that "in short, a citizenry was conceived in terms that allowed the American political animal to evolve into the *domesticated creature* of media politics." An invigorated democratic conception of civic identity, according to Wolin, "will require a citizen who fulfills his or her civic role by doing something other than *passively supporting those in authority"* (emphasis added).[14]

The analyses offered by Wolin and Hofstadter and others suggest clear parallels between the Augustinian interpretation of the Garden of Eden and the constricted vision of civic identity embodied in the Constitution. They both reflect the same bleak assumptions about human possibility, assumptions which preclude the need for embarking on any genuine educational effort whatsoever. Those who wielded institutional power defined ordinary people as incurably corrupted and therefore not suited to be educated out of their miserable condition, but suited only to obediently accept the instructions given to them by their natural superiors. In each instance, these foundational narratives of identity encouraged, above all, human passivity, enabling those in power to effectively manage the construction of meaning and identity in ways which benefited their vested interests.

The ideological imperative for *schooling passivity* was successfully encoded within the institution of public education during the nineteenth century. Despite some advances since then, the same basic imperative still reigns today, particularly for poor people of color. For quite some time, the liberal discourse celebrated the origin and development of public schooling in America as an unambiguous vehicle of equality, democracy, and progress. However, works such as Colin Greer's *The Great School Legend*, Bowles and Gintis's *Schooling in Capitalist America*, and Michael Katz's *Class, Bureaucracy, and Schools*, among others, all go a long distance toward resituating our perception of the origin and development of public schooling in America.[15] I believe the conservative direction of public school education that we see today reinforces their original arguments. That is to say, there exists a structural flaw within the dominant educational paradigm which liberal reform measures cannot rectify because class inequality constitutes the very structure of liberal capitalism. Accepting and extending this argument, I want to show how the liberal paradigm is also shaped by important symbolic and mythic associations in addition to its basis in economic class.

The scholarship noted above demonstrates that the movement toward a comprehensive public school system cannot be understood apart from the instrumental goal of producing an obedient labor force and implanting disciplinary values upon an increasingly restive urban proletariat in the northeast United States. As is well known, Horace Mann was forced to appeal to the rich in order to obtain the necessary funding for launching the common school movement. Today, corporate, profit-driven purposes and values continue to eclipse the education of alternative forms of "common sense" in which the purpose of public schooling is defined as that which promotes democratic civic education. Employing a discourse almost identical to Mann's, Daniel Webster wrote that public education is a "wise and liberal system of police by which property, and life, and the peace of society are secured."[16] Consistent with the attempt to insulate classrooms from exhibiting any trace of "Eve" (read: eros), educational historians show how women teachers in the nineteenth century had to be unmarried and virginal so as not to corrupt their students with the idea that they were sexual beings. Starting in the twentieth century, however, as gender-anxieties changed somewhat, women teachers then had to be married so as not to lead their students into temptation (either way, the objective was the same: to de-eroticize the classroom space).[17] In surveying nineteenth-century writings about the purposes of public schooling, such themes as *obedience, authority, police*, the threat of *internal commotions*, and the *protection of property* emerge as the central pattern of concern. The preoccupation with class-based and gender-based security during the founding moments of public schooling reveals the existence of an Edenic discourse of danger. These brief examples are far from exhaustive, yet they bespeak the presence of an underlying Augustinian imperative.

Christopher Lasch has written a trenchant analysis of Horace Mann and the origins of public schooling in America. Sympathetic yet critical, Lasch persuasively contends that Mann was a progressive "visionary" who should not be so easily dismissed as a political reactionary. Yet, even while recognizing his nobler intentions, Lasch offers a rather devastating epistemological critique of Mann's educational philosophy, aptly summarized by the subtitle of his essay, "Horace Mann and the Assault on Imagination."[18] Based on Lasch's analysis, it is clear that Mann's thought leads inexorably to the depoliticization and de-eroticization of the classroom space.

Because he believed so deeply that schools should be insulated from worldly controversy and any kind of political knowledge, Mann unwittingly recapitulates a Garden of Eden narrative by insisting that students must be protected against forms of knowledge which would induce their inevitable corruption. Lasch asserts:

Reading these passages, one begins to see that Mann wanted to keep politics out of the school not only because he was afraid that his system would be torn apart by those who wished to use it for partisan purposes but because he distrusted political activity as such. It produced an "inflammation of the passions." It generated controversy—a necessary part of education, it might be argued, but in Mann's eyes a waste of time and energy. Anything controversial was to be passed over in silence or, at best, with the admonition that "the schoolroom is neither the tribunal to adjudicate, nor the forum to discuss it."[19]

The institutionalization of Mann's educational logic, as an outgrowth of the Puritan world view, resulted in the severe de-privileging of affective learning, a development which atrophied the potential of democratic civic education. The classroom Mann envisioned was, by design, an emotionally arid one. Is it not disturbing that the chief architect of public schooling in America would have his educational philosophy described as an "assault on imagination"? Introducing controversy and passion and contestation in the classroom to provoke students to viscerally feel the moral and political principles at stake in the public issues of the day, represents an approach which is the very basis of critical pedagogy. But the value of inquiry is in no way encouraged within the dominant interpretation of the Garden of Eden or within Mann's classroom space; it is, rather, a quality met with stern punishment. To borrow from Freire's vocabulary, Mann lays the foundation for the banking method of education:

What is even worse is the way in which his bland tutelage deprived children of anything that might have appealed to the imagination or—to use his own term—"the passions." Political history, taught along the lines recommended by Mann, would be drained of controversy, sanitized, bowdlerized, and therefore drained of excitement. It would become mild, innocuous, and profoundly boring, trivialized by a suffocating didacticism.[20]

Although some might claim that this bias against passion and controversy has been overcome today, my experience in teaching high school and as a faculty member in a school of education suggests otherwise. Secondary textbooks, of course, are the most egregious examples of how politics and passion are systematically erased from the educational experience. The functional relationship between passion and democracy should no longer be ignored. Since the interminable process of "conscientization" is defined by a heightened awareness of the internal and external contradictions perceived in one's social reality, it follows that conflict and tension must be present within the learner in order to generate the necessary energy to propel consciousness upward, toward the perception of larger connections and higher unities. In this way, love in the form of eros is implicit in the process of *conscientization.*

As an abolitionist, pacifist, and social reformer, Mann was only too aware of the contradictions searing the fabric of American culture prior to the Civil War. Yet, sounding a lot like the Bishop of Hippo, such topics were "forbidden" from entering the public sphere of the classroom. This prohibition is consistent with the logic employed by the founders in their original design of American political identity. Eros=Knowledge=Danger. Immune from conflict, passion, and the ambiguities of political discourse, Mann envisioned the classroom as an Edenic space, existing apart from history and politics in a timeless realm of innocence.

Based on these shared symbolic patterns, albeit centuries apart in history, it's reasonable to contend that the foundational principles of American education and political identity grow out of a view of human nature exemplified in Augustine's interpretation of the Garden of Eden.

To pursue these connections, let us return to the text of Genesis and ask ourselves why Augustine condemned Eve for her "transgression." Why would an act of curiosity on Eve's part, a quest for knowledge, be so vigorously coded as evil? As discussed in chapter 1, it will be recalled that eros is elicited by one's ethical relation to one's ignorance, manifesting itself as a desire to know. Eros propels the process of questioning and functions as a catalyst in the interminable quest for knowledge. When Augustine defines Eve's quest for knowledge as evil, he repudiates the value of eros. Denying Eve space for the unfolding of her desire for knowledge *means* the denial of eros.

Pedagogically, Augustine lays the deep-structure for the banking pardigm of education.[21] In this framework, knowledge is located externally as in some static edifice, and education becomes a process whereby students habitually receive deposits of information from their all-knowing teachers, creating the conditions in which passivity is systematically schooled into the consciousness of students. The kind of open inquiry and restless searching which people require to develop into autonomous beings cannot readily occur within the logic of the banking system.

> "Have you eaten of the tree of which I commanded you not to eat?" The man said, "The woman whom thou gavest to be with me, she gave me the fruit of the tree and I ate." Then the Lord God said to the woman, "What is this that you have done?" The woman said, "the serpent beguiled me, and I ate." (Gen. 3:16 KJV)

In this pedagogical moment, the knowledge of the difference between good and evil—the kind of knowledge God seems to have, but which Eve desires—becomes a quality of knowing strictly off-limits to her. Significantly, Eve defies the received wisdom that there is a structure of knowledge organized vertically, beyond her lowly grasp. Eve's action suggests that knowledge is not organized vertically but horizontally, permitting her to attain knowledge on her own without prior external authorization. Her defiance provokes one God to anger:

> To the woman he said, "I will greatly multiply your pain in childrearing; in pain you shall bring forth children, yet your desire shall be for your husband, and he should rule over you." (Gen. 3:16 KJV)

The motifs of discipline, punishment, and habitual reception of imposed knowledge coalesce to form a social imaginary easily accommodated to external authority. As a pedagogical text, the dominant interpretation of the Garden of Eden is a prescription for developing *heteronomous* modes of being; that is, modes of being in which one lives according to rules set by an external authority.[22] The normalization of these cultural codes function to construct identities informed by a readiness to obey, a chronic absence of curiosity, a lack of passion, and thus a general restriction of both human agency and democratic forms of culture.

Who is Eve? What psychological qualities does her motivation symbolize? Before our inquiry turns to an analysis of the Gnostic interpretations of the meaning of Eve, it may be useful to take a closer look at why Augustine interpreted Eve's act as morally bankrupt. Instead of signifying an act of empowerment, Augustine views the taking of the apple as evidence of a dangerous "ontological conceit."[23] Eve symbolizes a kind of self against which Augustine was trying to cohere a new Christian identity. Specifically, Augustine criticized the pagan self for regarding itself as the ground of its own existence. In the *City of God*, he writes:

> Our first parents fell into open disobedience because already they were secretly corrupted; for the evil act had never been done had not an evil will preceded it. And what is the origin of our evil will but pride? And what is pride but the craving for undue exaltation? And this is undue exaltation when the soul abandons Him to whom it ought to cleave as its end, and becomes a kind of end to itself. The devil, then, would not have ensnared man in the open and manifest sin of doing what God had forbidden, had not man already begun to live for himself. It was this that made him listen with pleasure to the words, "Ye shall be as Gods," which they would have much more readily accomplished by obediently adhering to their supreme and true end by proudly living to themselves.[24]

In the context of the fourth-century Roman Empire, Augustine's project was to defend against the charge by non-Christians that the widening Christian movement was the main reason why the Roman Empire was in decline. *The City of God* was written to turn this accusation on its head. Augustine tried to accomplish this by identifying the polytheist/atheist pagan culture as the prime culprit for the moral decline of Rome. Augustine's great ambition was to institute a whole new form of selfhood, one that would be monotheistic, ascetic, confessing, and not prone to self-aggrandizement, in the sense that one would not forget that the ground of existence is anchored in God, not Man. Augustine ultimately bases his theological and political thought on a crucial distinction he makes between different types of desire and love.

The term Augustine uses to describe a pejorative form of desire, *concupiscence*, is the governing principle for the heathens who inhabit the City of the World (*Civitas Terrena*), a metaphorical space which he distinguishes from those who inhabit the City of God (*Civitas Dei*). In this view, there are two fundamental types of love intrinsic to each realm: *cupiditas* (amor mundi) as love of the world, and *caritas* (amor dei) as love of God. Augustine:

> Accordingly, two cities have been formed by two loves: the earthly by love of the self, even to the contempt of god; the heavenly by the love of god, even to the contempt of self. The former, in a word, glories in itself, the latter in the Lord. (*CG*, 14.13)

In this formulation, two modes of love are constructed as ontologically separable. This theme will be further explored when Augustine's conversion experience is discussed. While it is problematic to simply equate *eros* with *cupiditas* without taking note of certain distinctions, these valences of love can also be plausibly compared. Because of the dualism of good and evil which Augustine constructs between World and God, eros/cupiditas can generally be seen as allied forms of "worldly" love neither of which, in Augustine's thinking, contain any final ontological value.

According to Augustine, Eve failed to recognize that the moral geography of the Garden was rightfully organized on a vertical basis, and thus she should have renounced the possibility of authoring her own knowledge within the *Civitas Terrena*, in favor of receiving a morally superior knowledge, located outside and beyond, in the *Civitas Dei*. In the absence of an authoritative command not to disobey, not to confuse the two realms, Augustine was convinced that human beings, like the pagans he criticized, would inevitably forget the real ground of their own being and drift into godless narcissism. Augustine condemned Gnostics who advocated the blasphemous idea that God could be discovered or known from within. Gnostics rejected the notion that God could be so neatly separated from "this world" or from one's soul.

The reason the contradiction between the Augustinian and Gnostic understandings of Eve is crucial for critical pedagogy is that the dispute underscores two radically different definitions of eros. If one embraces the Augustinian view, then the eros which Eve embodied by seizing the forbidden fruit is a bad thing. Such a view implicitly supports a top-down, paternalistic, banking method of education. If, on the other hand, one favors the Gnostic view that Eve's transgression was a good thing, a symbol of spiritual awakening, such a view implicitly supports a problem-posing, horizontally-based, critical pedagogy grounded in inquiry. One of the key pedagogical principles at stake here, I believe, is the value which ought to be attached to questioning. There is no explicitly encouraged questioning within the banking model of education, nor is this value built into one of its contemporary technologies of control, *performance-based outcomes*; in contrast, the invitation to question defines problem-posing pedagogy, an approach which results in forms of knowledge that defy quantification.

Paradise Abandoned, Eros Recovered: Surveying the Gnostic Interpretations

For roughly 1,600 years the only knowledge we had of the Gnostics was obtained through Christian theologians who denounced them as heretics.[25] Representing a strong alternative to the nascent orthodoxy, the Gnostics prompted Church Fathers to draw clear and unambiguous boundaries between "true" Christians and other heretic sects. A central marker used to enable this boundary-drawing practice was whether or not one accepted the correct view of the meaning of Eve's intrepid behavior. The discovery at Nag Hammadi gives us the opportunity to evaluate Gnostic interpretations of the Garden of Eden directly, unmediated by their heavily vested opponents.

As Pagels makes clear in *The Gnostic Gospels* and *Adam, Eve, and the Serpent*, the Gnostics elude easy definition. The designation "Gnostic" stems from the Greek term *gnosis*, meaning "knowledge" or "insight."[26] One unifying feature of Gnostic theology was their emphasis on personal experience as the basis of the most genuine form of knowledge, knowledge acquired not so much by reason and abstract conceptualization as by experiencing the intuition of the mystery of the self. In this view, the human unconscious becomes consubstantial with the "Godhead," an ineffable entity which could be described metaphorically as a "divine spark" latent in the depths of one's being.[27] Mere belief in God was not enough for the Gnostics, they sought experiential encounter with the divine mystery, unalloyed by the gloss of doctrine. This stance put them on a collision course with the new hierarchy that was being constructed, a hierarchy whose power increasingly rested on the legitimacy of these new forms of church bureaucracy.

Gnostic Christians were suspicious of orthodox Christians who interpreted the Scriptures literally. Gnostics pointed out that the Garden of Eden story is rife with contradiction. For example, when God said, "You shall not eat of the tree of knowledge of good and evil, for on the day you eat of it you shall surely die," Gnostics noticed that Eve and Adam had indeed lived after this alleged transgression. Was God lying, they asked? Similar examples demonstrated to Gnostics that Genesis should be understood allegorically. Pagels describes the Gnostic hermeneutic approach:

> Certain Gnostic Christians suggested that such absurdities show that the story was never meant to be taken literally but should be understood as spiritual allegory—not so much history with a moral as myth with meaning. These Gnostics took each line of the Scriptures as an enigma, a riddle pointing to a deeper meaning. Read this way, the text became a shimmering surface of symbols, inviting the spiritually adventurous to explore its hidden depths, to draw upon their own inner experience—what artists call the creative imagination—to interpret this story. Consequently, gnostic Christians neither sought nor found any consensus concerning what the story meant but regarded Genesis 1-3 rather like

a fugal melody upon which they continually improvised new variations, all of which, Bishop Irenaenus said, were "full of blasphemy." (*Adam,* 63-64)

By celebrating ambiguity, the Gnostic allegorical method unsettles the orthodox boundaries between God and Self. This way of knowing diminishes the meaning of the Paradise/Fall idea, for this trope is predicated on a moral epistemology which denies worldly knowledge a place in the sacred. By disenchanting the world of its sacredness, the discursive value of eros was bound to evaporate, since eros represents, among other things, worldly desire. Because Gnostics called the orthodox separation between God and Human into deep question, the very foundation of the Paradise/Fall motif was severely undermined. From a Gnostic perspective, the orthodox telos of Paradise *lost* and *found* denied to the present moment the fullness of meaning it deserved. By embracing the *ultimate* value of the embodied present, Gnostics *abandoned* the Paradise idea, and by doing so, pried open space for privileging eros.

Further in line with the abandonment of Paradise, Gnostics rejected the concept of sin, original or otherwise, as the most important cause of suffering. Rather, they considered ignorance—lack of self-knowledge—as the central cause of suffering. Perhaps one of the most astonishing texts is the *Gospel of Philip*, where an unknown writer refers to the source of divinity in terms which must have horrified the custodians of truth working within the emerging Catholic hierarchy:

In the beginning, God created humanity. But now humanity creates God. This is the story of the world—human beings invent Gods and worship their creation. It would be more fitting for the gods to worship human beings. (quoted in *Adam,* 65)

Such allegorical interpretations threatened orthodox Christians and led to the violent suppression and erasure of Gnostic culture. In response to these types of "Christian" interpretations, Irenaeus compiled a five-volume treatise, *Refutation and Overthrow of Falsely So-Called Gnosis,* to argue that Gnostic teaching necessarily leads its followers to "an abyss of madness and blasphemy."[28]

Nowhere was this abyss of madness and blasphemy more evident than in the Gnostic readings of the Garden of Eden story. Most Gnostics saw this story as a psychological map describing the journey of individuals who experience a radical transformation of consciousness. On this reading, Eve becomes a symbol of spiritual awakening: eating the apple sparks an agentic process toward fuller humanization and self-knowledge. According to this narrative, the angry-god syndrome does not exist. Gnostic texts repeatedly show how Adam, as psyche, recognized the power of Eve, as spirit, to awaken them both to the world. One of these texts, "Reality of the Rulers," exemplifies Gnostic mythology:

> After the day of rest, Sophia (wisdom) sent Zoe (life), her daughter, who is called Eve, as an instructor to raise up Adam. When Eve saw Adam cast down, she pitied him, and said, "Adam, live! Rise up upon the earth!" Immediately her word became deed. For when Adam rose up, he opened his eyes. When he saw her, he said, "It is you who have given me life: you shall be called the Mother of the Living, Eve; for it is she who is my Mother. It is she who is the physician, and the woman, and She Who Has Given Birth." (quoted in *Adam*, 66)

In this remarkable reversal of meaning, Eve's "transgression" is transformed into a symbol of spiritual power. No longer a sinister act of original sin, here Eve represents the redemptive power of embodied knowledge. For all of these reasons cited, the Gnostic interpretations are eros-friendly inasmuch as they refer to the value of embodied knowledge, to the here and now, to the value of the feminine, and to the questioning process which permeates the mythic landscape. Pagels elucidates these patterns of Gnostic interpretation:

> The majority of known Gnostic texts depict Adam (not Eve) as representing the psyche, while Eve represents the higher principle, the spiritual self. Gnostic authors loved to tell with many variations, the story of Eve, that elusive spiritual intelligence: how she first emerged with Adam and awakened him, the soul, to awareness of its spiritual nature; how she encountered resistance, was

misunderstood, attacked, and mistaken for what she was not; and how she finally joined Adam in marriage, so to speak. (*Adam*, 66)

The serpent's symbolic currency is also greatly enhanced by the gnostic improvisational spirit. In *Reality of the Rulers*, the spirit which Eve personifies appears momentarily *within* the serpent for the pedagogical purpose of reconnecting Adam to Eve, psyche to spirit:

Then the Female Spiritual Principle came in the Snake, the Instructor; and it taught them, saying, "What did he say to you?" Was it, "From every tree in the Garden shall you sing; yet—from the tree of recognizing evil and good do not eat"? The carnal Woman said, "Not only did he say 'Do not Eat', but even, 'Do not touch it; for the day you eat from it, with death you are going to die.'" And the Snake, the Instructor, said, "With death you shall not die; for it was out of jealousy that he said this to you. Rather your eyes will open and you shall come to be like the gods, recognizing good and evil." And the Female Instructing Principle was taken away from the snake, and she left it behind. (*Adam*, 67)

In reading these passages, one can hardly avoid speculating what the dominant conception of selfhood in the West would look like today had the Gnostic world view been more integrated into Western culture. These long-lost yet now recovered Gnostic voices are valuable for many reasons. One main reason is that the high value attached to Eve stands in stark contrast to what became the dominant view of the feminine in the West. Considering that the devaluation of the feminine almost always means a devaluation of eros, we need to recover those voices which offer positive images of Eve. Such a recovery is necessary in order to grasp the conceptual overlap between eros and gender.

The notion of a "female instructing principle" also finds expression in another Gnostic text, "The Secret Book of John." In this text, Eve is referred to as the "perfect primal intelligence." In one passage Eve explains her identity: "I am the thinking of the virginal spirit... Arise and remember...and follow your root, which is I...and beware of the deep sleep" (quoted in *Adam*, 68). Here a pedagogical element is central to Eve's identity. Of course, the meaning of the concept, "I am the thinking of the virginal spirit," is open to interpretation, but it seems to refer to a quality of being which is aware of itself as processual, as something not bound by past patterns of thinking and systems of value. The pedagogical refrain, "beware of the deep sleep" is presented as the opposite of the virginal spirit, leading us to speculate that if Eve did not seize the apple, she would lose her virginal spirit, lose an awareness of self as a situated, yet ever *moving* process.

These various manifestations of Eve and/or the Serpent, as facets of soul, represent the psychological forces animating the process of self-emergence. However, within the Augustinian interpretive frame, since what is called for is the passive reception of knowledge from above, these inquiring dimensions of experience are preempted from unfolding, a symbolic economy that reflects an anti-erotic bias. In contrast, by focusing on the meaning of the Garden in terms of psychological processes of transformation, the Gnostics offered a fundamentally different picture of human nature from the orthodox interpretation. The differences are striking: one represses the value of the feminine, the other embraces it; one treats the value of obedience as an end in itself and warns against the acquisition of worldly knowledge, while the other is constituted by its possibilities, referring to self-knowledge as an interminable quest; one denigrates the value of eros, the other is infused with its power and promise. The anti-erotic/erotic dichotomy referred to earlier to mark the so-called Augustinian shift grows out of these broadly defined differences. Sequestered inside both of these interpretations are different conceptions of identity, of truth, and what it means to be and to create a self.

Augustine, Truth, and the Eros/Agape Problematic

No genealogy of the eros concept would be sufficient without exploring in more detail why Augustine came to regard eros so negatively and agape so positively. Such a profound shift in value can be discerned not only in

Augustine's interpretation of the Garden of Eden but also in his *Confessions*. A critical assessment of his autobiography provides further insight into why Augustine developed a militant animus against eros in favor of privileging agape as a valence of love. The analysis which follows has important implications for critical pedagogy. To accept Augustine's understanding of a purely self-absorbed eros, an eros morally inferior and separable from agape, in effect, is to stay housed within Augustine's patriarchal assumptions. The purpose of this concluding section therefore is to suggest that these two key valences of love should not be seen as separable or located along an ethical hierarchy of superior and inferior.

As Peter Brown points out, Augustine had two distinct conversion experiences. His first, at age 19 (373 C.E.), came after reading Cicero's *Hortensius*, a work which instilled an intense "zeal for wisdom" in the young Augustine. The second conversion, at age 32 (386 C.E.), inaugurated his Christian identity. Ten years later, Augustine wrote the *Confessions*, and then he completed *City of God* between 413–26 C.E.[29] A comparative analysis of these two conversion experiences reveals an intriguing tension in his life's trajectory between the eros and agape motifs.

Looking back at his young adulthood, Augustine describes the impact of Cicero:

> In the ordinary course of study I came upon a book by a certain Cicero, whose tongue almost all men admire but not his heart. This work contains his exhortations to philosophy and is called *Hortensius*. This book changed all my affections. It turned all my prayers to you, Lord, and caused me to have different purposes and desires. All my vain hopes forthwith became worthless to me, and with incredible ardor of heart I desired undying wisdom. How I burned, O my God, how I burned with desire to fly away from earthly things and upwards to you, and yet I did not know what you would do with me! (*Conf.,* 3.4)

Shortly after this period, Augustine was deeply influenced by Neoplatonism. Anyone familiar with Augustine's life recognizes that although he may have ultimately rejected eros, the trajectory of his life was underwritten by its sensual, questioning, and restless spirit. The

Confessions is nothing if not a chronicle of an intense knowledge quest as it developed over a lifetime. "What then am I, O my God? What is my nature?" (*Conf.* 10.17). Or, most revealingly: "*I have become a question to myself, and that is my infirmity*" (*Conf.*, 10.33, emphasis added).

Augustine recognizes that his ontological ground is less than solid, based as it is in the process of questioning. However, instead of affirming "the questioning" as a fundamentally good condition of being, he defines the process as an "infirmity"—a defect that must be eliminated. By coupling "questioning" with "infirmity," Augustine betrays an anti-erotic bias: eros is not about completion or the cessation of tension, but just the reverse. He seems to be suggesting that while eros may have ignited the knowledge quest, by itself it cannot transport him to that domain of absolute certainty he seems to require. The limitations of Neoplatonism and eros become increasingly apparent to him in the few years preceding his second conversion:

> Then indeed I clearly saw your invisible things, understood by the things which are made, but I was unable to fix my gaze on them. In my frailty I was struck back, and I returned to my former ways. I took with me only a memory, loving and longing for what had, as it were, caught the odor of, but was not yet able to feed upon. (*Conf.*, 7.17)

With eros, it seems, Augustine can detect the scent of God, but only with agape can his ontological appetite be fully and completely sated. Augustine comes to criticize eros on the grounds that it provides no release from the tensions endemic to the human condition. As discussed in chapter 1, eros inevitably means tension: tension between the seductive *idea* and *desire* for completion, on the one hand, and the *feeling* of incompletion and lack on the other. For Augustine, Neoplatonic knowledge may have pointed toward God but it still remained permanently anchored in the soil of the *Civitas Terrena*. Augustine came to the conclusion that Neoplatonism was not appreciably different from the pagans and their "ontology of conceit":

> Now I began to desire to appear wise. Filled up with punishment of my sins, I did not weep over them, but rather was puffed up with knowledge. Where was the charity which builds upon the foundation of humility, which is Christ Jesus? When would these books teach it to me? But that the Word became flesh, and dwelt among us, I read not there. (*Conf.*, 7. 20)

Augustine believed that in order to re-assemble a new self out of the fallen world, a qualitatively different valence of love had to be identified and privileged. The qualities of charity and humility he refers to above are qualities associated with agape. Anders Nygren's influential *Agape and Eros* reinforces the argument that eros was devalued within the Augustinian system in favor of agape. This influential twentieth-century Swedish theologian did much to strengthen the ethical hierarchy dividing eros from agape. Commenting on Augustine, Nygren asserts:

> He, more than any of the Fathers of the Early Church, has given a central place to Christian love in the sense of Agape. Augustine seems to be well aware that God's love to us must be distinguished from Eros-love. God's love is a love of mercy and fullness of goodwill. Eros-love ascends and seeks the satisfaction of its needs; Agape-love descends in order to help and to give. In Neoplatonism he finds human Eros which tries to take heaven by storm, but he misses God's Agape which descends, and without which Eros cannot attain to God.[30]

The imagery attached to eros and agape as fields of energy ascending and descending fits neatly with the ethical hierarchy Augustine constructs between the *Civitas Terrena* and the *Civitas Dei*. Before attempting to unsettle this conceptual framework, however, it's important to delve further into the rationale Augustine adopts to support his interpretation.

After his Christian-based conversion, Augustine places great import on the Incarnation of Christ Jesus. For the new Christian self that was Augustine, the Incarnation provided evidence that God's love had indeed "descended" to earth in the form of agape. Only the power of agape could deflate the ontological conceit of those selves "puffed up" with the false knowledge of the *Civitas Terrena*. In Augustine's view, the privileging of this counterfeit knowledge leads human beings to an ethos of self-sufficiency, independence, and pride. Augustine's ambivalence toward eros is described by Nygren: "Neoplatonism had taught him to know God and had kindled his love of God, but it had also called forth his pride."[31] Thus, to counter these sinful tendencies, the confessing self which Augustine designs is structured to continually remind itself of its dependence on a power and knowledge external to itself, located in the *Civitas Dei*.

Significantly, the dichotomy between *Civitas Terrena* and *Civitas Dei* becomes coterminous with the separation between body and mind. In order to inhabit the *Civitas Dei*, one must first renounce the body and its desires, which are mired in the *Civitas Terrena*. Eros was dangerous to Augustine since it was a source of person-centered, embodied knowledge, while agape denotes a compassionate, unconditional form of love which "descends" from an exogenous God. In the context of the Garden of Eden, since agape descends from a source above and beyond, it's a reception of love Eve "misses" by choosing instead to author her own knowledge.

Augustine describes his second and last conversion experience in agapic terms. The agonizing tension evidenced in his earlier statement, "I have become a question to myself, and that is my infirmity," was finally resolved. Autobiographies which recount conversion experiences constitute a fascinating discursive genre. By definition, the conversion marks a discontinuity in identity. One's identity is split in two, transformed into *before* and *after* the experience. The subsequent distancing between the old self and the new is played out in a number of symbolic arenas. In Augustine's case, an analysis of these symbolic truth strategies reveals a pattern instructive to the eros/agape problematic.

Augustine was increasingly doubt-ridden in the days leading up to his conversion. By his own account, his agony over certain existential questions manifested themselves as physical symptoms of pain, including involuntary bodily movements and gesticulations (*Conf.*, 8.20). Clearly, the absence of closure to the question of being haunted Augustine!

> Ponticianus told us this story, and as he spoke, you, O Lord, turned me back upon myself. You took me from behind my own back, where I had placed myself because I did not wish to look upon myself. you stood me face to face with myself, so that I might see how foul I was, how deformed and defiled, how covered with stains and sores. I looked and I was filled with horror, but there was no place for me to flee to away from myself. If I tried to turn my gaze from myself, he still went on with the story he was telling, and once again you placed me in front of myself, and thrust me before my own eyes, so that I might find out my iniquity and hate it. I knew what it was, but pretended not to; I refused to look at it, and put it out of my memory. (*Conf.*, 8.16)

Augustine's "true" self is hidden from his sight. The self which he took to be real is shown to be false. He attempts to repress the tension generated by this ontological rift and "put it out" of memory. God thus becomes a special kind of mirror, reflecting what Augustine is (depraved) and is not (perfect). The structure of this passage illustrates the confessional mode of being which serves as a vehicle to cohere an ascetic self. Again, the body emerges as the antithesis of the sacred:

> Many, perhaps twelve, of my years had flown by since that nineteenth year when by reading Cicero's *Hortensius* I was aroused to a zeal for wisdom. Yet still I delayed to despise earthly happiness, and thus devote myself to that search…But I, a most wretched youth, most wretched from the very start of my youth, had even sought chastity from you, and had said, "Give me chastity and continence, but not yet!" For I feared that you would heal me of that disease of lust, which I wished to have satisfied rather than extinguished. *(Conf.*, 8.17)

The time for Augustine to begin despising earthly happiness was rapidly approaching. He was now prepared to quit the body, to "extinguish" its demands and enticements once and for all. Only with his renunciation of earthly, erotic attachments would he be free from his "disease." These torments provide insight into Augustine's commitment to not merely marginalize eros but to suppress any hint of value which might be associated with its wide-ranging human qualities. The dominant conception of eros today, as a devalued set of epistemological qualities, reflects a strong Augustinian influence. In *The Passionate Life*, Sam Keen describes the present-day consequences for Western culture for having institutionalized Augustine's view of eros in the pivotal fourth century:

> Had Augustine not felt so guilty for loving his mistress, the Middle Ages might have recognized that sexual feelings were one of the delightful gifts of the Creator. As it was, Christianity fell into an anti-erotic posture: glorifying virginity, degrading women, linking sex to guilt, discouraging romance, denying the flesh, casting suspicion upon sensuality. In theological terminology, this was expressed in the doctrine of the superiority of agape (which Christians defined as God-given and selfless) over eros (which they thought of as impure and lustful).[32]

With both Augustine and the banking approach to education, it appears that guilt inevitably becomes a central category of analysis. The decisive moment in Augustine's conversion came while he sat near his friend Alypius, vexed by self-division:

> But when deep reflection had dredged out of the secret recesses of my soul all my misery and heaped it up in full view of my heart, there arose a mighty storm, bringing with it a mighty downpour of tears. That I might pour it all forth with the proper sounds, I arose from Alypius's side—to be alone seemed more proper to this ordeal of weeping—and went farther apart, so that not even his presence would be a hindrance to me. I flung myself down, how I do not know, under a certain fig tree, and gave free reign to my tears. Not indeed in these words but to this effect I spoke many things to you: "And you, O Lord, how long? How long, O Lord, will you be angry forever? Remember not your past iniquities." For I felt that I was held by them, and I gasped forth these mournful words, "How long, how long? Tomorrow and tomorrow? Why not this very hour an end to my uncleanness?" (*Conf.*, 8.28)

Incredibly, at this moment, Augustine suddenly hears the melody of children singing from a nearby house: "Take up and read. Take up and read" (*Conf.*, 8. 29). Augustine tried to regain his composure and make sense out of what the children had said: "I began to think most intently whether children made use of any such chant in some kind of game, but I could not recall hearing it anywhere" (*Conf.*, 8.28). Thinking that such a message might be an echo of divine intent, Augustine promptly returned to where he had been sitting next to Alypius and saw the book of the apostle lying there:

> I snatched it up, opened it, and read in silence the chapter on which my eyes first fell: "Not in rioting and drunkenness, not in chambering and impurities, not in strife and envying; but put you on the Lord Jesus Christ, and make not provision for the flesh in its concupiscences." (*Conf.,* 8.29)

Augustine interprets this passage to mean that he should renounce his body and give himself entirely to the *Civitas Dei*. With this, God's agape descends and Augustine's conversion experience crests:

> No further wished I to read, nor was there need to do so. Instantly, in truth, at the end of this sentence, as if before a peaceful light streaming into my heart, all the dark shadows of doubt fled away. (*Conf.,* 8. 29)

The agapic dimension of this experience is captured by the phrase, "a peaceful light streaming into my heart." Recognizing this experience as conversionary, he immediately sought out his mother, Monica, to tell her the good news. For his mother, a longtime Christian who once locked her son out of the house for becoming a Manichean, news of her son's conversion represented a clear fulfillment of her earlier prophecy. He tells us, "She was filled with exaltation and triumph" (*Conf.,* 8. 30).

The tensions and ambiguities which characterized Augustine's life before the conversion were suddenly gone: "All shadows of doubt fled away." The significance of the conversion experience for this inquiry is that it illuminates his earlier statement: "I have become a question to myself, and that is my infirmity." His post-conversion self, simply put, is no longer a question to itself. Now, Augustine can represent the Truth of his God authoritatively to the world, a personal conviction which is soon transformed into a universally binding imperative through the instrument of the Catholic Church. The salvational discovery quenched Augustine's thirst for *questioning* the ground of being; however, this should not be confused with the many post conversion *assertions* he makes about the ground of being. To clarify: Augustine tries to eliminate undecidability as an inherent feature of selfhood. Such a project is itself anti-erotic. As Samuel Skolnicov reminds us, while agape might *forgive*, only eros *educates*.[33]

After his conversion, Augustine was elevated to the influential position of bishop within the church hierarchy and used this power to institutionalize a unique conception of truth. As his prejudices about truth became incrementally normalized, the value of eros was correspondingly diminished on the symbolic level as a principle vital to the construction of identity. According to Peter Brown, Augustine's wisdom is not defined as an interminable, open-ended process, as would be the case if an eros concept were privileged, but rather, as a learning that is terminable, marked by an identifiable closure:

> One thing, however is certain: a wisdom without the "name of Christ" was quite out of the question. The name of Christ was applied to the Christian like a vaccination. It was the only guarantee of safety.[34]

Those who did not subscribe to Augustine's "Truth" simply failed to recognize authentic wisdom. The various ethical hierarchies which undergird Augustine's world view—mind/body, God/Human, sacred/profane, and Christian/Pagan—reflect a framework which can only "frame" otherness vertically, in terms of superior/inferior. For this reason, one would be hard pressed to find an ideology more congenial to the creation of an Imperial Self than Augustine's.[35] As a symbolic formation, the Imperial Self is educated to comply with the imperatives of official authority, an educational mode of production which perhaps reached its zenith in 1950s Cold War America when the dominant narratives of civic identity were steeped in rituals of obedience to the national security priesthood.

The discursive nets surrounding dominant images of eros in the academy and popular culture still bear the heavy stamp of Augustine's influence. Such negative images of eros, with its concomitant devaluation of the feminine, strengthen the heroic iconography of the Imperial Self. If our ethical view of otherness is to be fundamentally re-situated along an alternative conceptual axis, I submit that a critically theorized concept of eros can function as an effective counterpoise to the hegemony of the citizen-warrior model of civic identity. A positive revaluation of eros would disturb the masculinist basis of this dominant form of civic identity. This phase of the genealogy further suggests that the devaluation of eros we see today—evidenced by the marginalization of an eros discourse—is clear testimony to Augustine's institutional power and enduring cultural influence. The puritanization of the American classroom was a disciplinary project deeply indebted to Augustine's anti-erotic prejudices. As the inquiry proceeds, it will be useful to recall the ways in which these fourth-century representations of eros reflect both a patriarchal and an anti-democratic bias.

Notes

1. Peter Brown, *Augustine of Hippo* (Berkeley: University of California Press, 1967), 35–39. One prime example of this methodological difficulty in interpreting eros genealogically is the question of language. Although Augustine did not know Greek and did not specifically use "eros," "agape," or "philia" in his writings, he uses Latin terms such as "cupiditas," "concupiscence," and "caritas," which scholars have generally adopted to approximate the Greek terms. Similarly, within educational theory the use of eros is attributed to Rousseau (e.g., Joel Spring) even though he never uses the term in any of his writings, but rather uses *amour de soi* and *amour propre*. This inquiry attempts to come to grips with the difficulties posed by these translations across different languages and historical contexts.

2. Elaine Pagels, *Adam, Eve, and the Serpent* (New York: Vintage Books, 1988). Subsequent references from this work are cited in the text with the abbreviation *Adam*.

3. Anders Nygren, *Eros and Agape* (Chicago: University of Chicago Press, 1982). Paul Tillich, for one, rejects how Nygren (and Augustine) dichotomize eros and agape and offers a non-dualistic interpretation of the two motifs. In his *Love, Power, and Justice* (New York: Oxford University Press, 1960), Tillich writes: "Even more serious is the rejection of the eros quality of love with respect to God. The consequence of this rejection is that love towards God becomes an impossible concept, to be replaced by obedience to God. But obedience is not love. It can be the opposite of love" (31). In his *Systematic Theology* (Chicago: University of Chicago Press, 1963), we find another rejection: "If eros and agape cannot be united, agape toward God is impossible" (281).

4. Romand Coles, "Augustine's Critique of the Roman Pagan Self" in *Self/ Power/Other: Political Theory and Dialogical Ethics* (Ithaca, NY: Cornell University Press, 1992), 17–26.

5. William Connolly, *The Augustinian Imperative: A Reflection on the Politics of Morality* (London: Sage Press, 1993), xx.

6. Pagels, *The Gnostic Gospels* (New York: Vintage Books, 1979), 151.

7. St. Augustine, *Confessions*, trans. by Henry Chadwick (New York: Oxford University Press, 1991), 6.12, 6.15. Subsequent references to this work in the text are abbreviated *Conf.*

8. Karl Jaspers, *Plato and Augustine* (New York: Harcourt Brace, 1962), 110.

9. My interpretation of the elite/democratic contradiction, or paradox, at the core of the American negotiation of civic identify is indebted to many authors, among them Bruce Ackerman, *We the People: Foundations* (Cambridge: Harvard University Press, 1991); Jackson Turner Main, *The Anti-Federalists* (New York: Van Rees Press, 1961); William Appleman Williams, *America Confronts a Revolutionary World: 1776–1976* (New York: Morrow, 1976); Sheldon Wolin et al., *Athenian Political Thought and the Reconstruction of American Democracy* (Ithaca: Cornell University Press, 1992); Gordon S. Wood, *The Radicalism of the American Revolution* (New York: Vintage Press, 1991); and Howard Zinn, *A People's History of the United States* (New York: Harper, 1980).

10. Alexander Hamilton, John Jay, and James Madison, *The Federalist Papers* (New York: New American Library, 1961), 77–84.

11. Paul Ford, ed., *The Collected Works of Thomas Jefferson* (New York: Putnam, 1950), 12:1630.

12. Richard Hofstadter, *The American Political Tradition and the Men Who Made It* (New York: Knopf, 1965), 3–17; Eric Foner, "To Call It Freedom," in *The Story of American Freedom* (New York: Norton, 1998), 28–45.

13. Sheldon Wolin, "Democracy Without the Citizen," in *The Presence of the Past* (Baltimore: Johns Hopkins University Press, 1989), 190. For a critical analysis of the elite conception of civic identity within the still reigning national security paradigm, see John Marciano, *Civic Illiteracy and Education* (New York: Peter Lang Publishing, 1997), 31–46.

14. Wolin, 181–91.

15. Samuel Bowles and Herbert Gintis, *Schooling in Capitalist America* (New York: Basic Books, 1976); Colin Greer, *The Great School Legend* (New York: Basic Books, 1972); Michael Katz, *Class, Bureaucracy, and the Schools* (New York: Praeger Books, 1971).

16. Quoted in Bowles and Gintis, *Schooling in Capitalist America*, 160.

17. Jackie Blount, "Manly Men and Womanly Women: Deviance, Gender Role Polarization, and the Shift in Woman's School Employment, 1900–1976," *Harvard Educational Review* 66, no. 2 (Summer 1996): 318–38.

18. Christopher Lasch, "The Common Schools: Horace Man and the Assault on Imagination," in *The Revolt of the Elites* (New York: Norton, 1995), 141–60.

19. Lasch, 153.

20. Lasch, 154.

21. Paulo Freire, *Pedagogy of the Oppressed* (New York: Seabury, 1992).

22. Cornelius Castoriadis, "The Problem of Democracy Today," *Democracy and Nature* 8, no. 2, issue 8: 18–37. According to Castoriadis, democratic forms of living are tied to the project of autonomy, in that democracy requires an ethos whereby individuals "set rules for themselves," i.e., are self-authors (auto=self, nomos=law). People who are habituated to living by rules "set by others" are heteronomously oriented and thus ill-equipped for participating in or creating democratic culture. From an educational standpoint, the distinction between autonomy and heteronomy is analogous to the distinction between the problem-posing and the banking approaches to education. Genuinely autonomous individuals cannot easily be educated within a banking system, since this reigning system removes the capacity to question its own power and purposes.

23. Coles, 17–26.

24. St. Augustine, *The City of God*, trans. Marcus Dods (New York: Random House, 1950), 14.13. Subsequent references to this work in the text will be abbreviated *CG*.

25. Mircea Eliade, ed., *The Encyclopedia of Religion* (New York: Macmillan, 1987), 578–79.

26. F. E. Peters, ed., *Greek Philosophical Terms: A Historical Lexicon* (New York: New York University Press, 1967), 74.

27. R. M. Grant, *Gnosticism and Early Christianity* (New York: Columbia University Press, 1959), 8.

28. Pagels, *The Gnostic Gospels*, 32.

29. Brown, see chapter 3, "Education," and chapter 4, "Wisdom," 35–45.

30. Nygren, 472.

31. Nygren, 472.

32. Sam Keen, *The Passionate Life* (San Francisco: HarperCollins, 1983), 9.

33. Samuel Skolnicov, *Plato's Metaphysics of Education* (London: Routledge, 1988), 80.

34. Brown, 41.

35. David Campbell, *Writing Security: United States Foreign Policy and the Politics of Identity* (Minneapolis: University of Minnesota Press, 1992). My use of the terms "Imperial Self" or "National Security Self" refers to a type of character formation that conceives of otherness hierarchically—thus, as Campbell points out, it's a formation that *requires* external and internal enemies to constitute its own identity. Campbell makes interesting connections between the structural logic of Augustine's model of otherness, as it was applied not only to Pagans and Gnostics, but to dimensions of himself as well, to the model of otherness exhibited in the New World, as it was applied by Columbus to the indigenous peoples he encountered, and later by the Puritans to the Indians. This same structural logic is operative today, he argues, within the still reigning "national security" paradigm of identity and difference. An apt measure of the persistence of this paradigm, in my opinion, is simply to recall how quickly, after the USSR dissolved, that optimistic talk of a "peace dividend" evaporated. The problem is that in its dominant formation, national identity seems to require the production of enemies to secure its own fragile existence. Even though all national identities are imagined communities, "American" identity (having to be created *ex nihilo*) probably relies more on representational practices than other national identities do because of its claim to civic and spiritual universalism. The pedagogical question is: How should American civic identity be educated today both toward the state and toward cultural

difference, given the obvious historical patterns which suggest that the dominant formation *requires* an active roster of internal and external enemies? The rich yet problematic frontier discourse in American culture, in my opinion, provides the conceptual framework for coding the self/other difference. Can the symbolism of the American frontier be used today, pedagogically, to function as something other than a boundary dividing civilization from barbarism, or as a backdrop from which to sell cars and jeeps? Perhaps America's civic religion of possibility is tied symbolically to the iconography of the frontier, suggesting that the frontier as an organizing trope of American identity can be deployed in either a progressive or regressive fashion.

3

Rousseau on Love, Education, and Selfhood in *Emile*

Jean-Jacques Rousseau sees Eros as a driving force that creates the social person. In Rousseau's educational plan, Eros provides the psychological force for directing self-love to an understanding that an injury to another can also be an injury to oneself. This creates compassion, which leads to helping others.
—Joel Spring (1999)

Outlining the Modern Historical Context

Jean-Jacques Rousseau's *Emile, Or, On Education* is an outstanding modern representation of eros because it demonstrates the ways in which the themes of love and education are implicated in the construction of selfhood. These interrelated themes combine to form an historically anchored symbolic matrix, a framework which helps to explain how the trope of love gives coherence to the construction of identity within pedagogical contexts. For this reason, a genealogical analysis must pay close attention to the shifting historical frames within which the eros concept is defined and deployed. The modern, Enlightenment paradigm of education that Rousseau constructs is a bold departure, in some ways, from the Christian paradigm he inherited. Rousseau, as we shall see, turns his critical gaze toward the doctrine of original sin and to the assumption of an intrinsic human depravity and seeks to demolish the idea, root and branch. Since copies of *Emile* were burned by the French government in Paris only days after its publication in 1762, it is safe to say that Rousseau struck a raw nerve by drawing critical attention to a doctrine which institutional power had made sacrosanct.[1]

When gender is adopted as a unit of analysis, however, we see that the Christian and modern educational paradigms remain firmly ensconced within a set of patriarchal assumptions despite other notable differences. While Rousseau thematizes the power of what could be called eros in many positive ways, his invention of Sophie as a social pillar in the organization of society is tragic, for she fares no better than Augustine's Eve: both of their ontological vocations are severely restricted. This is not to say that Rousseau's response to the "woman question" is identical to Augustine's, for it is not, but only that the practical effect of Rousseau's educational philosophy means the same for women, in the end, as Augustine's pedagogy does. Broadly speaking, the purpose of this chapter is to sort out several interpretive complexities which arise when assessing representations of love and education conceived by this exemplary modern thinker.

This chapter maps Rousseau's purported use of the eros concept within the pedagogical context of *Emile* and other relevant texts. In this analysis, the first sections of the chapter focus on the methodological problems of translating ancient Greek discourse on eros to modern French equivalents, and on the uncertainties and epistemic boundary problems which issue when trying to negotiate these different linguistic and historically-based terminologies. In the concluding section, I examine Rousseau's gendered love discourse in Book V of *Emile* as it pertains to Sophie's education and position in society.

Situated in the early stages of modernity, Rousseau interpreted the role of love in education and theorized about its relation to the emerging *bourgeois self* in ways that generated social and political upheaval in the decades to come.[2] As a harsh critic of his society, Rousseau detested the modern trends he saw emerging in the mid-eighteenth century. According to Marshall Berman, Rousseau defined the emerging bourgeois self—the personification of modernity—as a vacant kind of "non-identity." The fatal flaw of this character-type was that its desires were not authentic, but externally derived. The bourgeois loved, but he learned to love and desire only what official others had preordained. No longer author of his choices, his artificial loves diminished him, binding him to symbolic webs of illusion about who he was and what he desired. Rousseau's critique of the bourgeois character formation is scathing. Though pessimistic about the historical trends he saw emerging in modernity, Rousseau maintained a belief in the capacity of human beings to transform themselves as well as to fundamentally reconstruct their social arrangements.

Rousseau's early writings focused on the problem of personal insincerity and the widening gap he observed between a "real self," on the one hand, and the "false persona" increasingly adopted by people in their social interactions on the other. Rousseau's speculations on the tricky question of defining what it means to be an authentic self are discussed quite perceptively in Marshall Berman's *The Politics of Authenticity: Radical Individualism and the Emergence of Modern Society.* In his view, Rousseau utterly rejected the modern bourgeois model of identity:

> Rousseau soon concluded that his contemporaries were not free enough to be capable of insincerity. The men of the metropolis seemed to lack the basic equipment for insincerity: they had no selves to conceal. If their social roles and forms of behavior were masks, there seemed to be no faces underneath.[3]

For Rousseau, one's desires had to be educated, negatively, *against* the vitiating influences of society, *against* a rising commercial culture that commodified one's very identity, and *for* the express purpose of revealing one's authentic self to oneself. The image employed is one in which an authentic self is seen to be buried beneath layers of historical accretion, beneath the "empire of opinion," as Rousseau liked to say. Once these layers are penetrated and seen for what they are, they can be shed, and individuals can then become the good and moral persons they "naturally" are. Thus, in a modernist counterpoise to Augustine's original sin metaphysic, Rousseau asserts that human beings are born good, and that the real source of corruption is located outside the individual, in society. This Rousseauian idea is expressed in his well-known phrase, "man is born free, but everywhere he is in chains."[4]

The same principle is sketched in *Emile:*

> Man's nature is like a young tree which, by chance, has been born in the middle of a great highway. If it were left to itself the traffic would crash into its every limb, mutilate its senses, and kill it before too long.[5]

Rousseau's political and educational thought is calibrated as a response to the predicament described above. The individual's desires and expectations must be honed, cultivated, and protected, like a tree on a highway, lest they be mutilated by the weight of social convention or diminished by the enticements offered by the commercial culture which increasingly defined the modern experience. In contrast to Augustine, Rousseau believes in the educability of the person, if by educability we mean a belief in the capacity of people to transcend themselves, to fundamentally change a condition of their being. One of the defining historical characteristics of modernity, in addition to its association with the rise of capitalism and the sanctification of profit, is an assumption that nothing is immune from sweeping transformation.[6] Such an assumption buttressed a belief in something called "progress," a multifaceted discourse which encapsulated a lot of powerful ideas about human perfectibility and civilizational development, not to mention presumptions about ethical and cultural superiority. As an ascendant secular discourse, the progress narrative tended to undermine the hegemonic idea that human beings did not have the potential to change. Rousseau's modern educational perspective is rooted in the assumption that human goodness and the potential for psychological and social transformation is both desirable and possible. Paradoxically, however, although Rousseau embraced the modern notion of human educability, he remained deeply suspicious of the general thrust of modernity in the aggregate.

The Problem of Interpreting Rousseau's Love Discourse: Reflections on Joel Spring's *Wheels in the Head*

Much of the emphasis developed in this chapter is prompted by a discussion of Rousseau's educational philosophy offered by Joel Spring.[7] Spring writes that Rousseau believed eros was a power which could be used to cultivate such virtues as compassion and citizenship, adding that eros was a dynamic activated as the sexual passions awoke during adolescence. In interpreting the eros concept not only in Rousseau's work but within the Western intellectual tradition generally, Spring proceeds to effectively reduce eros to sexuality, while, at the same time, he fails to mention anything at all about its crucial gendered dimensions. While I am supportive of Spring's main project in the book, I do have serious problems with the character of eros presented in his interpretation. In the following pages, I want to address these problems as well as explore the methodological, epistemological, and strategic dilemmas for critical pedagogy which are raised by Spring's partial (mis)reading of the eros concept. The passage below serves as a touchstone for my analysis:

> Jean-Jacques Rousseau sees Eros as a driving force that creates the social person. The birth of the sexual drives at adolescence, he argues, can lead a person to a life of vanity or one of compassion. In this case, the issue is not repression but channeling of Eros through education. In Rousseau's educational plan, Eros provides the psychological force for directing self-love to an understanding that an injury to another can also be an injury to oneself. This creates compassion, which leads to helping others. Without this education, Rousseau believes, Eros turns self-love into vanity, which results in people spending their lives devoted to their personal appearance and accumulation of wealth.[8]

An eloquent summary of the positive powers of eros! Spring deserves credit for drawing attention to its educational value, particularly given the continued marginalization of eros from mainstream educational discourse. However, a problem arises when one recognizes that Rousseau never used the term *eros* in any of his writings. Nor is there any note taken of the two concepts that Rousseau did in fact use*: amour de soi* and *amour propre*. These omissions may be understandable since within Spring's book discussion of eros occupies only a small part of a much larger canvas. But, still, several questions are raised: Can we so easily conflate the Rousseauian concepts of *amour de soi* and *amour propre* with "Eros"? And if there are notable differences, how do we account for them? What core qualities of eros does Spring privilege, and hence de-privilege, in order to anchor his representational scheme? Should critical pedagogy accept Spring's portrait of an eros-concept devoid of gendered associations?

Competing interpretive claims about eros raise necessary questions about what, exactly, eros is, and which of its various qualities should be deemed essential for any general yet theoretically nuanced representation. I want to clarify and, to some extent, disentangle Spring's conflation of eros with *amour de soi* and *amour propre* for the purpose of developing a more finely-tuned representation of the eros concept. Although Rousseau discusses these two concepts in other works, section IV of *Emile* will be used most extensively since it concerns the education of the hero of the novel, Emile, during his adolescence when the effects of eros are supposedly awakened. Equipped with a better understanding of *amour de soi* and *amour propre* in the context of the novel, we will then revisit Spring's portrait of eros for further analysis and clarification.

Overview of *Emile* and Rousseau's Educational Philosophy

Ostensibly a novel, *Emile* is nevertheless an educational treatise comparable in important respects to Plato's *Republic*. Both works are located at the thematic intersection where education, philosophy, and politics meet. It is important that readers encounter both of these texts more as a set of provocative "thought experiments" than as policy initiatives intended to be empirically implemented.

Given Rousseau's baseline assumptions about the tension-filled and paradoxical relation between the individual and society, the educational plan detailed in *Emile* calls for the removal of young Emile from Paris (the symbol of societal corruption) to the French countryside (where unnatural relations of domination are much less in evidence). According to Rousseau, only if one obtains critical distance from the effects of power endogenous to society during childhood and adolescence can the experience of "freedom" be actualized later on within society. To understand the logic of this framework, Rousseau's conception of the State and its relation to his definition of freedom require brief explanation. In the process of tracing these theoretical connections, the symbolic matrix Rousseau constructs between *amour de soi/amour propre*, education, and the politics of identity will begin to emerge.

A starting point for understanding Rousseau's modernist teleology is his belief in the notion that ontogenesis recapitulates phylogenesis; that is, the development of the species (as civilization) undergoes the same stages of development that individuals do.[9] This linear, developmental model is a foundational element of Rousseau's educational philosophy. For when Rousseau declares that what he calls Savage Man existed in a natural condition, he means that it was presocial, before social relations based on domination and interdependency had come into historical existence. As the sinews of "society" grow in scope and encompass a wider circle, as it were, one becomes increasingly dependent on others, thus diminishing one's freedom. However, according to Rousseau, despite this loss of a "state of nature," one is still endowed with the potential to develop capacities of reason and morality within the constraining society, an outcome which reflects the fullest expression of human freedom.[10]

Freedom for Rousseau is not personified by Savage Man, since in this stage, "freedom" comes as a *given* rather than as something which is *achieved*. In Rousseau's view, attaining freedom in modern times, in "mature" society, was an increasingly remote possibility. It is also seen as an unavoidably paradoxical state of being. *Emile* is a novel which teaches the principle that one must *learn to know the limits of freedom*, since the achievement of absolute freedom is unattainable. One should want only what one can attain and attain only what one wants. This explains why Emile (and Sophie) must come to know the boundaries of their possibility, and to acknowledge, albeit in radically different ways, the constraints endemic to each of their gendered lives. Thus, Rousseau's pedagogy embraces the paradoxical goal of cultivating in Emile what he calls a "well-regulated freedom" (*E*, 92). Rousseau believed the State grew out of a condition of mutual interdependence among people, who then collectively came to embody a "general will."[11] Since the State exists as the embodiment of the general will, Emile is intrinsically a social being, tied *ambivalently* to others. In a sense, the novel reflects an educational philosophy designed to provoke Emile to come to grips with this ambivalence.

The removal of Emile from society is necessary in order to permit natural educational processes to unfold unimpeded by the corrupting conditions of modern existence. In the absence of these societal pressures, Emile could avoid experiencing *amour de soi* and *amour propre* in their distorted forms and avoid splintering his loves and desires in all the wrong directions. In adopting this symbolic withdrawal from society, Rousseau expresses his concept of "negative education." (*E*, 94). Such a delay in learning all the wrong opinions, habits, and desires provides Emile the necessary time to anchor a self in the firm ground of the "natural" developmental stages of life. Only then, Rousseau argues, will the student come to hold in (his) possession the moral compass required to navigate through the shoals of bourgeois selfhood.

In *Emile*, Rousseau divides the human lifespan into five stages. The first section of the book consists of stages 1–3 (from infancy to age 15) and involves the education of Emile "removed" from society. In the second section, stages 4–5 (ages 15–20), we witness the "integration" of Emile back into society. Emile's social reintegration culminates in his marriage to Sophie and in his travels throughout Europe in order to learn a proper civic identity. As I will discuss in the final section of this chapter, Sophie's education is qualitatively different from Emile's: in addition to other differences, her education does not include European travel since, for Rousseau, females must forgo the development of their public and civic selves. With this broad-brush overview of *Emile* in mind, Rousseau's discussion of *amour de soi* and *amour propre* may now be understood within a wider context.

Amour de Soi *and* Amour Propre *in Book IV of* Emile

Joel Spring's interpretation of Rousseau's use of eros focuses on the onset of puberty when the "birth of the sexual drives can lead a person to a life of vanity or one of compassion."[12] A central theme in Book IV of *Emile* concerns the ways in which *amour de soi* and *amour propre* can assume positive or negative forms in the process of individual development. A literal translation of *amour de soi* (love of self) does not begin to convey the usages and nuances Rousseau attached to the term. At one level, Rousseau uses *amour de soi* in reference to a dynamic force with intention, aimed at the preservation of life. The power of this force binds the animate and inanimate in an ever widening circle; consciousness of this widening circle and the awareness that its energy could be redirected, pedagogically, is one example of how Rousseau links the trope of love to education. Rousseau:

> Amour de soi is a natural feeling which leads every animal to look to its own preservation, and which, guided in man by reason and modified by compassion, creates humanity and virtue.[13]

The ethical associations he attaches to *amour de soi* indicate the importance this wider, educated form of love has for Rousseau's political project of citizenship and community. In Platonic terms, such an image of a love-force contains both prephilosophical and philosophical dimensions. For example, a mother bear protecting her cubs is a manifestation of *amour de soi*, just as a human being choosing to commit oneself to help others is similarly an instance of *amour de soi*. The bear's *amour de soi* is instinctual, naturalistic, while the human being's *amour de soi* is ethical, assuming the form of a *choice*. Spring refers to Rousseau's "eros" awakening at puberty; however, it would appear from this definition that *amour de soi* actually *precedes* the hormonal rush that is adolescent sexuality. Writing in *Emile*, Rousseau accents another facet of *amour de soi*:

> The source of our passions, the origin and principle of all others, the only one born with man and which never leaves him so long as he lives is amour de soi—a primitive, innate passion, which is anterior to every other, and which all others are in a sense only modifications. (*E*, 212-213)

Here, *amour de soi* is the primal source of being, "anterior" to every passion, modifying all others that proceed from it. The statement that *amour de soi* can "never leave" someone so long as they are physically alive is not in line with Plato's emphasis, since in his conception, the mere fact of one's physical existence does not guarantee, in itself, a constant level of eros. But Rousseau also seems to present a model of *amour de soi* which could be said to exist along a continuum, from acts of sheer physical survival to its highest manifestation as an ethical, conscious transcendence.

In the exalted form of *amour de soi* (largely dependent on the educated recognition of human connectivity), love of others becomes a widened modification of loving oneself.[14]

Rousseau's use of *amour propre* (literally, *self-love*), is generally presented as a quality of being that is predisposed to mastery over others. According to Rousseau scholar N. J. H. Dent, the origin of *amour propre* "is rooted in a child's imperiously willful reaction to frustration by which he hopes to command other people and the world to his service."[15] In this way, *amour propre* owes its existence to the ego's struggle for constant recognition and confirmation in a terror-filled world. In defining *amour propre*, Rousseau also discusses these two concepts in binary terms, as representing ethically superior/inferior qualities:

> Amour propre, which makes comparisons, is never content and never could be, because the sentiment, preferring ourselves to others, also demands others to prefer us to themselves, which is impossible. This is how the gentle and affectionate passions are born of amour de soi and how hateful and irascible passions are born of amour propre. (*E*, 214)

It is intriguing that these two concepts are framed as oppositional in view of their near identical etymologies (love of self, self-love). In any event, passages like this lend credence to the view that *amour de soi* refers to an "instinct" to preserve life, a field of energy which can also be educated beyond instinct into a form of care for self and for others, while *amour propre* refers to a negative form of self-love amplified to vanity and a desire for control and domination.

Elizabeth Rappaport reaffirms this seeming polarity in her own interpretation of Rousseau. She claims that *amour propre* is a "pernicious principle" which "always" leads to negative consequences, containing no redeeming positive features. Rappaport claims that *amour propre* is not yet an "active principle" in the child.[16] Recall Spring's assertion that eros suddenly appears on the scene at puberty: if *amour de soi* is antecedent, as established, then whatever "emergence of eros" occurs at puberty must derive from *amour propre*. Yet this proposition is troubling, given *amour propre*'s purely negative coding. Since Spring's eros emphasizes its positive aspects, does he perhaps have *amour de soi* in mind rather than *amour propre*? Spring doesn't say which Rousseauian concept emerges at this crucial point, but rather advances an unproblematic "eros." When Spring posits the notion of a mechanical correspondence between sexuality and eros, it seems to me that his version of Rousseau's "eros" is actually Freud's concept of libido in linguistic disguise. Such a representation implies that levels of eros wax and wane according to the same model in which sexual energy waxes and wanes. According to this representation, levels of eros are not appreciably influenced by one's ethical relation to one's ignorance, or by one's relation to the feminine, whether this feminine is objectified as an "inferior other" or embraced as a positive and soulful presence. In this way, the meaning of eros is confined exclusively to the hydraulic images of sexuality. I submit this is a restrictive, mechanistic view of eros.

In an attempt to undermine the Augustinian view of human nature, as well as to clarify the separate qualities of *amour de soi* and *amour propre*, Rousseau writes:

> Let us set down as an incontestable maxim that the first movements of nature are always right. There is no original perversity in the human heart. There is not a single vice to be found in it of which it cannot be said how and from whence it entered. The sole passion natural to man is amour de soi and amour propre taken in an extended sense. This amour propre in itself or relative to us is good and useful; and since it has no necessary relation to others, it is in this respect naturally neutral. It becomes good or bad only by the application made of it and the relations given it. (*E*, 92)

When Rousseau talks about *amour propre* "taken in an extended sense," he refers to its potential to be educated and thus widened beyond the instrumentalities of an acquistive, narcissistic, domineering ego consciousness. Such a formulation is consistent with Rousseau's assertion: "Extend *amour propre* to other beings and it is transformed into virtue, a virtue which has its root in the heart of every one of us" (*E*, 242). In trying to untangle these discursive knots, it now appears that *amour propre* is not intrinsically negative, but it does appear that *amour de soi* is intrinsically positive. Furthermore, the idea that *amour propre* is "naturally neutral" suggests that an a priori existence eventually assumes good or bad form depending on one's context. This positive conceptualization of *amour propre* troubles the boundaries of the simple positive/negative binary we began the inquiry with.

In my research, I was startled to see such deep confusion among Rousseau scholars over the exact meaning and boundaries of these two key terms. N. J. H. Dent captures this confusion:

> Charvet writes that: "It may be wondered whether Rousseau means amour propre here rather than amour de soi…" And Horowitz quotes a passage starting: "Extend self-love…" and simply asserts without comment the phrase amour de soi after self-love although the text has amour propre.[17]

The confusion evidenced here over the very basis of these terms underscores the problem not only of distinguishing between these two concepts of love, but also the difficulty of simply placing both under the rubric of an eros principle. Certainly parallels exist between *amour de soi, amour propre*, and eros, but this should not mean, as it appears to mean for Spring, that a perfect symmetry exists between Rousseau's love discourse and "eros."

The internal linkage between these two concepts is illustrated within the text of *Emile*. In describing the trajectory of Emile's life, Rousseau says that "my Emile" has focused only on himself up to the age of puberty, at which time he now looks upon others. The "first sentiment" aroused within him is to compare himself with others and to desire to be "in the first position" (*E*, 235). At this point, according to Rousseau, *amour de soi* turns into *amour propre*. Rousseau argues that puberty is the critical point at which the passions, ignited by a nascent sexuality and awareness, can potentially give birth to the development of a moral sensibility. Rousseau thus conceives of adolescence and the onset of *amour propre* as a crisis point in Emile's education, representing danger and opportunity. For Rousseau, puberty is the psychological stage which necessarily leads one to face the existential reality of Others. Up to this age, Emile's negative education has been all about his relation to physical things in his immediate, natural environment. Now, however, Emile's education will concern itself foremost with his ethical relations to human beings. This education must be arranged in such a way that feeling and compassion rather than vanity and domination become the organizing principles of identity formation.

The key that unlocks Emile's latent capacity to transform *amour propre* toward positive ends are those passions which are projected outward toward others. In the case of the so-called petulant *amour propre*, this projection is rooted in comparing oneself to others for the purpose of achieving precedence. Yet, as we have seen, this is not an inherent outcome but rather the one which typically prevails. Rousseau implies that *amour propre* can be channeled in the right direction if students are exposed to the existence of human suffering:

> At sixteen the adolescent knows what it is to suffer, for he himself suffered. But he hardly knows that other beings suffer too. *To see it without feeling it is not to know it* [emphasis added]; and as I have said a hundred times, the child, not imagining what others feel, knows only his own ills. But when the first development of his senses lights the fire of his imagination, he begins to feel himself in his fellows, to be moved by their complaints and to suffer from their pains. It is then that the sad picture of suffering humanity ought to bring his heart the first tenderness it has experienced. (*E*, 222)

Here we observe an intriguing causal connection between the onset of sexuality and the imaginative function. This passage probably serves as the basis of Spring's summary of Rousseau's eros cited earlier. Rousseau's privileging of feeling over "disembodied vision" as a basis for knowledge corroborates many feminist arguments. Yet, we must be careful not to reproduce strict feeling/thinking, body/mind antinomies when attempting to symbolize discursive eros. While eros cannot be understood apart from an embodiment, neither should it be conceived of as restricted to the body. Rousseau discusses the imperative of cultivating and provoking Emile's imagination in order to spark a positive manifestation of *amour propre*:

> Thus, no one becomes sensitive until his imagination is animated and begins to transport him out of himself. To excite and nourish this nascent sensibility, to guide it or follow it in its natural inclination, what is there to do other than to offer the young man objects on which the expansive force of his heart can act—objects which swell the heart, which extend it to other beings, which make it find itself everywhere outside of itself—and carefully to keep away those which contract and concentrate the heart and tighten the spring of the human I? (*E*, 226)

For Rousseau, the bourgeois self is deluded in its own self-conception, unable as a "tightly constricted I" to get outside the orbit of its own egotistical demands. The metaphors used to describe a better, alternative form of identity merit attention: "expansive," "swell," "heart," "extend," and "finding itself everywhere outside itself." Rousseau's *Emile* is an attempt to show a way out of the prison walls which surround the modern, bourgeois self. Rousseau conceptualizes a social person who is in society but not of society. It was in this paradoxical, tension-filled space where authenticity and freedom were to be actualized. With this broad overview of section IV of *Emile*, we are now positioned to further consider Spring's use of eros to describe *amour de soi* and *amour propre*.

I appreciate Spring's effort to revalue eros as a useful concept for critical pedagogy. On this crucial point, we agree that the eros concept needs to be integrated into the theoretical inventory of critical pedagogy. The question is, what kind of eros? Before thematizing a generalized eros over the heads of various thinkers who did not specifically employ the term, we would do well to take pause. Such a methodological move may be acceptable, but only after certain methodological and epistemological questions and caveats are fully considered. In this passage Spring links eros to sexuality:

And, similarly to Rousseau and Hall, Freire believes that Eros can motivate people to a state of compassion for fellow humans, which, in this case, means a desire to free all people. By linking the state of consciousness to Eros, Freire continues the Western tradition of locating the desire to know the truth and to be free in the interplay between sexuality and society.[18]

Although I agree that something we call "eros" may be deeply implicated in these social processes, I do not agree that eros should be reduced to sexuality at the expense of other valid associations. We need to exercise a finer sense of discernment about the boundaries of eros. I suggest that in constructing more nuanced representations of eros, critical pedagogy also needs to develop what could be called a secular love literacy. Such a literacy would entail the development of a capacity to conceptualize different valences of love, from eros, agape, and philia to *amour propre* and *amour mundi*, to mention a few signifiers which hold great potential to educate new forms of civic identity rooted in the humanist tradition.

Spring's summary definition of eros also invites critical analysis: "Eros was the Greek god of erotic love. Eros is also an aggregate of basic instincts and needs, sublimated impulses caused by instincts and needs, and impulses to protect the body and mind."[19] I respectfully submit this is an inadequate epistemological foundation from which to develop a critically informed concept of eros. Spring's "aggregate instinct model," for example, sounds more like Freud's concept of libido than Plato's philosophical eros. Here's the main point: Eros is itself a contested concept and we need to acknowledge the politics of its representation, as a first step. We should do this not only in the interest of sound scholarship but also to underscore the richer textures of the concept. Lost in Spring's definition, for example, is any discussion of eros's gendered attributes. Of course, when eros is reduced to instinct, need, and impulse, there is no space to talk about the feminine associations of eros, or to consider one's ethical relation to ignorance as a factor in triggering the absence or presence of eros within an individual life. The sense of eros as that which entices us toward a vision of the good is similarly discounted in Spring's treatment.

What is at the center of this epistemic uncertainty is the difference between Freud's view of eros, which Spring tacitly embraces, and Plato's view, which I believe is much preferable. Rollo May, a particularly astute observer of both Freud and Plato, offers this view:

> Even after introducing eros, Freud defined it as a push from behind, a force coming out of chaotic, undifferentiated, instinctive, energy-sources along predictable and prescribable paths...Whereas for Plato, eros is entirely bound up with the possibilities ahead which "pull" one; it is the yearning for union, the capacity to relate to new forms of experience...The culture in which Freud studied, thought, and worked was an alienated one, and that alienation is revealed in his definitions of love and sex...This may partly account for his confusion of his eros with Plato's.[20]

May disagrees with those who equate Freud's eros with Plato's, including Freud himself, who liked to refer to "the divine Plato." My criticism of Spring's representation of eros can be understood in the context of the distinction sketched above between Plato and Freud on the nature of eros.

When Spring refers to a *singular* God of Eros, in effect, he effaces Eros's *pluralistic* mythological parentage, an oversight which is bound to lead to a one-dimensional interpretation of the concept (see chapter 1). Moreover, recall that eros is represented as an "in-between" (metaxu), a third term holding opposites together. This dimension, attributed to eros by Plato, is not part of Rousseau's theoretical stance toward *amour de soi* and *amour propre*. Therefore, the multiple, ambiguous, ironic, daimonic, and gendered qualities often associated with eros unfortunately fall beneath Spring's epistemological radar. Although this may be a hard pill for some to swallow, to me it's clear that Plato's sophisticated representation of eros is far more sympathetic to the aims of critical pedagogy than the "libidinized" and mechanistic eros which Spring attributes to Rousseau and Freire.

In the next section we shall continue to track expressions of *amour de soi* and *amour propre* as they occur in Book V of *Emile*. The critical emphasis will be to read gender into Rousseau's love terminology as it relates to Sophie, Emile's pre-arranged wife.

Sophie's Choice? An Analysis of Rousseau's Love Discourse

Rousseau's will to dominate and control women—what might be called his passion for patriarchy—is nowhere more clearly expressed than in the three passages below, taken from Book V of *Emile*:

> The entire education of woman must be relative to man, to please them, to be useful to them, to be loved and honored by them, to rear them when they are young, to care for them when they are grown up, to counsel and console, to make their lives pleasant and charming, these are the duties of women at all times, and they should be taught them in childhood. (*E*, 45)

> In the union of the sexes each contributes equally to the common aim, but not in the same way. From this diversity arises the first assignable difference in moral relations of the two sexes. One ought to be active and strong, the other passive and weak. One must necessarily will and be able; it suffices that the other put up little resistance. Once this principle is established, it follows that woman is made especially to please man. (*E*, 46)

> If woman is made to please and be subjugated, she ought to make herself agreeable to man instead of arousing him. (*E*, 47)

It is a testament to the power of the female image in Western thought that two seemingly dissimilar thinkers like Augustine and Rousseau would nevertheless share the same kind of gendered essentialisms. Just as Augustine framed Eve as the embodiment of danger and sought to deny her the pursuit of erotic knowledge, Rousseau likewise invents Sophie, whose "ontological vocation" is bonded to purposes outside her own authorship, a subordinate condition the passages above make clear.[21]

In an etymological reversal dripping with cruel irony, the *wisdom* which *Sophie* is supposed to embody has nothing whatever to do with the philosophic quest or the project of autonomy. The only wisdom Rousseau wishes for Sophie is for her to learn a private identity and accept her subordinate location in society, a location which excludes participation in the activity of philosophy and politics.[22] Sophie's psychological development is quite narrowly prescribed not because Rousseau thinks women are incapable of attaining the highest possible moral and intellectual development, but because if women were to receive an open-ended and creative education the patriarchal structure of the family and society would likely crumble. For Rousseau, the patriarchal family was naturalized as the linchpin of civilization. The separation in the kind of education each sex ought to receive needs to be understood within the context of Rousseau's high valuation of the private, domestic sphere. If women did not anchor the domestic sphere, no community and feeling of mutual interdependence embodied in the collective "general will" could ever materialize. Still, even if Rousseau's educational and "ontological apartheid" is grounded in the best of intentions, its capacity to create the conditions in which community and mutual interdependence might develop is far from obvious.

In contrast, Plato's educational theory fares much better according to contemporary standards of sex and gender equality. A cardinal principle in Book V of the *Republic*, illustrated when Plato said women ought to be included within the sphere of philosophy, is that consciousness is consciousness and bodies should not be seen as determinative when evaluating the educational potential of the sexes.[23] Indeed, if one were to reflect back on Plato's figure of *Diotima* and compare her subversive gender narrative to Augustine's *Eve* or to Rousseau's *Sophie*, one recognizes how substantially different Plato is from these thinkers insofar as assigning value to the feminine is concerned.

The crucial point for Rousseau is the fact that women give birth and are the "natural" caretakers of their children, a condition which should thus determine their function and education in life. According to this logic, it would be "contrary to nature" for Sophie to receive the same education as

Emile. As the novel makes plain, Emile is to be granted infinitely more latitude for intellectual creativity and open-ended educational inquiry than Sophie. While Emile is encouraged to define his own purposes, at least within the parameters of his tutors' guidance, Sophie has her trivial purposes prescribed for her in nauseating detail. Says Rousseau:

> To be a woman means to be coquettish, but her couquetry changes its form and its object according to her view. Let us regulate her views according to those of nature, and women will have the education which suits her. Little girls love adornment almost from birth. Not satisfied with being pretty, they want people to think they are pretty. In fact, almost all little girls learn to read and write with repugnance. But as for holding a needle, that they always learn gladly. Once this path is opened, it is easy to follow. Sewing, embroidery, and lacemaking come by themselves. (*E*, 365)

The curriculum for males, as we have seen, is designed to provoke a paradoxical "well-regulated freedom," a condition which grows out of a tension-filled negotiation between the private and public spheres. The curriculum for women consists of a privatized, male-led regime of discipline and control designed to solidify the *fragile* stability of the patriarchal family structure. I say fragile because Rousseau saw the imperative to educationally reproduce what would not reproduce "naturally" on its own, namely, the patriarchal model of family. If this model of the family is in fact natural, why the imperative to deny Sophie a genuine education? Therein lies one of Rousseau's contradictions.[24] Ironic to see how Rousseau repudiates the doctrine of original sin but turns round to restrict Sophie's self-determination much as Augustine restricted Eve's. Modern eros may be positively coded with Rousseau, but its positive zone of activity is to be regulated on the basis of sex.

Foremost among Rousseau's patriarchal assumptions is the idea that women should be denied a public, civic identity. An apt symbol of this bias occurs when Sophie's education does not include the opportunity for European travel. The itinerary for Emile's continental trip consists of excursions to various capitals for the purpose of educating a larger, civic identity: "Now that Emile has considered himself in his physical relations with other beings and in his moral relations with other men, it remains for him to consider himself in his civil relations with his fellow citizens" (*E*, 455). To permit Sophie to eat the forbidden fruit of Paris or London or Athens would be tantamount to creating the preconditions for social chaos. The problem facing Rousseau was this: Who would function as the existential pillar of the family and, by extension, the *state*, if the mother/wife was off studying dance and politics at the Sorbonne? The impossibility of imagining alternative familial arrangements led Rousseau to conclude that the social structure of society would degenerate if woman's ontological vocation were not strictly circumscribed. Rousseau's educational philosophy is steeped in a nature discourse. His arguments rest on a perceived ability to accurately read what "nature intended." A terse example of this nature discourse is seen when Jean-Jacques lays down the law for Sophie: "When Emile became your husband, he became your master, it is the *will of nature* that you should obey him" (*E*, 478).

Rousseau's position on the education of Sophie has been interpreted by many as evidence that he assigned an inferior status to women's educational *potential*. Penny Weiss, however, argues that Rousseau's sex-roled education is more complex than it appears. For example, Weiss shows how Rousseau consistently questions the concept of a fixed human nature and therefore treats the family not as a natural formation but as something which needs to be strictly constructed for "society's interest." Significantly, in some passages, Rousseau's sexual differentiation is not grounded in appeals to nature or biology, but in what he saw as the necessary limitations each sex would have to learn in order to create a community based on mutuality. But he also contradicts this "non-essentialist" position in other passages. As Weiss concludes, the inequality at the root of Rousseau's educational program is at odds with the very mutuality and community that he wants his sexually-differentiated educational system to bring about.[25]

This brief overview of Book V is intended to situate Rousseau's love terminology in the context of his gendered educational philosophy. We are now better positioned to explore how *amour de soi* and *amour propre* relate to the education of Sophie. Although the previous section concluded on a note of caution that these two signifiers should not be so easily equated with eros, it will also be recalled that similarities exist between them at a broad level of analysis. Therefore, I want to make the limited assertion that *amour de soi, amour propre*, and eros are similar insofar as all three concepts are deemed crucial to the educational project and to the construction of identity. Is Rousseau's discourse of love, so indispensable to theorizing Emile's education, also present in his discussion of Sophie's education?

There are thirty-five combined references to *amour de soi* and *amour propre* in the entire text of *Emile*, excluding footnotes (*E*, 497). Yet, there are only four references to these concepts in Book V, and none of these references involve Sophie. Rather, each instance discusses how these concepts might apply to Emile's life. Thus, *Rousseau's love discourse is absent from Sophie's educational experience.* This absence is important and could be read in a number of ways. First, it underscores the vital role *amour de soi, amour propre*, or a "generalized eros" plays in the denouement of a truly educative process. Emile's education is undeniably superior to Sophie's: his education is conceptualized in terms of the presence of a love discourse; her education is conceptualized in the absence of a love discourse.

If one appreciates that Rousseau's love terminology is deeply connected to his notion of authenticity, it follows that Sophie's education would have no use for such potentially transformative energies since the aspiration of "authentic selfhood" is not an option for her. Sophie has no choice or possibility beyond her function as a site of reproduction. The *discursive absence of eros* in Book V of *Emile*, then, could be read as the single most defining feature of an intrinsically *inferior* education. Eros signifies the motive force propelling forms of education that are flatly denied Sophie.

This omission also suggests the additional threat females might pose were the educational qualities of eros integrated into their experience. Why do Augustine and Rousseau both want to keep women in check? One could surmise that there is something about the qualities contained within eros which threaten the patriarchal structure of power. On the basis of this historical pattern, perhaps we could speculate that the power of eros is often perceived to undermine any structure of power which is hierarchically or vertically organized. If this is indeed the case, the conceptual affinities between eros and democracy merit further analysis (see chapter 5).

In her commentary on *Emile*, Jane Martin refers to the male principle of education as "developmental" and the female educational principle as one of "reproduction."[26] Again, a generalized eros is present in the developmental model and absent in the reproductive model, an interpretive scheme which is analogous to Freire's problem-posing and banking models of education. The symbolic matrix Rousseau constructs around love, education, and selfhood in *Emile* reflects a discursive snapshot of the tensions and contradictions residing within the historical frame we know as early modernity.

There is a continuity between Augustine and Rousseau in that they posit the notion of a recoverable self, but the internal selves they sought to recover were at once radically different, yet, in terms of gender, virtually identical. Gazing into his deepest self, Rousseau did not see an original sinner, but sinister accretions of social convention. Unlike Augustine and his concept of original sin, Rousseau believed these colonizing overlays could be uncovered through education, and something good would be found: the authentic self. This radical reversal—from seeing oneself as the locus of evil, to seeing "society" as the ultimate source of corruption—represents the sea change in perception that defined modernity. Yet, *sea change*—a metaphor describing historical discontinuity and subsequent shifts in perception—is an image that tends to obscure those historical features within a period which remain continuous, such as the motif of fear and control surrounding eros and women. Like Eve, Sophie is not permitted to eat from the tree of knowledge in Rousseau's societized garden: eros and the promise of the soul's possibility are experiences available only to Emile.

Rousseau's modern representation of eros can be understood in terms of its paradoxical relation to the medieval/Christian paradigm from which it emerged. Rousseau codes what could be called a generalized eros in very positive ways, highlighting the indispensability of the concept to the pedagogical construction of a wider, more humane form of civic identity. Yet, despite this notable advance beyond Augustine, Rousseau develops what might be called a "zonal eros," an eros whose zone of educational activity is restricted to males only. Not until the twentieth century would the politics of representation surrounding eros be seriously challenged; only then would discursive eros begin to be unbound from its patriarchal moorings.

Notes

---

1. N. J. H. Dent, *A Rousseau Dictionary* (Cambridge: Blackwell Publishers, 1992), 106.

2. The Rousseauian discourse on authenticity can be assessed in Marshall Berman, *The Politics of Authenticity: Radical Individualism and the Emergence of Modern Society* (New York: Atheneum Books, 1970). See also Alessandro Ferrara, *Modernity and Authenticity: A Study of the Social and Ethical Thought of Jean-Jacques Rousseau* (Albany: SUNY Press, 1993); Madan Sarup, *Identity, Culture, and the Postmodern World* (Athens: University of Georgia Press, 1996); and Judith Shklar, *Men and Citizens: A Case Study of Rousseau's Social Theory* (London: Cambridge University Press), 1969. Berman writes: "It was only in the second generation of the Enlightenment, through Rousseau, that the search for authenticity came into its own" (75).

3. Berman, 136.

4. Jean-Jacques Rousseau, *The Social Contract* (London: Penguin, 1968), 49.

5. Jean-Jacques Rousseau, *Emile, Or, On Education* (New York: Basic Books, 1979), 5–6. Subsequent references from this work are cited in the text with the abbreviation *E*.

6. Thomas C. Patterson, *Inventing Western Civilization* (New York: Monthly Review Press, 1997). For a fuller discussion of the hallmarks of modernity, see "The Idea of Progress," 32–36.

7. Joel Spring, *Wheels in the Head: Educational Philosophies of Authority, Freedom, and Culture From Socrates to Human Rights* (New York: McGraw-Hill, 1999).

8. Spring, 155.

9. Jean-Jacques Rousseau, *Discourse on the Origin and Foundation of Inequality Among Mankind* (Indianapolis: Hackett Publishing Company, 1987), 37–59.

10. Rousseau, *Discourse*, 60–81.

11. Rousseau, *The Social Contract*, Book II, "The General Will," 69–100.

12. Spring, 155.

13. Rousseau, *Discourse*, 34.

14. N. J. H. Dent, *Rousseau* (Oxford: Basil Blackwell, 1988), 143–45.

15. Dent, *Dictionary*, 33–36.

16. Elizabeth Rappaport, "On the Future of Love: Rousseau and the Radical Feminists," in *Women and Philosophy*, ed. Carol Gould and Max Wartofsky (New York: G. P. Putnam's Sons, 1976), 195–96.

17. Dent, *Dictionary*, 35.

18. Spring, 156.

19. Spring, 154.

20. Rollo May, *Love and Will* (New York: Norton, 1969), 88.

21. This Freirean concept explains quite well what Sophie is denied. Her ability to "become more fully human" is not an option. For a definition of "ontological vocation," see Paulo Freire, *Pedagogy of the Oppressed* (New York: Seabury, 1993), 25–26.

22. Jane Martin, "Sophie and Emile: A Case Study of Sex Bias in the History of Educational Thought," *Harvard Educational Review* (August, 1981): 357–77; Susan Moller Okin, *Women in Western Political Thought* (Princeton: Princeton University Press, 1979), 135–45.

23. For a discussion of this theme, see Gregory Vlastos, "Was Plato a Feminist?" and Arlene Saxonhouse, "The Philosopher and the Female in the Political Thought of Plato" in *Feminist Interpretations of Plato*, ed. Nancy Tuana (University Park: Pennsylvania State University Press, 1994), 11–23, 67–85.

24. For an excellent feminist interpretation of Rousseau's contradictions on the subject of gender, see Penny Weiss, *Gendered Community: Rousseau, Sex, and Politics* (New York: New York University Press, 1993); in particular, "Producing Gender: Sex, Freedom, and Equality in *Emile*," 10–35. For an exploration of Rousseau's pedagogical paradoxes, see Donald Finkel and William Ray Arney, *Educating for Freedom: The Paradox of Pedagogy* (New Brunswick: Rutgers University Press, 1995).

25. Weiss, *Gendered Community*, 30–35.

26. Martin, 357–72.

4

Postpatriarchal Representations of
Eros in the Twentieth Century

With the transformation from sexuality into Eros, the life instincts
evolve their sensuous order, while reason become sensuous to the
degree to which it comprehends and organizes necessity in terms of
protecting and enriching the life instincts.

—Herbert Marcuse (1955)

Given that critical pedagogy seeks to transform consciousness, to
provide students with ways of knowing that enable them to know
themselves better and live in the world more fully, to some extent it
must rely on the presence of the erotic in the classroom to aid the
learning process.

—bell hooks (1994)

As educators, we need to recover the ways in which the twentieth century
is a chronicle of horror.[1] Only by encouraging this recovery will our
pedagogical conceptions in general and the aims of peace education in
particular be sufficiently anchored in the recognition of the human capacity
for hate and aggression. If these capacities are systematically ignored
within the curriculum, as they currently are, we squander the opportunity
to educate at the deeper levels of consciousness and identity. In this regard,
the emergence of certain aspects of postmodern theory can be seen as a
positive development, since this intellectual turn has disturbed many of the

grand narratives inherited from the Enlightenment. The comforting belief in the inevitability of "progress," for example, or the equally comforting idea of a unitary rational subject, governed exclusively by reason, have been fairly shattered by some of the most horrific events of the twentieth century, symbolized by the names of places such as Auschwitz, Bergen-Belsen, Hiroshima, and Nagasaki. The relevant point here is that the ongoing human potential for dehumanization should not be obscured by the intoxicating triumphalism of global capitalism, the reigning narrative which lulls all too many into a state of forgetfulness about the social injustices daily enacted as a consequence of religious consumerism and the ongoing militarization of American society.[2] At this juncture, in the year 2000, it is worth asking what themes and categories future commentators may invent to help frame the time-span currently organized under the rubric of "the twentieth century."

Of course, the politics of memory production should never be overlooked, especially with respect to the historical coding of eros. The powerful are always advantaged in representing what values and categories of explanation will be deemed true and objective, and thus what myths of cultural heroism will be valorized or forgotten. The institutionalization of epochal labels, such as The Age of Enlightenment or the Dark Ages, both reflects and perpetuates a social authority to construct meaning and to frame what counts as knowledge and truth. The exercise of such power carries vast consequences for the social construction of identity. Within the liberal/modern paradigm, for example, eros is a category which does not exist.

Despite the obvious perils in advancing a paradigmatic analysis of large blocs of Western history, I want to assert that an underlying cause of much of the human suffering evidenced in the twentieth century can be traced, in large measure, to the historic patterns of meaning which have been imposed on the eros concept. The patriarchal stamp imposed on eros at the *discursive* level, as a negative value, has filtered down and instantiated itself in our bodies and minds, on the *experiential* level.[3] This is not to say that an entire century should be reduced to any one interpretive framework (a position which would be absurd) but simply that insight into certain aspects of contemporary history can be obtained by the use of such an interpretive model. To clarify this assertion, let's briefly explore two instances in which a postpatriarchal representation of eros can be used as a heuristic device to illuminate aspects of historical events frequently left unattended by conventional analyses.

Eros and the Nazi Devaluation of the Feminine

Consider the Nazi/German genocide of European Jewry, 1941–45. Few doubt this event to be the most egregious historical example of the capacity of human beings to reject and dehumanize the other. As the critical theorists of the Frankfurt School, among others, have observed, the Nazi movement drew its strength from a masculine ideal predicated both on the repression of sexuality and positive images of the feminine.[4] Arguably, therefore, part of that repression which enabled "ordinary Germans" to dehumanize European Jews was the *prior existence of a psychological alienation within themselves*, whereby an over-determined masculinity, buttressed by official propaganda, devalued various feminine qualities within the familiar terms of German culture.[5] An impressive body of scholarship demonstrates that an intensified masculinity and corresponding suppression of the feminine is always associated with acute forms of nationalism.[6] Without the state, after all, there could be no war, if by "war" we refer to the institutionalization of state violence.[7] Since schools are state-sponsored, part of their undiscussed mission is to produce compliant citizen-warriors, an objective most effectively accomplished in the context of emotionally arid educational climates. As one reflects upon the educational meaning of the Holocaust, as well as other instances of state-sponsored violence, such as the American war in Vietnam and the emotionally-repressive Cold War culture that preceded it,[8] the more one is convinced that the Holocaust and the dehumanization which lurks at its core is not a problem specific to "Germans" that somehow ended in 1945. Rather, such dehumanization constitutes a universal potential not so much eliminated as acknowledged and hopefully educated, since everybody carries the ongoing capacity for hate and aggression.

For this reason, the renegotiation of the self/other relation is the most urgent ethical and pedagogical challenge facing American teachers today. When viewed from this vantage point, the politics of representation surrounding the eros concept assume cardinal importance. If the patriarchal devaluation of "eros-qualities" goes unchallenged, we squander the opportunity to theorize a gender-balanced conceptual basis for imagining a future untethered from the imperatives of the national security state. As Horkheimer and Adorno declared in *The Authoritarian Personality*: "If fear and destructiveness are the major emotional sources of fascism, then eros belongs mainly to democracy."9

Reading Columbine Through the Lens of the Eros Principle

Consider also the carnage at Columbine High School on April 20, 1999, in Littleton, Colorado. Press and media reports in the wake of the violence said the teenagers who did the killing selected that day because it was Adolph Hitler's birthday. Their intended symbolism, I think, is not insignificant but an important clue that confers a kind of meaning to their actions. As one media pundit after another gave their analyses of the causes of youth violence in America and what could be done to remedy this problem, I was distressed by the narrow boundaries of analysis reflected in these discussions. Legislative remedies such as adopting tighter gun control laws, "moral" remedies like posting the Ten Commandments, or technical-security solutions calling for the mass introduction of gun-detectors into the schools only serve to mystify the American romance with violence. As a counterpoise to the conventional approach, I think it's useful to read the

Columbine episode through the lens of the eros concept. For example, had Harris and Klebold felt a prior web of connection to people, whether peers or parents, the vital precondition for enabling murderous violence, namely, social disconnection and pervasive nihilism, would not have developed in the first place. What are the sources of their rage and disconnection? How can gender as a unit of analysis throw light on the social dynamics of what they were disconnected from, as well as what they were connected to?

Apparently, the marginalization these teenagers experienced was not based on class, race, or cruel aesthetic judgments, but on the high symbolic currency of the *jock culture* at Columbine. The social hierarchies enacted every day in high schools across the nation mirror the enactment of hierarchies reflected in the wider culture.[10] The computer games which served as the defining social space and imagined community of the "trench coat mafia" were also cited as a contributing factor in promoting the slide toward violence. Needless to say, the "warrior dreams" which took hold of these two boys were produced by a multiplicity of factors, some of which have been articulated in the media; other factors, however, have been less articulated, such as questions concerning their negotiation of gender and sexuality issues within that specific school culture.[11]

Indeed, it is now confirmed that the ridicule leveled at Harris and Klebold was laced with homosexual association, not terribly surprising in a school dominated by jock culture. In an exclusive issue of *Time* magazine ("The Columbine Tapes"), one male student at Columbine High School, identified as a football player, described Harris and Klebold this way: "They're a bunch of homos, grabbing each other's private parts. If you want to get rid of someone you tease 'em. So the whole school would call them homos, and when they did something sick, we'd tell them 'You're sick and that's wrong.'"[12] No one familiar with high schools can doubt the pervasive character of this discourse, a discourse which separates a superior "us" from an inferior "them." A culture of intolerance can incite extreme acts of both internal and external aggression. In responding to the Columbine incident, Harvard psychiatrist James Gilligan notes that,

"Nothing stimulates violence as powerfully as the experience of being shamed and humiliated."[13] According to an alternative interpretation of this violent episode, which some Columbine parents support, the rage these teenagers felt did not stem primarily from their respective family situations but, significantly, arose *from within the school culture itself.*

By reading Columbine critically through the lens of the eros principle, questions of psychological connection/disconnection and the negotiation of gender and sexual identity emerge as important areas of inquiry. If cultural images of eros—feeling, connection, emotion, and vision of the good—were revalued and represented along more positive lines, beyond the limits imposed by patriarchy, perhaps such incidents of dehumanization would be less likely to occur. Considered at the level of educational policy, such a revaluation of eros qualities could lead to the implementation of a K-12 curriculum geared more toward learning the "horizontal" skills of conflict resolution than the "vertical" skills of hero warriors; more toward learning models of civic identity founded on tolerance and respect for diversity than on discourses of danger and other rituals of enmity.[14] The type of common sense that values only knowledge which is quantifiable also impedes the oft-repeated goal of "celebrating diversity" within the curriculum. If, for example, schools were to elevate music and art to the same level of value as the now *iconic* athletic culture, new space would be opened for identity to be imagined beyond the narratives of cultural heroism prescribed within the dominant jock imperium.

I introduce the disparate events of the Holocaust and the Columbine episode not only to highlight the negative consequences which flow from a devalued and distorted concept of eros, but also because these two examples pose serious interpretive dilemmas about how we should go about integrating an eros concept into pedagogical theory and practice. For example, I began the study by defining eros rather broadly as "passion and connection." The problem with this understanding, however, is that one may feel passionate and connected to the wrong things. People may feel passionate about going to the mall to buy stuff, but indifferent to the realities of social injustice in their own communities. Many Germans in the 1930s felt love toward Adolph Hitler and were righteous about their anti-Semitism. Put somewhat crudely, "desire" may thus be turned toward destructive or consumerist ends, and/or it can be turned toward constructive and peaceful ends. Sigmund Freud believed that for most individuals these two tendencies, eros and the death instinct, were not separable but generally "alloyed" in varying degrees.[15]

Given the heavy weight of the past on the institutions and ideas which structure our thinking and feeling, it's especially difficult to educate desire toward constructive ends. Complicating this pedagogical process, the emotion of anger must to some extent be regarded as something positive and cultivated as a healthy response to many situations. Some anger, it should be acknowledged, flows out of love, such as the indignation one feels when witnessing suffering and injustice. How to account for the emotion of anger with its curious connection to love? Is eros inherently good? Should destructive forms of passion be given another name, or should these instances be regarded as "eros," too? Since eros generally signifies qualities like feeling, receptivity, connection, emotion, and so forth, does this mean that the concept is intrinsically feminine? If this is the case, do females have special access to eros?

In this chapter, I want to analyze these questions primarily from the standpoint of feminist theory and pedagogy. Compared to other academic fields, feminist literature stands at the forefront in terms of the volume and quality of work published on the subject of eros. The striking insurgent quality evidenced in many of these writings derives from a penetrating critique of how patriarchal power (mis)shapes representations of eros and what these misrepresentations mean in terms of the social construction of identity. In the final section of the chapter, I discuss how the development of an eros-informed pedagogy could be enhanced if the practitioners of Socratic and feminist pedagogy understood that their frameworks were connected at the deepest levels of analysis.

Feminist Accounts of Eros: Disrupting the
Dominant Dichotomies

Although discussed in previous chapters, it bears repeating that today's dominant world view is predicated on a set of dichotomies (or binary oppositions) which frame the patterns of consciousness within which we think, feel, and know. These organizing structures are not static or petrified in time but, rather, can be compared to the characteristics of a coral reef, *alive* and *shifting* despite their appearance as *inanimate* and *solid*. Although these conceptual structures are historical accretions, lineaments of the past insinuated in our present, they nonetheless require a "performative" dimension on our part to provide the symbolic oxygen of renewed meaning. Thus, the perpetuation of these structures depends in large part on levels of unconscious, performed complicity. These "historical accretions" can be defined as an internalization of mental patterns that function to channel conceptual thought along certain prescribed routes. To illustrate this point, consider how, for centuries, the idea that females were incapable of reason came to be regarded as a self-evident truth within western culture. Now we can see how such a "fact" was really an historically-instituted *ideological imposition* that was collectively internalized. If one were to take an ahistorical view of these binaries, however, and project a universal or natural quality onto them, there would be no point in attempting to de-link eros from the logic of patriarchy, since that logic would be seen to reflect an unchangeable part of nature. A key assumption in this study is that the binaries outlined below are historically shifting constructs, sites of interpretation that are subject to contestation and reconceptualization.

Superior/Inferior

reason/passion	**public**/private
mind/body	**self**/other
masculine/feminine	**male**/female
spirituality/sexuality	**analytic**/synthesizing

The binaries present themselves to the human eye on a horizontal plane, yet within the dominant strands of Western thought, these oppositions have consistently been interpreted according to a vertical model, whereby an ethical hierarchy is constructed on the basis of historically instituted power relations. Thus, within the logic of patriarchy: eros *as passion* drags reason down and is inferior; eros *as embodied* drags the mind down and is inferior; eros *as feminine* reflects "the other" and is inferior; eros *as private experience* has no place in the public sphere and is inferior; and finally, eros *as sexuality* corrupts spirituality and is thus inferior. These and other assumptions underpin patriarchal culture. Our identities are tethered to its logic.

The impact of this patriarchal structuring of experience on the education of civic identity is immense. As Megan Boler affirms, "within Western patriarchal culture, emotions are a site of social control."[16] That emotions are a site of social control is a theme consistent with the thesis of this book, inasmuch as eros, as an emotional signifier, has also been "socially controlled" throughout its discursive history. The exercise of institutional power to control or inhibit patterns of human emotion within public schools obviously is a power which carries profound public effects, despite the dominant coding of emotion as a purely private effect. In the following pages, I want to bring the public dimensions of eros into relief. One of the central features of eros, as a concept, is that it defies tidy classification on either side of the binaries noted above; thus, the eros concept can promote the aims of critical multiculturalism since it exposes the limitations of dualistic thinking.

In Audre Lorde's brief but influential essay, she describes the erotic as a power which is tragically obscured within a culture that reduces eros to sexuality. While not denying that eros and sexuality are linked in some ways, she insists that any understanding is incomplete when eros is conflated with sex:

> The erotic is a resource within each of us that lies in a deeply female and spiritual plane, firmly rooted in the power of our unexpressed or unrecognized feeling. In order to perpetuate itself, every oppression must corrupt or distort those various sources of power within the culture of the oppressed that can provide energy for change. For women, this has meant a suppression of the erotic as a considered source of power and information within our lives. We have been taught to suspect this resource, vilified, abused, and devalued within western society.[17]

Lorde codes eros as "deeply female" and "spiritual," representing an internal energy which can potentially become a source of empowerment, particularly if it is "seen" or "felt" apart from its patriarchal trappings. The rejection of one essentialism (eros is sexuality) appears to be replaced by two additional essentialisms, namely, that eros is "female" and "spiritual"; the latter designation can plausibly be read as unambiguously "good." But, from the standpoint of critical pedagogy, is it advisable to regard eros as female and good? Similar assumptions about the nature of eros are reflected in the work of Haunani-Kay Trask, whose concept of a "feminist eros," while essentialist, is still valuable because she elevates eros to the level of an educational principle:

> As an alternative vision, the feminist eros is a challenge to patriarchal power, the quintessential power of men over women. I argue that this version of feminist power is explicitly beneficent, taking as its model the nurturing power of the mother, of her active gentleness. There is an emphasis in the feminist eros on the exchange and sharing of authority, on the equality of the self among the equality of others. In the social realm, compassion and reciprocity are esteemed above manipulation and domination.[18]

Trask discusses the need to reformulate notions of power, since the experience of power within the context of patriarchy is defined in terms of "manipulation," "domination," and "control." Implicit in her feminist eros is an alternative understanding of power itself. Certainly this attractive definition of eros supports the argument that eros should be seen as the educational principle of democracy, since its expression undermines vertical structures of power, a *movement* which defines the moral basis of democracy. However, at issue now is the question of whether eros should be seen as something gendered female, as well as something which is unambiguously good. Both Lorde and Trask appear to link eros *not* to the feminine, but to females; in addition, both writers describe an eros which is, in essence, unambiguously good. Lorde makes this linkage clear:

> When I speak of the erotic, then, I speak of it as an assertion of the lifeforce of women; of that creative energy empowered, the knowledge and use of which we are now reclaiming in our language, our history, our dancing, our loving, our work, our lives.[19]

To be sure, this discourse tends to locate men outside the sphere of eros. I believe that such a conceptualization, while understandable given the history of patriarchy, is still untenable when judged from the standpoint of critical pedagogy. Why limit the powers of eros to women only? While it is true that eros *may* find a more hospitable climate of expression within female bodies owing to gendered narratives of socialization, the argument which holds that eros can find expression only in female bodies strikes me as inaccurate and pedagogically unproductive. Yet there is a pattern of interpretation among some feminist writers which reflects this bias. Cheryl Hall identifies the theoretical and political problems which flow from this strand of interpretation:

> What these writers are unable to do as a result of this particular strategy is to challenge the oppositions that have been set up between masculinity and eros and masculinity and femininity. In these passages, eros is still not considered a quality "belonging" to men, and as such, the quality is still used to help distinguish a class of people called "men" from a class called "women."[20]

What also gets folded into this gendered dichotomy are ideas about what is "natural" to women (eros and emotion) and to men (reason and thinking). Hall contends that a revaluation of eros, absent an alteration in the larger binary between woman's alleged nature and man's alleged nature, would ultimately turn out to be a pyrrhic victory for feminist-minded people. A more radical challenge to the core epistemology of patriarchy would be to argue that, whatever eros is, it is equally available to women and men. Since the reality of patriarchal hegemony means the construction of an overly masculinized self, the remedy would seem to call for an integration into the hegemonic self of that which it is lacking. What is lacking, especially from the standpoint of men, are the qualities located under the rubric of the feminine: sensitivity, receptivity, connectedness, and so on. While the strategy pursued by Trask and Lorde would seem to offer benefit to women who reclaim their repressed eros within, so to speak, these acts of individual liberation would not alter the larger problematic binary. For example, according to this essentialized view, while women might reclaim eros, such a conception would allow men to continue to distance and objectify women and eros as the liminal other. The nature discourse upon which patriarchal hegemony rests would go undisturbed. Hall observes:

> In a world where hierarchy does exist, where men still do have social power, insisting on associating eros with women (and not men) may make it more difficult to effectively revalue eros, for unless and until a quality is associated with those in power it will still be valued less than those qualities that are. The strategy thus jeopardizes the success of revaluing both eros and women. Such a goal would be better reached by attempting to break the link between the two—by working against claims that eros is a particularly feminine trait—than by reaffirming it.[21]

In this formulation, by breaking the link between "eros and women," new space is opened for men to access structurally repressed dimensions of their own being. The key phrase in Hall's argument is that eros should not be seen as a "peculiarly feminine trait." While the history of eros as a symbolic motif demonstrates that it has been identified as both male and female, defined in the context of patriarchal values, its close association with the body and desire has given eros a feminine cast. I believe this association need not be denied, but at the same time a critical pedagogy of eros must be clear that "feminine" and "masculine" are gendered qualities which are not intrinsically rooted in either sex, but psychological qualities and potentialities within all human beings.

While bell hooks's writings consistently foreground variables of race, class, and gender, her coding of eros indicates that it is not essentially sexed, raced, or classed, but rather a potential quality that is universal to human beings. She writes that eros is a force that can "provide an epistemological grounding informing how we know what we know."[22] Megan Boler's argument that emotions have historically been a site of social control within educational structures is vividly reinforced by hooks's analysis of pedagogical eros. When one takes into consideration the ideological underpinning of American public school education, particularly reflected in the writings of Horace Mann, the question of "how we know what we know" is answered very clearly. Passion, emotion, feeling, controversy, imagination, and laughter are "surgically removed" from the classroom, with the consequent narrowing of the boundaries of the self that is produced within its spaces. As I maintained in chapter 2, the public space of the classroom was envisioned as an "innocent" space, "unsullied" by political conflict, ambiguity, imagination, passion, and the "corruptions" of "the body":

> Professors rarely speak of the place of eros or the erotic in our classrooms. Trained in the philosophical context of Western metaphysical dualism, many of us have accepted the notion that there is a split between body and mind. Believing this, individuals enter the classroom to teach as though only the mind is present, and not the body. To call attention to the body is to betray the legacy of repression and denial that have been handed down to us. The public world of institutional learning was a site where the body had to be erased, go unnoticed. Repression and denial make it possible for us to forget and then desperately seek to recover ourselves, our feelings, our passions in some private place—after class.[23]

Such exercises of emotional control ordain a "modern" rather than a "postpatriarchal" subject. As an antidote to this disciplinary climate, the integration of an eros concept into critical pedagogy would help de-puritanize American self-conception. Still, difficult theoretical problems remain. One of the main problems in trying to revalue eros derives from the fact that it is discursively ensnared in nets of patriarchal value. Thus the dualisms which undergird these categories cannot be effectively evaluated in isolation, "solved" one at a time, since they are part of a mutually informed system.

Case in point: the mind/body dualism identified by hooks prohibits a revaluation of eros insofar as this categorical separation easily bleeds into the assumption that reason (as mind) and passion (as body) are mutually exclusive qualities. It will be recalled from chapter 1 that Plato's adroit use of feminine imagery in the *Symposium* and *Phaedrus* was intended to subvert and reject this assumption, replacing it with a view that reason absent passion, or eros, was reason *unfulfilled*. Audre Lorde, in the same way, uses a wonderful image to help us grasp, metaphorically, how eros "spreads into" reason. She describes in her youth (1940s) how government-issued sacks of margarine came to her family white in color, but contained an "intense yellow pellet" which would be massaged through the margarine, until gradually the yellow permeated the entire mass. "I find the erotic such a kernel within myself. When released from its intense and constrained pellet, it flows through and colors my life with a kind of energy that heightens and sensitizes all my experience."[24]

Herbert Marcuse's attempt to bridge eros and reason reflects a similar insight and metaphoric strategy. In *Eros and Civilization*, he discusses how a liberated eros extends beyond the sexual. Marcuse sometimes uses libido and eros interchangeably, but it should be borne in mind that part of his project in *Eros and Civilization* is to explicitly separate himself from Freud's mechanistic understanding of libido:

> However, the process just outlined involves not simply a release but a transformation of libido: from sexuality constrained under genital supremacy to eroticization of the entire personality. It is a spread rather than an explosion of libido—a spread over private and societal relations which bridges the gap maintained between them by a repressive reality principle.[25]

The phrase, "the eroticization of the entire personality" mirrors the same process Lorde describes. By whatever name, both images convey a deepening of meaning. In this instance, I am reminded of Diotima's admonition to Socrates that only if he could "let go in the right way," would he be able to actually *know* the mysteries of eros. On my reading, this was a signal for him to let go of the arid, logical, masculinist, mindlocked ways of knowing that he allegedly championed. Thus, all of these thinkers are describing a crucial dimension of eros, not only how a humane concept of reason requires eros for fulfillment but the ways in which eros can spread over the canvas of everyday life. The spreading transforms, or educates, the energy itself. This image of transformation is crucial to Marcuse, for it provides a basis from which to make the provocative claim that under proper conditions, eros can develop its own morality

> Under non-repressive conditions, sexuality tends to grow into Eros—that is to say, toward self-sublimation in lasting and expanding relations (including work relations) which serve to intensify and enlarge instinctual gratification. Eros strives for "externalizing" itself in permanent *order*. With the transformation from sexuality into Eros, the life instincts evolve their sensuous order, while reason becomes sensuous to the degree to which it comprehends and organizes necessity in terms of protecting and enriching the life instincts.[26]

Marcuse's attempt to profile the dynamics of a "new rationality" unsettles a cluster of patriarchal binaries. In *Eros and Civilization*, Marcuse employs different labels to name the same basic thing. He refers to "libidinal rationality," to "sensuous order," to the "rationality of gratification," and to how "reason becomes sensuous." By insisting that *order* is a characteristic of eros, Marcuse shatters conventional epistemology which relegates passion, emotion, and feeling to the *disorderly*, irrational, and inferior. Once again, we ought to pay close attention to the implications that these alternative accounts of eros and reason have for revisioning civic identity.

If we accept Marcuse's notion that eros moves toward "expanding relations" in its trajectory toward higher orders of being (a theme present in the writings of Plato, Rousseau, and various feminist theorists), it behooves educators to make this energetic movement a site of analysis, in order to help educate its development. This genealogy shows that the energy and movement in question—the trajectory of eros, if you will—can potentially assume a constructive or destructive form. Because of this historically consistent pattern of representation, a constructive education of eros holds the promise of widening the circle of human identification, in effect blurring the boundaries erected between self and other. In this way, again, eros is seen as an energy and movement which cannot be so easily contained within conventional understandings of the self/other dichotomy. Indeed, rigid lines of demarcation between private and public are also disturbed when this "widening quality" of eros is taken into account. The widening I refer to here, as that which transports identity from the individual realm to an identification with the social realm beyond the orbit of the ego, is clearly a phenomenon with profound political implications for the progressive reconstruction of American self-conception.

Feminist theologians are interested in the theme of eros for its capacity to fulfill spiritual values. Since critical pedagogy and liberation theology share the same underlying narratives of transformation, it is appropriate to explore how these thinkers represent the eros concept. Carter Heyward's analysis supports the claim that Augustine helped institute a strict dichotomy between sexual and spiritual passion, paving the way for the notion that eros is "less godly" than "disembodied" *agape*. Obviously it is impossible to revalue eros if one remains tied to the logic of the dominant discourse. Carter Heyward introduces an alternative way of knowing eros:

> The erotic is our most fully embodied experience of the love of God. As such it is the source of our capacity of transcendence, the "crossing over" among ourselves, making connections between ourselves in relation. The erotic is the divine spirit's yearning, through our bodyselves, toward mutually empowering relation, which is our most fully embodied experience as God as love.[27]

In this passage one can almost hear the sound of icons falling as patriarchal divisions between God and human and body and mind come tumbling down. Eros becomes the sacred agent of "right relation" and "mutuality," two of Heyward's central theological principles. "Mutuality is our shared experience of power in relation."[28] It is crucial to note that this experience of power, according to Heyward, cannot be a "power-over" but must be seen and felt as a "power-with," as something "good." Postponing the question of whether eros is uncritically idealized in Heyward's representation, the defining features of her eros appear to share a striking affinity with democratic forms of culture.

Clearly, one of the main threats to democratic culture is the radical rejection of otherness, the magnification of difference into Difference. Any culture whose dominant model for conceptualizing otherness is vertical in structure contradicts democratic forms of relationship and association; forms which are, in theory, understood horizontally on the basis of an ethical belief in social and political equality. Of course, *vertical* and *horizontal* are only metaphors, but sequestered inside them are two vastly different ways of experiencing power and two vastly different "structural and emotional guides" for encountering the other. In their analyses and metaphoric inventories, Lorde, Trask, Heyward, and other feminist writers foreground the liberatory and democratic strands of eros. I think these accounts accurately represent the potential or ideal form which the powers of eros may help actualize. However, acknowledging this potential, the problem which still remains is the education of eros. Given the social orchestration of desire and the ongoing possibility that identity can devolve into selfish and destructive forms of desire—what Plato called *epithymia*; Rousseau, petulant *amour propre*; Freud, the death instinct; Marcuse, *thanatos*; and Fromm and Freire, necrophilia—critical pedagogues must take seriously the theme of educating the desires.

With its roots in the feminist "consciousness-raising" groups of the 1960s, feminist pedagogy has directly confronted the educational problem of the emotions. For the purposes of this study, these efforts are valuable to consider because they reflect a recognition that within the context of patriarchal hegemony, one's relation to the affective domain of consciousness is "controlled" by the internalization of categories and values characteristic of the modern/liberal/patriarchal paradigm. This recognition led to an acute awareness early in the movement that women's desire and emotions were colonized, or, to use a Platonic metaphor, "turned in the wrong direction." In the passage below, Berenice Fisher does not mention eros explicitly, but her analysis resonates with it implicitly:

> In theoretical terms, we cannot simultaneously claim that all feelings are socially conditioned and that some feelings are "true." We should be more consistent to acknowledge that society only partly shapes our emotions, leaving an opening where we can challenge and change the responses to which we have been socialized. That opening enables the consciousness-raising process to take place and gives us space in which to reflect on the new emotional responses that our process evokes.[29]

When Fisher refers to "the new emotional responses that our process evokes," the contemporary relevance and political radicalism of feminist pedagogy is made clear, for this reference indicates that one's landscape of desire ought to become a site of pedagogical inquiry. Similarly, Kathleen Weiler refers to the "goal of making students themselves theorists of their own lives by interrogating and analyzing their own experience."[30]

The most powerful and transformative forms of education are those that provoke students to reflect upon the social orchestration of their desire. Actively trying to provoke fundamental change in the consciousness and identity of students raises the question: On what grounds do we justify such radical interventions? Is there a democratic way to negotiate the asymmetrical power relation between teacher and student? Ursula Kelly explores many of these predicaments in her book, *Schooling Desire*:

> While it strikes me as necessary to reclaim eros, it is necessary to reclaim it cautiously. Such caution demands, minimally, that we ask continually of ourselves and our pedagogies what the sources of our passions and desires are, what effects our passions and desires have on others, and in what ways our passions and desires might interface with desiring others in productive and unproductive ways. I suggest it is our responses to these questions wherein lies the specificity of an

erotic character of our pedagogies. For this reason alone, it is important to analyze responses to cultural texts of teaching as a means of locating a reflexive sense of personal eros and teaching.[31]

The cautionary note Kelly expresses reminds us that unlike the dominant banking approach, radical pedagogies are designed to liberate both souls and societies. The incredibly ambitious nature of critical pedagogy requires that its practitioners remain constantly aware of their own potential hubris. This is particularly the case for white men, whose privileged location within patriarchal culture can make it difficult to grasp how their own authoritative interventions on behalf of a liberatory ideal can nevertheless function to silence and oppress others.

As Kathleen Weiler has shown, feminist consciousness-raising groups developed a non-dominative pedagogical method while retaining a strong commitment to personal and social transformation. The vertical model of education in which an all-knowing teacher narrated the contents of education to passive students was replaced by a horizontal model of teacher authority, in which students transformed themselves into the subjects rather than the objects of the educational process. This was accomplished by encouraging the participants of the CR groups to speak their mind and express feelings, anger, and so on, without fear of being judged by others or by a teacher/leader positioned as the unquestioned arbiter of truth.[32] Translated into mythological terms, feminists decided to step outside the moral geography of the Garden of Eden (at least outside the dominant interpretation). The educational goal of "reclaiming eros," therefore, is an activity which can best occur when vertical understandings of teacher authority are critically encountered within the classroom space. By reconfiguring operations of power within classroom settings and by moving away from the vertical model, new space is opened for students to name the world and to imagine a different one. The fact that this restructuring of power cannot be fully achieved, given the entrenched institutional hierarchies teachers work within, does not mean the project is futile and shouldn't be attempted. All that teachers can do is move decisively yet reflectively in this direction, keeping in mind that, like democracy, critical pedagogy will always remain an unfinished historical project.

The patriarchal structures and value system analyzed in this chapter have been shown to prohibit the discursive revaluation of eros. Thus far in the study, eros has been loosely framed as a discourse, experience, event, relation, gender, principle, as a template of affective epistemological qualities, and as a critical unit of analysis. Sometimes eros is referred to as an ontological condition, a mode of being that propels the meaning-quest and search for knowledge and truth, instilling within individuals the "pull" of future-directedness. Several qualities of eros are profiled by Maxine Greene when she conceives of education "as a process of futuring, or releasing persons to become reflective, of provoking people to repair lacks and to take action to create themselves."[33] Taken together, these multiple strands highlight eros's function as an *educational principle*.

Megan Boler's excellent study on the discursive history of emotion is valuable for many reasons, but for the purpose of defining eros, her definition of emotion as a unit of analysis may be used to illuminate the similarities and differences between these two signifiers.[34] As a tentative proposition, I suggest that emotion be understood as a wider ontological braid within which eros resides as a separate educational strand. For example, if someone said they are experiencing boredom, this experience reflects a negative emotion—as in "I feel bored." But this particular emotion, however, must be distinguished from the emotion of eros, which, in addition to its embodiment as feeling, includes a specific kind of value attachment, a zestful future-directedness, an animated desire to make larger connections and create novel meanings. So while eros reflects a set of emotions, I submit that these emotions are best identified by their educational resonances.

Toward a Feminist/Socratic Conversation

Feminist and Socratic pedagogy share many of the same structural and normative features; yet these similarities are generally overlooked. For an eros discourse to reach a new level of critical mass, I believe the conventional antipathy between feminist and Socratic pedagogy needs to be bridged. First of all, both frameworks thematize eros as a symbol of transformation. Both approaches foreground dialogue and consider it a valid source of knowledge and truth. Both privilege the emotional, imaginative domain of consciousness as that which propels the truth-quest. Both introduce a pedagogical imperative whereby the authority of the teacher is deconstructed. Both question prevailing truth regimes, drawing critical attention to the connections between power and knowledge in the construction of identity. Both grasp ignorance not as a quantitative deficiency, as a lack of empirical knowledge, but view ignorance as a qualitative relation, something we perform moment to moment. In this way, ignorance is above all an ethical relation, a fertile terrain pregnant with educational possibility. In view of these conceptual similarities, I contend that a sound basis exists for reconceiving the very terms in which the feminist/Socratic conversation takes place.

In *Feeling Power*, Megan Boler criticizes the Socratic admonition to "know thyself" as an approach which turns critical reflection into a solipsistic exercise, into what she calls "New Age, liberal navel-gazing." I agree with Boler that the practice of critical reflection should not be divorced from the practice of examining the reproductive links between identity and political culture. According to Boler, "to honor these complexities requires learning to develop genealogies of one's positionalities and emotional resistances."[35] But this is precisely what Socratic pedagogy attempts to do! One problem I have with Boler's discussion is that Socrates is implicitly cast as the demon, as somehow providing the ideological blueprint for the production of uncritical navel-gazers. Such a representation requires one to ignore a contextualized reading of the Socratic texts. In my view, the frequent caricature of Socratic pedagogy as an unselfconsciously patriarchal, conservative, and anti-democratic educational philosophy is misguided. Those in critical pedagogy should take seriously Wendy Brown's argument that the Socratic/Platonic project was intended to subvert the patriarchal iconography of ancient Athens, as well as Martha Nussbaum's interpretation of Socrates as a demophile.[36]

To justify these claims, it is important to recall the special relation which exists between eros and ignorance. In the *Symposium*, Diotima describes the power of eros as something which is elicited out of a condition of ignorance, but only when the individual acknowledges the condition of unknowing as intolerable.[37] In other words, the intense desire to know can only arise from a prior realization that one does not know: a lack that aches. As the Parable of the Cave illustrates, however, people often do not care if they don't know. What governs this caring and not caring? A recurring theme in this book has been the idea that eros is elicited (or not) by one's ethical relation to one's ignorance, by how one relates to and experiences the *aporias* intrinsic to selfhood. In a pedagogical approach anchored in self-interpretation, that is, anchored in a critical analysis of desire and how power works on identity, mapping one's ignorance becomes a crucial ethical practice. This pedagogical drama is played out by Socrates in the *Meno*.

At the outset of *Meno*, Socrates is posed the (in)famous question: "Can you tell me, Socrates, if virtue can be taught?" This question sets the stage for, as some would have it, the great dissimulation, the feign of ignorance cloaking the Socratic will to power "I am so far from knowing whether virtue can be taught or not that I do not even have any knowledge what virtue itself is." Meno refuses to accept Socrates' confession of ignorance: he wants instead for Socrates to deliver a clever-sounding lecture, to impart to him a truth which he obviously locates outside himself. Meno says, "But how do you mean that we do not learn, but what is called learning is recollection? Can you teach me how this is so?" To this Socrates replies:

"Meno, you are a rascal. Here you are asking me to give you my 'teaching,' I who claim there is no such thing as teaching, only recollection."[38] To this, Shoshana Felman responds:

> Socrates, that extraordinary teacher who taught humanity what pedagogy is, and whose name personifies the birth of pedagogics as a science, thus inaugurates his teaching practice, paradoxically enough, by asserting not just his own ignorance but the radical impossibility of teaching.[39]

In denying his vocation as teacher, in effect deconstructing his authority, Socrates deftly shifts the focus of inquiry from what he does or doesn't know to something quite different, namely, a critique of the quality of Meno's search. Meno responds to Socrates' line of questioning rather sluggishly. In doing so, Meno symbolizes an attitude toward learning which reflects a dissociation from one's lived experience. Although Meno *says* he desires to know what virtue is, Socrates begins to suspect that Meno's "desire to know" is abstracted from his own situatedness, a characteristic which virtually guarantees that his questions will be superficially motivated. Socrates sees Meno as a pedagogical problem because Meno wants to be filled with an externally derived knowledge and truth. Socrates wants Meno to look at his situatedness first. As Finkel and Arney write: "He chooses to take Meno seriously even though Meno is not taking himself seriously."[40] Socrates' dialogue with Meno, while not extensive, still contains important implications for grasping the fertility of ignorance as a concept and for grasping how tenets of Socratic pedagogy overlap with feminist pedagogy.

In the very first pages, for example, Socrates attempts to connect Meno's personal history and experience to the question which Meno has posed to Socrates. This is an important move. Rather than answering Meno's abstract question directly, Socrates instead wants to ground the dialogue by having Meno "locate" himself first. Socrates tells Meno he knows who his lover is, knows that he admires the sophist Gorgias, and knows that he is from Thessaly and not Athens. By refracting Meno's question about virtue back onto Meno's biography, provoking him to interrogate his own historical embeddedness, Socrates is pursuing exactly what Boler refers to as a "pedagogy of discomfort." Meno soon becomes uncomfortable and evasive and only wants to genuflect at Gorgias's feet, declaring that surely *he* knows what virtue is. Socrates is blunt: "Let's leave him out of this since, after all, he isn't here. What do you yourself say virtue is?"[41] Finkel and Arney develop this key pedagogical theme:

> Socrates makes Meno's biography relevant to the conversation because he wishes not to discuss the issue of virtue in the abstract, but the question of virtue in the concrete embodied presence that these two men are enacting before one another. After only a few lines of this dialogue, the question is no longer: Can virtue be taught? Instead, it is shifting toward the concrete question: Can Meno be taught virtue? He is telling Meno that it is time now to consider himself seriously, if he is going to ask such serious questions.[42]

This specific feature of Socratic pedagogy is central to feminist pedagogy and to what Boler calls "collective witnessing." As she defines it, "in contrast to the admonition to 'know thyself', collective witnessing is always understood in relation to others, and in relation to personal and cultural histories and material conditions."[43] My point is that Socrates does not conform to the solipsistic or conservative representations which are frequently attributed to his pedagogy. I believe that Boler's notions of "collective witnessing," on the one hand, and "pedagogy of discomfort," on the other ("to engage in critical inquiry regarding values and cherished beliefs"), are both eloquently and perceptively expressed. I want to suggest, however, there is a bit of "reinventing the wheel" operative in the introduction of these two categories since the conceptual underpinning of both are traced directly to Socratic pedagogy. First, Socrates is summarily discarded, then his educational categories are appropriated! I am not saying that feminist pedagogy should regard Socrates as a close ally, but only that the significant overlap between Socratic and feminist pedagogy be acknowledged.

Kathleen Weiler's brief history of women's consciousness-raising groups makes clear that a non-hierarchical structure constituted the basis of these learning communities. Feminist pedagogy has inherited this structural characteristic. Some critics have argued that although Plato obviously privileges dialogue, his dialogue is rooted in hierarchy. Yet, as we have seen in the *Meno*, if Socrates creates a hierarchy by continually referring to his own ignorance and by denying his ability to teach anything, it's certainly an odd-looking hierarchy. This interpretive dilemma reveals Socrates to be a friend of democratic political culture. To illustrate, I want to return to Socrates' assertion: "there is no such thing as teaching." Socrates' conviction that he is not or could not be a teacher is intertwined with his notion of ignorance. In her cogent analysis of this Socratic riddle, Felman quotes Sigmund Freud's similar reference to the impossibility of psychoanalysis: "At an early stage I had accepted the *bon mot* which lays it down that there are three impossible professions—educating, healing, governing—and I was fully occupied with the second of them." For Felman, these vocational doubts incite questions which every teacher ought to consider:

> If teaching is impossible, what are we teachers doing? How should we understand—and carry out—our task? And why is it that two of the most effective teachers ever to appear in the intellectual history of mankind regard the task of teaching as impossible? Indeed, is not their enunciation of the impossibility of teaching itself actively engaged in teaching, itself part of the lesson they bequeath us? And if so, what can be learned from the fact that it is impossible to teach? What can the impossibility of teaching teach us?[44]

The active self-subversion of one's authority as a teacher, which Socrates encourages, is a pedagogical and political move consistent with the precepts of a democratic political education. This is the case because democracy requires the education of autonomous individuals as against heteronomous individuals. My use of autonomy here should not be confused with solipsistic or individualistic orientations to the world, but rather, in line with democratic theorist Cornelius Castoriadis, "autonomous" is used to describe a mode of being in which one "authors" one's own rules and laws, in contrast to the heteronomous individual whose rules and laws are derived from external sources.[45] Socrates wants others to be author of their own truths, and to the extent they conceive of him as "the teacher," they merely re-enact narratives of dependence, whereby the location of truth and knowledge is externalized, a predisposition which preempts more authentic searches of their own. How can a student ever become her own teacher unless and until this hierarchy is exposed and transcended?

Few commentators explain the political radicalism of the Socratic/Platonic educational paradigm as well as Wendy Brown:

> Platonic epistemology and pedagogy are intricately bound to Platonic politics. The content of Platonic truth, its *political* radicalism, is in part why the road to truth is not paved solely with dialectic, reason, or logic. The myths, allegories, stories, and images in the dialogues appeal to the dimensions of Socrates' companions that are not necessarily articulate but that feel, sense, and yearn.[46]

The feeling, sensing, and yearning valences of eros are described by Plato through the use of feminine symbolism. Diotima refers to the beautiful image of *soul pregnancy* to approximate the expectant, about-to-give-birth intentionality of consciousness. In the *Theatetus*, Socrates calls himself a "midwife"; in the *Gorgias*, Callicles ridicules Socrates as "effeminant"; while in the *Meno*, Socrates *takes care not to treat Meno as yet another instance to win someone over and exert a kind of power-over,* via lecture, but as a person who has a location in history, who can inquire, and whose educational potential is boundless. These educational patterns lead Wendy Brown to describe Platonic pedagogy as "maternal."[47] The development of an eros-informed critical pedagogy will be enhanced if practitioners of Socratic and feminist pedagogy recognize that at some of the deepest levels of analysis, their theories share many of the same structural and normative features. The creative tension generated by a renewed Socratic/feminist conversation could only clarify the question of what eros is and how it can best be integrated into critical pedagogy.

Kal Alston elaborates on the educational importance of eros in terms of its ability, as a concept, to synthesize the epistemic, social, and moral demands of teaching:

> To dissociate knowledge and its pursuit from love seems almost natural in the context of current talk about the "science" of education, but that naturalness is sheer illusion. The relation of love to teaching seems immediately problematic. In part this is due to the philosophies of love that sentimentalize or biologize it. Like friendship, love has been removed from consideration as a form of human association that has powerful possibilities apart from its private significance, making claims for its place as a public good dubious. However, it will be argued here that love (eros) is precisely the kind of relationship that is required to coalesce the social and moral demands of teaching with the epistemic ones.[48]

In this formulation, Alston contends that eros is a "form of human association" that informs not only how we know, epistemologically, but what this knowledge comes to mean for students and teachers morally and ethically in terms of its potential to transform lives. The fact that Alston would refer to eros as something which embraces all of these foundational categories reaffirms the proposition that eros is indeed the transformative principle of education. Developing a critical literacy about the multifaceted qualities of eros, therefore, can provide an effective framework for teachers who wish to radicalize their pedagogical interventions.

Notes

1. For an indispensable discussion of this theme, see Theodor W. Adorno, "Education After Auschwitz," in *Critical Models: Interventions and Catchwords* (New York: Columbia University Press, 1998), 191–204. "Every debate about the ideals of education is trivial and inconsequential compared to this single ideal: never again Auschwitz. One speaks of the threat of a relapse into barbarism. But it is not a threat—Auschwitz *was* this relapse, and barbarism continues so long as the fundamental conditions that favored the relapse continue largely unchanged. That is the whole horror...Any reflection on the means to prevent the recurrence of Auschwitz is darkened by the thought that this desperation must be made conscious to people, lest they give way to idealistic platitudes. Nevertheless the attempt must be made, even in the face of the fact that the fundamental structure of society, and thereby its members who have made it so, are the same today as twenty-five years ago. Millions of innocent people—to quote or haggle over the numbers is already inhumane—were systematically murdered. That cannot be dismissed by any living person as a superficial phenomenon, as an aberration of the course of history to be disregarded when compared to the great dynamic of progress, of enlightenment, of the supposed growth of humanitarianism (191–92).

2. For an excellent analysis of how recent increases in military spending impact social programs, see "Congress Moves to Boost Military Spending," *Weekly Defense Monitor*, vol. 3, issue 14 (Washington, D.C., Center for Defense Information, April 8, 1999): 6–7. For a startling look at how American military expenditures eclipse the military expenditures of its nearest competitor (Russia = $55 billion, United States = $288 billion) as well as the rest of the world, see "U. S. Share of World Military Spending Growing," *Weekly Defense Monitor*, vol. 3, issue 44 (Washington, D.C., Center for Defense Information, November 11, 1999): 5.

3. Ursula Kelly, *Schooling Desire: Literacy, Cultural Politics, and Pedagogy* (New York: Routledge, 1997), 22; Roger Simon, *Teaching Against the Grain: Texts for a Pedagogy of Possibility* (South Hadley, Mass.: Bergin and Garvey, 1992), 40.

4. Erich Fromm, "Psychology of Nazism," in *Escape From Freedom* (New York: Holt, 1941), 205–38; Wilhelm Reich, *The Mass Psychology of Fascism* (New York: Farrar,

Straus and Giroux, 1934); George Mosse, *The Image of Man: The Creation of Modern Masculinity* (New York: Oxford University Press, 1986); Lynn Abrams and Elizabeth Harvey, "Driving the Message Home: Nazi Propaganda in the Private Sphere," in *Gender Relations in German History: Power, Agency and Experience from the Sixteenth to the Twentieth Century* (Durham: Duke University Press, 1997), 189–207.

5. George Mosse, *Nationalism and Sexuality* (Madison: University of Wisconsin Press, 1985); Klaus Theweleit, *Male Fantasies 1: Women, Floods, Bodies, History* (Minneapolis: University of Minnesota Press, 1987).

6. Wendy Brown, *Manhood and Politics: A Feminist Reading in Political Theory* (Totowa, N.J.: Rowman and Littlefield, 1988).

7. Anthony Giddens, "Nation-States and Violence," in *Social Theory and Modern Sociology* (Cambridge: Polity Press, 1987), 166–82.

8. Margot A. Henrikson, *Dr. Strangelove's America: Society and Culture in the Atomic Age* (Berkeley: University of California Press, 1997).

9. Theodor Adorno and Max Horkheimer, *The Authoritarian Personality* (New York: Norton, 1950), 976.

10. Michael Messner, *Power at Play: Sports and the Problem of Masculinity* (Boston: Beacon Press, 1992).

11. William James Gibson, *Warrior Dreams: Paramilitary Culture in Post-Vietnam America* (New York: Basic Books, 1992).

12. *Time* (December 20, 1999), 50–51.

13. As quoted in "The Columbine Tragedy: Countering the Hysteria," *The Humanist: A Magazine of Critical Inquiry and Social Concern* (July/August 1999): 7–10.

14. For a superb study analyzing conflict resolution models in the United States, see Megan Boler, "Taming the Labile Student: Emotional Literacy Curricula," in *Feeling Power: Emotions and Education* (New York: Routledge, 1999), 79–107.

15. While discussing Freud, I choose not to use the term "Thanatos" to describe the "death instinct," since it's not reflected in any of his texts, though the term is widely attributed to him. Ernest Jones remarks: "It is a little odd that Freud himself never, except in conversation, used for the death instinct the term Thanatos, one which has become so popular since." See Ernest Jones, *Freud, Life and Work*, III (London: Hogarth Press, 1961), 295. For a discussion of how eros and the death instinct are "alloyed," see "Why

War?" *The Freud/Einstein Letters, International Journal of Group Tensions,* 1 (Jan/March 1971): 9–26. Freud writes, "It seems as though an instinct of the one sort can scarcely ever operate in isolation; it is always accompanied—or, as we say, alloyed—with an element from the other side, which modifies its aim or is, in some cases, what enables it to achieve its aim" (p. 19).

16. Boler, preface to viii–xxv.

17. Audre Lorde, "Uses of the Erotic: The Erotic as Power," in *Sister/Outsider* (Freedom, Calif.: The Crossing Press Feminist Series, 1984), 53.

18. Haunani-Kay Trask, *Eros and Power: The Promise of Feminist Theory* (University Park: University of Pennsylvania Press, 1986): preface to viii–xi.

19. Lorde, 60. Audre Lorde does make implied references to this same power existing within men, too; however, what I am criticizing is the tendency to collapse eros with females, not the feminine.

20. Cheryl Hall, "Uses of the Erotic: Contemporary Feminists and Plato on Eros, Power, and Reason" (Ph.D. diss., Princeton University, 1993), 59.

21. Hall, 60.

22. bell hooks, "Eros, Eroticism, and the Pedagogical Project," in *Teaching to Transgress* (New York: Routledge, 1994), 195.

23. hooks, 191–92.

24. Lorde, 57.

25. Herbert Marcuse, *Eros and Civilization* (Boston: Beacon Press, 1955), 201–02. See also Joan Landes, "Marcuse's Feminist Dimension," *Telos* (1979), 158–86. Landes quotes Marcuse from a lecture he gave in 1974: "Perhaps the [women's movement] is the most important and potentially the most radical political movement we have" (158).

26. Marcuse, 222.

27. Carter Heyward, *Touching Our Strength: The Erotic as Power and the Love of God* (San Francisco: Harper and Row, 1989), 89. For a non-theological, yet "spiritual" account of eros, see Susan Griffin, *The Eros of Everyday Life* (New York: Anchor Books, 1995).

28. Heyward, 90.

29. Berenice Fisher, "The Heart Has Its Reasons: Feeling, Thinking, and Community-Building in Feminist Education," in *Women's Studies Quarterly*, XV: 3&4 (Fall/Winter 1987): 48.

30. Kathleen Weiler, "Freire and a Feminist Pedagogy of Difference," *Harvard Educational Review* 61:4 (November 1991): 462. See also Carolyn Shrewsbury, "What is Feminist Pedagogy?" *Women's Studies Quarterly* XV: 3&4 (Fall/Winter 1987): 6–14.

31. Kelly, 130.

32. Weiler, 455–60.

33. Maxine Greene, *The Dialectic of Freedom* (New York: Teachers College Press, 1988), 22.

34. Boler, xix–xx.

35. Boler, 178.

36. See Wendy Brown, "Supposing Truth Were a Woman: Plato's Subversion of Masculine Discourse," in *Feminist Interpretations of Plato*, ed. Nancy Tuana (University Park: Pennsylvania State University Press, 1994), 158–79; and Martha Nussbaum, "Socratic Self-Examination," in *Cultivating Humanity* (Cambridge: Harvard University Press, 1997), 15–49.

37. Plato, *Symposium*, 204a. Subsequent references to this work are cited in the text with the abbreviation *Sym.*

38. Plato, *Meno*, 70a–71b.

39. Shoshona Felman, "Psychoanalysis and Education: Teaching Terminable and Interminable," in *Jacques Lacan and the Adventure of Insight* (Cambridge: Harvard University Press, 1988), 69.

40. Donald Finkel and William Ray Arney, *Educating for Freedom: The Paradox of Pedagogy* (New Brunswick: Rutgers University Press, 1995), 171.

41. *Meno*, 71d.

42. Finkel and Arney, 172.

43. Boler, 178.

44. Felman, 70.

45. Cornelius Castoriadis, "The Problem of Democracy Today," *Democracy and Nature* 3: 22–24.

46. Brown, 167.

47. Brown, 168.

48. Kal Alston, "Teaching, Philosophy, and Eros: Love as a Relation to Truth," *Educational Theory* (Fall 1991): 385–86. For another perspective, which argues that progressive political change in the United States, including educational reform, requires a critically theorized love discourse to fulfill it aims, see bell hooks, "Love as the Practice of Freedom," in *Outlaw Culture: Resisting Representations* (New York: Routledge, 1996), 243–50.

5

Eros as the Educational Principle of Democracy

The soul of the ordinary man and woman hides vast recesses of intensity. The sadness of much human life lies in the disproportion between this intensity and the accidental or unworthy objects on which people so often lavish their intense commitments. That this reserve capacity for devotion and obsession can be tapped productively, for the good of the community, has always been the major tenet of the American religion of possibility. Democracy, Americans understand, depends upon *demophilia*, love of the people.
—West and Unger (1998)

If fear and destructiveness are the major emotional sources of fascism, eros belongs mainly to democracy.
—Horkheimer and Adorno (1950)

Eros, Education, and Democracy

One of the chief obstacles to deepening and extending the democratic project is the liberal/modernist educational paradigm. The fundamental problem with this dominant paradigm lies in its crucial devaluation of eros, broadly understood as passion and connection. This devaluation carries severe consequences for educating democratic citizens, yet liberal narratives do not raise serious questions about their anti-democratic underpinnings. Indeed, the absence of such questions today is barely noticed, an apt measure of liberal hegemony. Instead, we learn that liberalism is virtually synonymous with democracy and functions as its principal enabler. This comforting assumption invites critical analysis. Such an analysis must illuminate the anti-erotic prejudices of the liberal knowledge system and articulate the ways in which a greater understanding of the conceptual affinities between eros and democracy can help educators invigorate democratic forms of education. Once we grasp that liberal epistemology is conceptually unable to "see" eros as a meaningful category and value it as a vital dimension of education, we begin to understand the limitations it has in terms of its capacity to educate for democracy.

Rollo May writes that "eros is a *state of being*," a form of desire which provides the condition of possibility for seeking union with our highest potentialities, however interminable that process may be.[1] Although eros is notoriously difficult to define in any reductionistic sense, its broad contours can be generally discerned. For example, the symbolic association of eros with qualities such as passion, connection, questioning, community, empathy, and a vision of the good, not to mention its perpetually incomplete character, gives the concept a rich inventory of meanings. The various qualities attributed to eros, significantly, inform the associational dimensions of democracy. Taken together, these qualities and meanings clearly approximate Dewey's definition of democracy as a *state of being*, "a form of moral and spiritual association."[2] It is noteworthy that in his biography of America's most influential philosopher, Robert Westbrook concludes that Dewey's concept of democracy is at odds with the main tenets of liberalism.[3]

As I argued in the introduction of this book, few if any educators can deny that what we call eros enables education to occur: in this sense, eros is the radical of the educational moment, the square root of its power. If we can acknowledge that the experience of eros constitutes the heart of education, why not take the next step and elevate eros to its proper status as an organizing principle of education? The elevation of eros to an organizing principle would enable students and teachers alike to better grasp the non-economistic meanings and purposes of education. For this elevation to occur, one must first identify, understand, and ultimately abandon certain commonsense assumptions characteristic of the liberal paradigm.

A dominant strand of liberal thought, for example, is that passion ought not play any role in politics or education. We have seen in chapter 2 how Horace Mann sought to create a kind of *cordon sanitaire* around the public space of the classroom so that "reason" (the mind) could reign supreme over the passions (the body). According to the liberal conception, the public realm is thus designed to be an emotionally neutral space, a feature which seeks to bracket out the role of passion rather than confronting the pedagogical task of actually educating the passions or desires. This epistemological prejudice includes the devaluation of feeling, emotion, imagination, and wonder, all qualities which can be reasonably organized under the rubric of an eros principle. Benjamin Barber argues that liberalism does support, in various ways, a weak or "thin" version of democracy, but its epistemology and register of values render it unable to provide a framework for the development of "strong" democracy:

> Liberal democracy is based on premises about human nature, knowledge, and politics that are genuinely liberal but that are not intrinsically democratic. Its conception of the individual and of individual interest undermines the democratic practices upon which both individuals and their interests depend. Liberal democracy is thus a "thin" theory of democracy, one whose democratic values are prudential, and thus provisional, optional, and conditional—means to exclusively individualistic and private ends. From this precarious foundation, no firm theory of citizenship, participation, public goods, or civic virtue can be expected to arise.[4]

Because most educators operate unselfconsciously within the liberal paradigm, the overwhelming majority of teachers emphasize the state-centric and electoral aspects of democracy as if these dimensions represent the heart of what democracy is. By thus defining democracy preeminently by its institutionality, students are miseducated to conceive of democracy as a purely mechanical routine whose principal mode of expression is voting. As John Dewey, Sheldon Wolin, Cornel West, C. Douglas Lummis, and Benjamin Barber, among others, have written, the nucleus of democracy is not the state, but is rather an individual and collective *state of being*.[5] The qualities and values that define democracy as a mode of being, such as questioning, the desire to know, to revise, to envision a perceived good, and to participate in a community, all grow out of the emotional soil of eros. The cumulative force of these affinities permits us to reassert that eros is the educational principle of democracy.

To arrange the various sections of this chapter into a coherent picture, I will address these two complex signifiers from several analytical standpoints. In the following pages, I explore what a classroom would look like if these two principles were joined together in pedagogical concert. I also attempt to disentangle eros and democracy from the public/private dichotomy, since too rigid an adherence to this conceptual framework obscures their affinities by locating them in separable categories. This task is not accomplished by abandoning the public/private distinction wholesale, but rather by examining the profound similarities eros and democracy share in terms of their epistemological and ontological overlap, *beneath their discursive organization*. Since feminist scholars have contributed enormously to the discourse on eros, I include an analysis of how power and gender differentials shape representations of eros and what these patterns imply about developing an "eros-informed" democratic pedagogy.[6] I conclude by examining some of the crucial paradigmatic issues at stake in the progressive reconstruction of democratic culture in the United States.

Snapshot of an Eros-Informed Democratic Classroom

In describing what a classroom would look and feel like when eros and democracy are understood in pedagogical concert, one should avoid attaching too much importance to any formulaic or de-contexualized prescriptions. What follows, therefore, is not so much a discussion of a particular method, but an impressionistic snapshot, so to speak, which tries to capture the images and associations of eros as they are tied together by a normative commitment to democracy as an historical project.

Let us begin by describing a classroom in which eros is *absent*. In this classroom, colored grey, there is no sharing of oneself with others by either the students or the teacher; education, in other words, is a solipsistic affair. Most students don't hear the voices of those next to them, not to mention voices from across the room: students here are not provoked to encounter others across their differences. In this classroom, people are guarded and cautious. Since individualism reigns, there is no emergent community identity arising from a sense of shared mutuality. There is no enthusiasm in the class (except perhaps to exit), for the subject under study bears little to no connection to the student's lived experience. There is no *élan vital*, no intense interest taken in the work of others. Nor is there a trace of irony in this humorless space. People are polite and contained, with no messy spillover: no emotional strife, no moments of dissension or awkward silences, and no affection. The "knowledge" which the teacher/clerk dutifully deposits in the minds of his/her students is religiously factual and thus disembodied.

There is, however, a significant degree of Order in this classroom. Everyone appears to know their place in the undiscussed hierarchy. The teacher, unwaveringly Objective, actively encourages students not to ask any questions about the structure of power within the classroom or the basis of her real or imagined authority. The rows of desks remain in neat, straight lines. Although this space is filled with individual souls, the absence of eros and a shared vision of the good (however the good is envisioned and contested) means the classroom experience is defined by an emotional void. Of course, this classroom is not only profoundly boring, it's also profoundly anti-democratic, even if what is being taught is the virtue of voting.

At a broad level, "eros" refers to a kind of intersubjective vitality: a kind of social climate generated when trust and sharing and participation through dialogue transforms academic work into a fully awake yet contentious enterprise (after all, democracy is not about agreement but largely how to disagree in a venue of contestation and equality). In this classroom there is no apathy, no absence of passion; the teacher leads, but not narcissistically. On another level, this classroom is infused with a culture of equality where the enactment of hierarchies is viewed with suspicion; thus democratic teachers tend to deconstruct their own authority, ironically. An erotically democratic classroom is one in which people *actively* listen to one another. As Jim Garrison puts it: "Dialogues across difference *are* disturbing. Listening is dangerous. It places us at risk and leaves us vulnerable, so why listen?...Because others may have what we need in thought, action, and feeling, and we might not even know it."[7] As an intensification of empathy, genuine listening contains both erotic and democratic components. Democracy also requires dialogue on a frank basis about the role of power in social existence, including its effects on the production of knowledge and identity.[8] Because these uniquely democratic questions cut to the marrow of identity and tend to expose what is frequently ignored in social life, they have the potential to elicit eros, as the desire to know.

At yet another level of analysis, classrooms can be seen as sites where prototypical forms of democratic association and community are made possible by a "lessening of difference" between self and other and world. Audre Lorde, for one, identifies this lessening of difference between people and the world as one of the most valuable capacities of eros.[9] When Freire constructs the moral distinction between being *in* the world as opposed to being *with* the world, he acknowledges the dynamic widening of identity which only the "revolutionary futurity" of eros can energize.[10]

In considering the education of these democratic dispositions, it is difficult to escape the conclusion that the liberal devaluation of passion in education and politics represents a structural limitation in terms of its capacity to reproduce democratic forms of culture. For the dispositions and habits which sustain democratic culture, such as a passionate engagement with the world or an intense indignation at the perception of social injustice, are qualities virtually impossible to cultivate within the dominant (liberal) way of knowing. Freire gives cogent expression to the challenge many teachers face whose practice is all too often ensnared in the consequences of liberal hegemony:

> We must dare, in the full sense of the word, to speak of love without the fear of being called ridiculous, mawkish, or unscientific, if not anti-scientific. We must dare in order to say scientifically, and not just as mere blah-blah-blah, that we study, we learn, we teach, we know with our entire body. We do all these things with feeling, with emotion, with wishes, with fear, with doubts, with passion, and also with critical reasoning. However, we never study, learn, teach, or know with the last only. We must dare so as to never dichotomize cognition and emotion. We must dare to learn how to dare in order to say no to the bureaucratization of the mind to which we are exposed every day.[11]

Every associational quality crucial to democratic political culture grows out of the emotional soil of eros. If teachers aspire to radical democratic education, they need to familiarize themselves with the symbolic currents of eros and inform their pedagogical practice accordingly. In understanding eros as an overarching educational principle, much-needed coherence is brought to the project of educating democratic citizens.

Disentangling the Epistemological and Ontological Overlap

Horkheimer and Adorno are eloquent in describing the conceptual linkages between eros and democracy: "If fear and destructiveness are the major emotional sources of fascism," they maintain, "*eros belongs mainly to democracy*" (emphasis added).[12] Given these authors' insights into the psychological roots of the fascist personality formation and its proclivity to dehumanize "the other," their statement deserves to be taken seriously.

For if indeed "eros belongs to democracy," we need to reflect upon this provocative assertion in all its depth and complexity.

First of all, notice that the conventional division between public (democracy) and private (eros) is implicitly disturbed and represented as an undivided effect, an ontological similitude which suggests that neither signifier can be accurately categorized as entirely public or private. Although these thinkers do not elaborate on this intriguing conceptual affinity in their book, this interpretive absence needs to be filled. For example, if the major emotional sources of fascism are fear and destructiveness, eros may be seen to represent the *emotional currents of love* that a democratic culture obviously requires. When one acknowledges the supreme challenge the achievement of strong democracy poses to imperfect human beings, and considers the demanding moral and spiritual qualities this form of association requires to sustain itself, it should not be surprising that the development of a critically theorized love discourse would be necessary to enable and help fulfill the democratic vision.

The affinity between eros and democracy has far-reaching educational implications for a pluralist society like the United States. Eros is an educational principle consistent with the tenets of critical multiculturalism not only because it has historically been coded as that which defies hierarchical distinctions, but also because its qualities are uniquely endowed to disrupt the historic nexus between violence and national identity. The lively and critical eros discourse which is now emerging should therefore be seen as an historical antidote to the "violent cartography" of the national political imaginary.[13] If people come to know and value eros, first discursively and then experientially, its unique qualities make it especially difficult to dehumanize the other and use the radical rejection of otherness as a fulcrum for the construction of one's own "superior identity."

At the most basic level, the epistemological and ontological overlap between eros and democracy could be framed in the following way. Epistemologically, they are alike in the sense that both eros and democracy symbolize ways of knowing which share the same patterns of value and signification. These patterns have been identified in previous chapters, and they will be further clarified in the pages ahead. Ontologically, they are alike in their recurring historical representation as two separate yet highly related "*states of being.*"

The Question of Questioning

For Cornelius Castoriadis, democratic dispositions are enabled only by the development of a kind of self-reflection which includes a passionate engagement with the world: a feeling of intense responsibility for the present and future quality of social life and public affairs. Castoriadis posits a form of political reflection as the nucleus of actually existing democracy. According to this perspective, democracy hinges on what he calls "political self-reflectiveness," a mode of questioning resonant with a passion for public affairs. Thus, by linking love of the world (*astynomos orga*) to a concept of self-reflection, Castoriadis transcends hegemonic narratives which separate reason from passion.[14] Such a passion-friendly conception of political knowledge also pries open space for the articulation of a theory of eros, which similarly denotes the affective, imaginative, communicative, intersubjective, and dynamic strands of human experience.

A particular etymological reading of *democracy* supports his definition of political self-reflectiveness:

> We must return to the original meaning of the word democracy. Democracy does not mean human rights, does not mean lack of censorship, does not mean elections of any kind. All this is very nice, but it's just second—or third—degree consequences of democracy. Democracy means the power (kratos) of the people (demos). If we think deeply about these words, some substantial questions emerge. First of all, what is the demos, who is the demos, who belongs to the demos? Then, what does power mean? And the fact that the very characterization, the very term, that defines this regime produces these questions, shows the special nature of this regime, which is born at the same moment with the philosophical inquiry,

as opposed to other forms of government in which such questions cannot be born. Democracy, by its name already, produces questions and problems.[15]

Castoriadis does not explicitly discuss the implications these questions have for pedagogical theory. But for the purposes of this inquiry, the main pedagogical point is fairly clear: democracy, among other things, is fundamentally about learning how to question power. He also indicates that these signifiers, democracy and love of wisdom, are two functionally related processes. Since eros has historically been associated with philosophy and the examined life, the effort by Castoriadis to link one questioning regime to another reinforces the view that the conceptual mutuality between eros and democracy exists on several levels. The historical coincidence of these *two regimes of questioning* represents another curious similarity which could easily provide further grist for our conceptual mill. However interesting it might be to enter into debate about the "origins" of philosophical eros and democracy, this inquiry is focused more on identifying their diverse affinities and speculating about what this *cumulative pattern* means for future efforts to reconstruct democratic political education.

Democratic questioning functions to distinguish education as a liberatory project from education as a disciplinary project. Indeed, the formulation of the democratic questions noted above constitutes a sound basis for the project of *educating* as opposed to *schooling* the desire of nascent citizens, a critical distinction which Ursula Kelly perceptively develops.[16] Of course, educating for democracy is a form of political education which is most certainly an imposition. But then, imposition is endemic to the educational project. A more fruitful question posed by this predicament is whether or not a meaningful distinction can be made between a democratic political education, on the one hand, and a politicized education, on the other. I contend that a democratic political education *educates* rather than *schools* desire, if, in line with Castoriadis, students develop a civic literacy for asking questions about the power/knowledge/truth relationships in their political and educational culture.

A genealogy of the eros motif from ancient to contemporary times demonstrates that eros has consistently been interpreted as constitutive of the process of questioning.[17] Eros is not about the closure of learning but is rather a metaphor for the energy motivating the question itself. That which propels the knowledge quest has been repeatedly attributed to eros: a desire to grasp ever larger connections and meaning between self and other and world. If Castoriadis is correct in saying that democracy is constituted by questioning, we can extend this point and assert that questioning is constituted by eros, as the desire to know. In a sense, then, eros can be seen as an ontological predicate of forms of experience conducive to democratic culture. To reaffirm Horkheimer and Adorno's assertion, we could say that the "emotional sources" which give rise to democratic forms of life, in the first instance, belong mainly to eros.

Eros, Democracy, and Sensuous Rationality

Sheldon Wolin's conception of democracy is related to the eros motif in ways which throw light on the notion that eros fulfills rather than destroys reason. The editors of *Athenian Political Thought and the Reconstruction of American Democracy* attempt to retrieve aspects of democracy generally forgotten in today's discourse:

> Democracy bears within it a moment of revolution, and Wolin argues that for any political order to remain genuinely democratic, it must nurture, rather than suppress, the seeds of its own transformation. Democracy violates constitutions, and constitutional democracies need to welcome their own violation if they would continue to be democratic.[18]

This remarkable description is suggestive of the mutuality between eros and democracy insofar as eros has also been described as a fluid, structureless structure.[19] Both eros and democracy have been feared, owing to this perception of their uncontainable and ungovernable qualities.

Significantly, Wolin extends an explicit criticality to this space deemed so crucial to democracy. In doing so, Wolin describes democracy as a self-critical and interminable movement, deliberately privileging its cultural rather than constitutional dimensions. In contrast to Wolin, Castoriadis, Barber, and others, conventional understandings of democracy usually emphasize its institutionality, its capacity to establish orderly constitutions such as the liberal republicanism extolled in the *Federalist Papers*. One consequence of this view for citizenship education is that it becomes overly attached to a state-centric/corporatist concept of democracy, which, in its shallowest yet all too frequent incarnation, restricts citizenship to a rather hollow legal status. In making these distinctions between different qualities of democracy, Wolin deserves extended quotation:

> Instead of a conception of democracy as indistinguishable from its constitution, I propose accepting the familiar charges that democracy is inherently unstable, inclined toward anarchy, and identified with revolution and using these traits as the basis for a different, *a*constitutional conception of democracy. Instead of assuming that the "natural" direction, the telos, of the democratic encounter with the political is toward greater institutional organization and that the problem is to adapt democracy to the requirements of organization, we might think of democracy as resistant to the rationalizing conceptions of power and its organization which for centuries have dominated western thinking and have developed constitutionalism and their legitimating rationale. This democracy might be summed up as the idea and practice of rational disorganization.[20]

Wolin's concept of democracy as the idea and practice of "rational disorganization" merges two opposing tendencies. These tendencies exist in tension and resist final closure. Wolin's theoretical move here is not unlike Marcuse's effort in *Eros and Civilization* to eroticize reason and transcend the passion/reason dichotomy by deploying the concept of "sensuous rationality."[21] Both of these paradoxical formulations are attempts to transcend excessively dichotomous patterns of thought characteristic of the liberal paradigm. Throughout its discursive history, with the exception of its prephilosophical and Augustinian representations, eros has been coded as that which can potentially instantiate a critical or reflective dimension. As Freire previously asserted, the educational privileging of love, or eros, should not be taken to mean that it stands in binary opposition to something called reason. Castoriadis's discussion of political self-reflectiveness, fueled as it is by *astynomos orga*, demonstrates that he is similarly rejecting the idea of an emotion/cognition dichotomy. In addition, many feminist scholars, such as bell hooks and Kathleen Weiler, specifically discuss eros as that which promotes rather than destroys critical reason.

Eros has been located on alternate sides of countless antinomies: female/male, feminine/masculine, mind/body, public/private, and spirituality/sexuality, to mention a few. In the *Symposium*, for example, Diotima tells Socrates that eros is "barefoot and homeless," as the offspring of poverty as well as plenty. Yet eros is also responsible for the "building of cities" and cooperative projects for the public good.[22] Plato's recurring descriptions of eros as existing "in between" poverty and plenty and ignorance and knowledge are examples of how, conceptually, eros escapes binary logic. As a heuristic device, then, the concept of eros is useful in terms of its capacity to disturb unselfconscious patterns of dualistic thought.[23]

While eros eludes simple and reductionistic definition, the contours of a generalized eros can be discerned in the work of liberation theologian Leonardo Boff. While referencing a liberation theologian to define eros may give some readers pause, in fact there are clear parallels to be drawn between liberation theology and critical pedagogy.[24] Interestingly, Wolin's definition of democracy as an unfinished reflective process is astonishingly similar to how Boff defines the main features of eros:

> The best way of representing the human spirit for us is to consider it as Eros, because the life of the spirit is never represented as something ready-made and finished, but rather as a process and project of execution, deepening, retreating

and recovering, searching out new molds, and rising above and beyond every determination.[25]

Boff interprets eros as an incomplete form in motion. In terms of its searching, future-directed purpose, this representation of eros is consistent with the features of democracy advanced by Castoriadis, Wolin, and others. Broadly speaking, the characteristics and concepts these authors identified as most valuable to democracy—"political self-reflectiveness," "moment of revolution," "seeds of its own transformation," and "rational disorganization"—are homologous to aspects of eros. Indeed, for many democratic theorists, democracy is defined by its revisable, unfinished movement, its buoyancy, and its explicit criticality.

These broad similarities of form must also be investigated in their qualitative and affective dimensions. Like Marcuse, Boff posits the existence of an historical tension between logos and eros. Boff rejects the Cartesian principle *cogito, ergo sum* that dominates contemporary thought. He argues that by positing the exclusive loci of identity within the thinking mind, human agency is restricted. Boff contends that the eros principle must be privileged if a wider understanding of what it means to be human is to emerge. His privileging of feeling over thinking subverts the epistemology of the dominant educational paradigm:

> The base experience is feeling. Not the *cogito, ergo sum* (I think, therefore I am), but the *sentio, ergo sum* (I feel, therefore I am); not Logos, but Pathos, the capacity to be affected and to affect—affectivity. Eros does not only imply a feeling, but a co-feeling, a consent, not only being conscious of the passion of the world, but having compassion. Everything that is tied to Eros must see with fantasy, with creativity, bursting forth toward the new, the surprising, the wonderful.[26]

In his analysis, Boff does not fall into the trap of supposing that eros is coterminus with the body while logos is strictly of the mind but, rather, sees both as principles in mutual tension. Just like Marcuse, Boff argues that the "historical task" of our present epoch is to redress the imbalance brought about by the historical forgetting of eros.

Eros as an educational principle should not, therefore, be imagined as a completely unmoored eros, unmediated by critical reflection. Recall that Marcuse's metaphor of "sensuous rationality" represents a creative tension between two opposing tendencies, just as Wolin's "rational disorganization" approximates a similar convergence. On the metaphoric level, then, in addition to other significant conceptual affinities, eros and democracy evince identical structural tensions. In this connection, they both share the distinction of sometimes being feared for their respective excesses: "mob rule" in the case of democracy and "*epithymia*" (as unreflective, base desire) in the case of eros. However, the point is that when both these conditions are properly educated, their "anarchic" and "ungovernable" energy can be transformed onto a higher plane, toward a vision of the good.[27] In terms of revaluing eros, Marcuse's concept of "sensuous rationality" is particularly useful, since it disturbs the reason/passion dichotomy at the basis of liberal epistemology.

Dewey, Eros, and Prophetic Pragmatism

John Dewey's representations of democracy privilege forms of association which exude many signs of eros. Dewey wrote very little on eros, per se—but he still foregrounds qualities such as communion, creativity, critical inquiry, and the art of communication, to mention a few—which could plausibly be organized under the heading of an eros principle.

Jim Garrison shows how Dewey displays an implicit theory of eros in his emphasis on the democratic negotiation of the good and in his revaluation of experiential and creative forms of learning.[28] In *The Public and Its Problems*, Dewey defines democracy in freewheeling cultural terms:

Democracy will come into its own, for democracy is a name for a life of free and enriching communion. It has its seer in Walt Whitman. It will have its consummation when free social inquiry is indissolubly wedded to the art of full and moving communication.[29]

In this passage, Dewey's ideal democracy is approximated by a set of dynamic and expansive metaphors consistent with those employed by Castoriadis, Wolin, and Boff. Notice in Dewey's brief formulation, democracy is a movement, a "life of free and enriching communion," actualized when "free social inquiry" is wedded to the "art of full and moving communication." Social inquiry, moreover, becomes democratic only when informed by the "art" of "full and moving communication." These Deweyan themes of democratic culture are clearly linked to eros. Jim Garrison asserts how Dewey advocated a theory of knowledge from a deeply democratic standpoint:

Everyone can only see from the various standpoints they have occupied, including what they remember of where they have been, where they think they are, and where they imagine they are going. The power of imagination lies in its capacity to multiply perspectives rapidly. Dewey thought that reality is infinitely complex but that mortals can only gather a finite number of perspectives. Thus finite creatures can grow wiser only if they share perspectives, for seeing things from the standpoint of others also allows us to multiply perspectives. That is why Dewey thought dialogues across differences were essential for those who desire to grow. When a single standpoint excludes others the result is a distorted view of reality.[30]

Significantly, for those who desire to grow wiser, "dialogue across difference" is seen as indispensable to that process. What form of educational power is capable of creating the conditions of possibility to enable the "art of full and moving communication"? From Sappho and Plato to Rousseau and Marcuse and forward to contemporary feminist pedagogy, it is eros which has been identified as the power and energy which informs the deepening and widening of identity.

Dewey also identifies the democratic impulse as that which must "break existing public forms."[31] This expansive image is consistent with

Wolin's "aconstitutional" definition of democracy as well as his description of democracy as containing a "moment of revolution" and the "seeds of its own transformation." Once again, the metaphors and characteristics used to describe democracy replicate characteristics frequently ascribed to eros. Thus far, four interwoven strands have surfaced as common to both democracy and eros: (a) a dynamism and movement, (b) an extension of identity, (c) an element of critical reflection, and (d) a manifest lack of completion.

According to Cornel West, Dewey searched unsuccessfully for a new language to describe democracy.[32] West contends that some of the labels Dewey attached to democracy—"new individualism," "renascent liberalism," "the great community"—ultimately proved inadequate because they did not properly emphasize the cultural aspects of radical democracy:

> These candidates are inadequate primarily because they fail to capture the most crucial aspect of Dewey's vision: the need for an Emersonian *culture* of radical democracy in which self-creation and communal participation flourish in all their diversity and plurality. For Dewey, the aim of political and social life is the cultural enrichment and moral development of self-begetting individuals and self-regulating communities by means of a release of human powers provoked by novel circumstances and new challenges. He thought that the crisis of American civilization was first and foremost a cultural crisis of distraught individuals, abject subjects, and ruptured communities alienated from their own powers, capacities, and potentialities.[33]

Accepting the validity of West's thesis permits us to view the essence of Dewey's democratic vision—its cultural terrain—as constituting a web of association and identity practice whose actualization is enabled by the questing energies of eros. West's language of crisis accurately mirrors Dewey's analysis of American culture. In this analysis, we see *distraught* individuals, *abject* subjects, *ruptured* communities, seemingly alienated from their own powers and potentialities. It is instructive to note that in profiling this malaise, every example involves the separation of the individual from others and from one's own internal powers: a measure of the absence of eros.

Cornel West concludes his brilliant genealogical analysis of American pragmatism by articulating a theory of "prophetic pragmatism." This powerful pedagogical vision tacitly affirms how closely entwined the concept of eros is to both democracy and critical pedagogy. West defines prophetic pragmatism as a new kind of "politically explicit" cultural criticism, one whose uniquely American practice brings philosophy down to earth, so to speak, for the purpose of expanding democratic political culture:

> Prophetic pragmatism, with its roots in the American heritage and its hopes for the wretched of the earth, constitutes the best chance of promoting an Emersonian culture of creative democracy by means of critical intelligence and social action. I have dubbed it "prophetic" in that it harks back to the Jewish and Christian prophets who brought urgent and compassionate critique to bear on the evils of their day. The mark of the prophet is to speak the truth in love with courage—come what may.[34]

In this pedagogical formulation, prophetic pragmatism involves the exact same kind of passionate and critical engagement with the world and its power relations that is so pronounced in the writings of Freire and Castoriadis. West's construction of this concept, as a vocational heuristic intended to strengthen realms of democratic culture, carries profound implications for teachers. On my reading, the language West employs to describe prophetic pragmatism could be organized under the rubric of an eros principle: *hope for the wretched of the earth, culture of creative democracy, compassion, truth, love, courage.* Since West references aspects of Plato sympathetically in his writings, he may agree with the proposition that eros, understood as an educational principle, could bring additional clarity to the main precepts of prophetic pragmatism.

Another attractive component of prophetic pragmatism is its capacity to embrace mobile epistemological standpoints, a necessary feature of any social theory purporting to extend democratic political culture. For example, in defining the concept, West says it "neither requires a religious foundation nor entails a religious perspective, yet prophetic pragmatism is compatible with certain religious outlooks."[35] Of course, if teachers were to understand their vocational identity in the context of prophetic pragmatism, in effect, they would be transgressing the boundaries of the liberal educational paradigm, since within its logic, the principles of *objectivity* and *political neutrality* are seen as both desirable and sacrosanct. When eros and democracy are understood pedagogically in the context of prophetic pragmatism, however, the principles of objectivity and political neutrality are positively desanctified. This abandonment of objectivity and political neutrality is not intended to license a pedagogy of reverse indoctrination, but rather, to encourage a critical posture to all forms of domination, including our own. Based on his own agonizing dilemmas, Dewey well understood the dangers of professionalizing philosophy: it could easily become de-politicized, alienated, and increasingly irrelevant to the social problems of the day. In response to what Dewey called the "intellectual timidity" of American culture, he put forth a "plea for speculative audacity."[36] The effort to educationalize eros and illuminate its connection to prophetic pragmatism is a response to this plea.

Conclusion. Eros as Counter-Paradigmatic Principle: The Education of Desire and the Future of Democratic Culture

The various accounts of eros and democracy surveyed in this inquiry support the claim that their metaphoric inventories are strikingly similar. I have traced their patterns of signification: dynamic, transformational, non-hierarchical, dialogical, communal, critical, each containing dimensions of incompletion and future-directedness. In acknowledging the affinity between what could now be described as *two states of being,* the question is no longer if eros belongs to democracy but in what sense it belongs and what these conceptual linkages mean in terms of educating for democracy.

I began the discussion by saying that within the dominant epistemology eros and democracy are posited as conceptually separable. Yet this inquiry demonstrates that both signifiers, despite their bifurcation through hierarchies of public/private, reason/passion, masculine/feminine, are nevertheless joined at the level of ontology. The rigidity of these dualisms, however, function to block our perception of the eros/democracy conceptual affinity. The intimate relationship between eros and democracy cannot be adequately explained within the liberal paradigm.

The idea that democracy is fundamentally a state of being expresses a conceptualization that Douglas Lummis urges us to retrieve:

> I have sought to argue that democracy is better described not as a "system" or a set of institutions but as a state of being and that the transition to it is not an institutional founding but a "change of state."[37]

By "change of state," Lummis refers to a transformation in consciousness. How should such a transformation be understood and provoked? In bell hooks's discussion of eros, there is a clear link made between eros and the transformation of identity, inasmuch as the mobilization of educational eros provokes a self-reflective process whereby an emerging self faces new and agonizing choices between competing truth narratives. From this and other descriptions we see that eros and democracy are similarly agonistic, as the quality of *incompletion* defines both: just as the process of self-knowledge is interminable, so too is democracy as an historical project.

Key anomalies of the liberal paradigm can be transcended if eros is acknowledged as the educational principle of democracy. This study shows that the most obvious "anomaly" which diminishes the liberal capacity to fulfill the democratic promise is its vital devaluation of emotion. Megan Boler persuasively describes how the dominant liberal epistemology has created an educational climate in which the emotions, as source of power, are routinely ignored:

Almost anyone who has spent time in a classroom can attest that the felt and expressed emotions, and the emotional dynamics of groups, shape the project of learning and the classroom environment. Yet how often do educators and cultural theorists ask: How do emotions define what counts as knowledge? How do emotions inform our ethical values and actions? How are social hierarchies established through unspoken emotional rules, and injustices perpetuated through unexamined rules of emotional expression? The phenomenon of the ignorance of emotion, and the unpopularity of this subject, is worthy of its own study.[38]

This passage exposes the anomaly of the liberal knowledge system when one realizes that the associational qualities so crucial to democracy grow out of the feeling or affective domains of the whole person (as opposed to the notion that one's *mind* represents the exclusive locus of identity). By dissociating mind from body, liberal epistemology erases any value that an eros principle might have for concepts of reason, politics, and education. Liberal epistemology ignores emotion. As Nancy Rosenblum observes, "Liberalism has vigorously warded off everything affective, personal, and expressive."[39]

As personifications of the liberal paradigm, Rene Descartes' "I think, therefore I am" and Immanuel Kant's principle of "pure" reason symbolize ways of knowing which devalue eros and embodied knowledge generally. As readers will recall, Leonardo Boff offered a non-liberal alternative to Descartes by his privileging of *sentio, ergo sum*. With respect to Kant, Robin May Schott claims that eros as a principle of knowledge is completely absent from his concept of pure reason and objectivity. Her critical interpretation of Kant provides a generalized definition of eros and explains how his classically liberal epistemology represents a suppression of the erotic:

In focussing on the suppression of eros in Kant's thought, I am invoking a specifically un-Kantian term. My use of eros here is purposely broad, encompassing a range of meanings including feelings, desires, sensual pleasures, and explicit sexual activity. Because of the perceived threat to rational control posed by emotion, desire, and sexuality, a fundamental opposition has been established between eros and cognition. The hostility toward sensuality manifest in Kant's view of objectivity [is] correlated with his dismissal of women as sexual beings, who were incapable of rational thought.[40]

To the extent that this epistemological bias is reproduced in the schools as common sense, it instantiates a character formation profoundly at odds with democratic culture. We may speculate that the liberal bias against radical democracy is curiously related to its bias against eros: significantly, both share the distinction of being described as threats to control and order. What is the meaning of this similitude? Could fear of an "ungovernable" feminine principle form the basis of liberal epistemology?[41] Carol Pateman takes note of how this patriarchal fear is typically expressed: "Women have a disorder at their very centers—in their morality—which can bring about the destruction of the state."[42] Without embracing an essentialist view of women or eros, it is plausible to speculate that a revaluation of eros would be tantamount to the revaluation of the feminine, a paradigmatic transition in meaning which would have far-reaching (and positive) consequences for democratic culture. Anthony Giddens argues that the democratization of personal and intimate relations necessarily entails a move toward the feminine principle, in that the "transformation of intimacy" is described in terms of horizontal (co-equal) rather than vertical (superior/inferior) social relations.[43] Such a formulation lends further credence to the idea that eros is associated with democracy, insofar as eros has been associated with feminine qualities as well as represented as non-hierarchical in its effects.

As Thomas Kuhn observed, paradigm shifts occur when conventional assumptions about what is taken to be known lose their capacity to explain rapidly changing circumstances.[44] Eventually the crisis of explanation leads to a decisive break with the value of the old categories and their now unedifying orthodoxies. A new structure of knowing begins to coalesce around alternative knowledge claims located outside the logic of the old paradigm. We are immersed in this crisis of explanation now. A host of educational contradictions are emerging in classrooms across the country which cannot be resolved within the logic of the reigning liberal orthodoxy.

Consider, for example, the immense powers brought to bear on American youth today to love consumption as a way of life, a learned disposition which is accompanied by an inevitable dissolution of *public* identity and *public* meaning. Nowadays, most schools are not engaged in producing critically reflective democratic citizens; they are far more engaged in the *mass production of idiocy*. I use this phrase with precision: the ancient Greek etymology of *idios* refers to a "purely private person," one who could participate in the polis as a citizen, but did not.[45] Citizenship education is thus being supplanted not only by thin conceptions of democracy, but increasingly by sophisticated corporate pedagogies of advertising which make the fetishization of commodities appear normal, desirable, and unproblematically good.[46] Mass advertising thus becomes a site where desire is not so much educated, as schooled, unreflectively. The liberal orthodoxy, however, cannot respond to these developments, since the motif of "educating desire" is located beyond the educational pale for them. In contrast, critical pedagogy can educate desire by drawing attention to its social orchestration and by transforming corporate iconography into a site of political analysis. If we as public intellectuals don't develop a critical theory about *educating the desires*, corporations will continue to exercise this educational power even more comprehensively than they do now.[47]

In response to this paradigmatic crisis, we should recognize eros as a principle indissolubly connected to associational forms of democratic culture and citizenship. I submit that a strategy of organizing a counter-paradigm around a broad heading such as eros is a sound basis for extending and deepening democratic education. Educating for democracy, it turns out, actually implies the education of eros since these concepts share so many affinities. Garrison elaborates on the tricky theme of educating eros:

> Distinguishing objects of mere desire, the apparent good, from the desirable, the genuinely good, is the education of Eros. Such an education teaches eros to strive for the genuinely good, and should be considered essential to the education of

good teachers. We need to talk about the education of Eros, the education for wisdom. It is particularly important that we recognize Eros as a creative poetic force that makes novel meanings and eventually makes us who we are.[48]

The politics and pedagogy of defining "the good" across difference is a tension-filled process which constitutes one of the most valuable elements of democratic political education. To a considerable degree, negotiating this vastly complex pedagogical process *is* the education of eros, since the creation of "novel meanings" always signals a shift in the direction, or intent, of one's desire. This language may sound foreign to our modern sensibilities. Paradoxically, however, the *new* paradigm for citizenship education will come into existence only to the extent that educators reconvene the *ancient* conversation of educating the desires. To encourage such a conversation will be to step outside the boundaries of the liberal/modernist educational paradigm.

Who among us is best equipped to step outside the dominant paradigm of education? According to Kuhn's analysis of the history of scientific revolutions, it is precisely *younger* people and others operating at the margins of disciplinary boundaries who most frequently dare to resist the dominant forms of common sense. Those who are disenchanted with how the prevailing purposes of education are defined, for example, will be most likely to see problems from new vantage points and on this basis create extraordinary new approaches for redefining educational meaning. Although Kuhn refers to "scientists" in the passage below, his description of the symptoms that precede paradigmatic transformation should be of interest to every teacher in America:

Confronted with anomaly or with crisis, scientists take a different attitude toward existing paradigms and the nature of their research changes accordingly. The proliferation of competing articulations, the willingness to try anything, the expression of explicit discontent, the recourse to philosophy and to debate over fundamentals, all these are symptoms of a transition from normal to extraordinary research.[49]

If America is to enact the best version of itself, educationally, politically, and culturally, the rich conceptual affinities that link eros to democracy need to be drawn out and further clarified. While it is clear that additional work is required to better thematize the eros/democracy connection, at least one crucial point stands out as a result of this inquiry: The reconstruction of common sense in American education can proceed most effectively and lucidly on the basis of eros as the educational principle of democracy. "Recourse to philosophy" and "debate over fundamentals," indeed!

Notes

1. Rollo May, "What Is Eros?" in *Love and Will* (New York: Norton, 1971), 72–94. For a cogent argument supporting the idea that an educational concept of love—anchored in eros, philia, or agape—is absolutely vital to the development of citizenship education, see Shin Shiba, "Hannah Arendt on Love and the Political: Love, Friendship, and Citizenship," *Review of Politics* (Summer 1995): 505–35.

2. John Dewey, *Democracy and Education* (New York: Macmillan, 1916): 240.

3. Robert Westbrook, *John Dewey and American Democracy* (Ithaca: Cornell University Press, 1991): xv–xvi, 33–58. Westbrook argues that Dewey's theory of democracy "failed to find a secure place in liberal ideology," his views were "set apart" from the liberal mainstream, and that American liberal theory represents a "rejection of Dewey's democratic faith." For an overview of some of the important responses to Westbrook's thesis, see Richard Brosio, "Democratic Theory and Practice: Dewey and Beyond," in *A Radical Democratic Critique of Capitalist Education* (New York: Peter Lang, 1994): 503–546.

4. Benjamin Barber, *Strong Democracy: Participatory Politics for a New Age* (Berkeley: University of California Press, 1984): 4. For another perspective which supports this thesis, see Anne Phillips, "So What's Wrong With Liberal Democracy?" in *Engendering Democracy* (University Park: The Pennsylvania State University Press, 1991): 147–68.

5. J. Peter Euben, *Corrupting Youth: Political Education, Democratic Culture, and Political Theory* (Princeton: Princeton University Press, 1997); Sheldon Wolin, "Norm and Form: The Constitutionalizing of Democracy," in *Athenian Political Thought and the Reconstruction of American Democracy* (Ithaca: Cornell University Press, 1994): 29–58; C. Douglas Lummis, *Radical Democracy* (Ithaca: Cornell University Press, 1996); Jean Bethke Elshtain, *Democracy on Trial* (New York: Basic Books, 1995); James Garrison, *Dewey and Eros: Wisdom and Desire in the Art of Teaching* (New York: Teachers College Press, 1997); Benjamin Barber, *An Aristocracy of Everyone: The Politics of Education and the Future of America* (New York: Oxford University Press, 1992); Cornel West, *The American Evasion of Philosophy: A Genealogy of*

American Pragmatism (Madison, University of Wisconsin Press, 1989); Cornel West and Roberto Unber, *The Future of American Progressivism* (Boston: Beacon Press, 1998); Anne Phillips, *Engendering Democracy* (University Park: The Pennsylvania State University Press, 1991); and Ellen Meiksins Wood, "Demos Versus 'We, The People': Freedom and Democracy: Ancient and Modern," in *Demokratia: A Conversation on Democracies, Ancient and Modern* (Princeton: Princeton University Press, 1996): 121–38.

6. Ursula Kelly, *Schooling Desire* (New York: Routledge, 1997); bell hooks, "Eros, Eroticism and the Pedagogical Process," in *Teaching to Transgress* (New York: Routledge, 1994): 191–99; Audre Lorde, "Uses of the Erotic: The Erotic as Power," in *Sister/Ousider* (Freedom, Cal.: The Crossing Press, 1984): 53–59; Susan Griffin, *The Eros of Everyday Life: Essays on Ecology, Gender and Society* (New York: Anchor Books, 1995); Regina Barreca and Deborah Deneholz Morse, eds., *The Erotics of Instruction* (Hanover: University Press of New England, 1997).

7. Jim Garrison, "A Deweyan Theory of Democratic Listening," *Educational Theory* 46:4 (Fall 1996): 429–51.

8. S. Sara Monoson, "Frank Speech, Democracy, and Philosophy: Plato's Debt to a Democratic Strategy of Civic Discourse," in *Athenian Political Thought and the Reconstruction of American Democracy* (Ithaca: Cornell University Press, 1994), 172–97. The authors in this volume interpret Socrates as a demophile, further testament to the eros/democracy conceptual affinity.

9. Lorde, 56.

10. Paulo Freire, *Pedagogy of the Oppressed* (New York: Seabury, 1992), 52–67.

11. Paulo Freire, *Teachers as Cultural Workers: Letters to Those Who Dare Teach* (Boulder: Westview, 1998), 3.

12. Theodor Adorno and Max Horkheimer, *The Authoritarian Personality* (New York: Norton, 1950: 976. For a useful overview of the eros/thanatos tension, see Martin Jay, *The Dialectical Imagination: A History of the Frankfurt School and the Institute of Social Research, 1923–1950* (Boston: Little, Brown, 1973), 86–112.

13. See Michael J. Shapiro, *Violent Cartographies: Mapping Cultures of War* (Minneapolis: University of Minnesota Press, 1997); David Campbell, *Writing Security: United States Foreign Policy and the Policies of Identity* (Minneapolis: University of Minnesota Press, 1992); Anders Stephanson, *Manifest Destiny: American Expansion and the Empire of Right* (New York: Hill and Wang, 1995); and Richard

Drinnon, *Facing West: The Metaphysics of Indian-Hating and Empire Building* (Minneapolis: University of Minnesota Press, 1980).

14. Castoriadis, "The Problem of Democracy Today," in *Democracy and Nature* 3: 18–37.

15. Castoriadis, 21–22.

16. Ursula Kelly, *Schooling Desire*, 123–38.

17. For various historical representations (listed in chronological order), see Anne Carson, *Eros the Bittersweet* (Princeton: Princeton University Press, 1986); Plato, *Symposium* 204d; Anders Nygren, *Eros and Agape* (Chicago: University of Chicago Press, 1932); Jean-Jacques Rousseau, *Emile*, Allan Bloom, ed. (New York: Basic Books, 1979), 223; Joel Spring, *Wheels in the Head: Educational Philosophies of Authority, Freedom, and Culture from Socrates to Paulo Freire* (New York: McGraw-Hill, 1994); and Kal Alston, "Teaching, Philosophy, and Eros: Love as a Relation to Truth," *Educational Theory* (Fall 1991): 385–95.

18. J. Peter Euben, John R. Wallach, and Josiah Ober, eds., "Introduction," *Athenian Political Thought and the Reconstruction of American Democracy* (Ithaca: Cornell University Press, 1994), 21.

19. Plato, *Symposium*, 203c.

20. Wolin, 37.

21. Herbert Marcuse, *Eros and Civilization* (Boston: Beacon Press, 1955), 222–28.

22. Plato, *Symposium*, 178d, 202a–12c.

23. Garrison, *Dewey and Eros*, 7.

24. See Thomas Oldenski, "Critical Discourses of Liberation Theology and Critical Pedagogy," in *Liberation Theology and Critical Pedagogy in Today's Catholic Schools* (New York: Garland Publishing, 1997), 61–93.

25. Leonardo Boff, *St. Francis: A Model of Human Liberation* (New York: Orbis Books, 1984), 11–12.

26. Boff, 11–12.

27. Plato, for example, in Book VIII of the *Republic* (561b), criticizes "democratic man" as being ruled by unruly desires. Wolin (1994) writes that democracy is "inherently

formless." These characteristics which *do not conform* account for the charge that eros and democracy can be ungovernable. The point is that both eros and democracy require educating (yet another similarity).

28. Garrison, 129–32.

29. Dewey, *The Public and Its Problems*, 213.

30. Garrison, 14–15.

31. Dewey, *The Public and Its Problems*, 255.

32. West, 69–111.

33. West, 103.

34. West, 232–33.

35. West, 233.

36. John Dewey, "Philosophy and Civilization," in *Philosophy and Civilization* (New York: Minton, Balch, 1931), 12.

37. Lummis, *Radical Democracy*, 159.

38. Megan Boler, "Disciplined Emotions: Philosophies of Educated Feelings, *Educational Theory* 2 (Spring 1997): 203–27.

39. Nancy L. Rosenblum, *Another Liberalism: Romanticism and the Reconstruction of Liberal Thought* (Cambridge: Harvard University Press, 1987), 4.

40. Robin Schott, preface to *Cognition and Eros: A Critique of the Kantian Paradigm* (Boston: Beacon Press, 1988), vii–viii. See also chapter 9, "Kant's Fetishism of Objectivity," 115–36.

41. See Helen Haste, *The Sexual Metaphor* (Cambridge: Harvard University Press, 1993); Carolyn Merchant, *The Death of Nature* (San Francisco: Harper and Row, 1980); and Susan Bordo, "The Cartesian Masculinization of Thought," *Signs* 11 (Spring 1986): 439–56.

42. Carol Pateman, *The Disorder of Women* (Stanford: Stanford University Press, 1989), 18.

43. Anthony Giddens, "Intimacy as Democracy," in *The Transformation of Intimacy* (Stanford: Stanford University Press, 1992), 94–96; 184–203.

44. Thomas Kuhn, *The Structure of Scientific Revolutions* (Chicago: University of Chicago Press, 1962).

45. The etymology of *idios* is taken from Arlene Saxonhouse, "The Philosopher and the Female in the Political Thought of Plato," in *Feminist Interpretations of Plato* (University Park: Pennsylvania State University Press, 1994), 79.

46. For several excellent critiques of corporate iconography, see Kalle Lasn, *Culture Jam: The Uncooling of America* (New York: Morrow, 1999); Henry Giroux, "Consuming Social Change: The United Colors of Benetton," in *Disturbing Pleasures: Learning Popular Culture* (New York: Routledge, 1994); Michael Shapiro, "Images of Planetary Danger: Luciano Benetton's Ecumenical Fantasy," *Alternatives* 19 (1994): 433–54; and Michael Eric Dyson, "Be Like Mike?: Michael Jordan and the Pedagogy of Desire," in *Reflecting Black: African-American Cultural Criticism* (Minneapolis: University of Minnesota Press, 1993), 64–74. For a provocative analysis of how an increasingly commodified world (mis)shapes student identity and educational purpose, see Mark Edmundson, "On the Uses of a Liberal Education: I. As Lite Entertainment for Bored College Students," *Harper's Magazine* (September 1997): 39–59.

47. In a parallel development, Megan Boler warns about the proliferation of "emotional literacy" programs (based largely on Daniel Goleman's *Emotional Intelligence*, 1995) and states that many of these programs are being transformed into blueprints for corporate ladder-climbing. She writes: "Only in rare instances do these curricula address questions of social hierarchies or power relations in relation to emotion. Who gets to decide what counts as good and appropriate emotional behavior for the next generation? For theorists who have hopes of intervening in educational policy, one primary challenge is to distinguish progressive from conservative emotional literacy programs. I believe we are the best people for this job" (227).

48. Jim Garrison, "Deweyan Prophetic Pragmatism, Poetry, and the Education of Eros," *American Journal of Education* 103 (August 1995): 408–09.

49. Kuhn, 90–91. The relevant passage reads as follows: "Almost always the men who achieve these fundamental inventions of a new paradigm have been either very young or new to the field whose paradigm they change."

Bibliography

Adorno, Theodor W. "Education After Auschwitz." In *Critical Models: Interventions and Catchwords* (New York: Columbia University Press, 1998), 191–204.

Adorno, Theodor, and Max Horkheimer. *The Authoritarian Personality*. New York: Norton, 1950.

Alston, Kal. "Teaching, Philosophy, and Eros: Love as a Relation to Truth." *Educational Theory* (Fall 1991): 285–95.

Apple, Michael. *Cultural Politics and Education*. New York: Teachers College Press, 1996.

Arendt, Hannah. "The Crisis in Education." In *Between Past and Future* (New York: Viking Press, 1968), 173–96.

Augustine, St. *The Confessions*. Translated by John K. Ryan. New York: Doubleday, 1960.

———. *City of God*. Translated by Rex Warner. New York: Penguin, 1963.

Ballard, Edward. *Socratic Ignorance: An Essay on Platonic Self-Knowledge*. The Hague: Martinus Nijhoff, 1965.

Barber, Benjamin. *An Aristocracy of Everyone: The Politics of Education and the Future of America*. New York: Oxford University Press, 1992.

———. *Strong Democracy: Participatory Democracy for a New Age*. Berkeley: University of California Press, 1984.

Berman, Martin. *The Politics of Authenticity: Radical Individualism and the Emergence of Modern Society*. New York: Atheneum Books, 1970.

Boff, Leonardo. *St. Francis: A Model for Human Liberation*. New York: Crossroad Publishing, 1984.

Boler, Megan. "Disciplined Emotions: Philosophies of Educated Feelings." *Educational Theory* 2 (1997): 203–227.

———. *Feeling Power: Emotions and Educators*. New York: Routledge, 1999.

Bowles, Samuel, and Herbert Gintis. *Schooling in Capitalist America*. New York: Basic Books, 1976.

Bremmer, Jan. *The Early Greek Concept of the Soul*. Princeton: Princeton University Press, 1983.

Brown, Peter. *Augustine of Hippo*. Berkeley: University of California Press, 1967.

Brown, Wendy. "Supposing Truth Were a Woman: Plato's Subversion of Masculine Discourse." *Political Theory* 16 (November 1988): 594–616.

Campbell, David. *Writing Security: United States Foreign Policy and the Politics of Identity.* Minneapolis: University of Minnesota Press, 1992.

Campbell, Joseph. "The Mythology of Love." In *Myths to Live By* (New York: Bantam, 1973), 152–73.

Carson, Anne. *Eros the Bittersweet.* Princeton: Princeton University Press, 1986.

Castoriadis, Cornelius. "The Problem of Democracy Today." *Democracy and Nature*, no. 8 (1995): 18–35.

———. *Philosophy, Politics, Autonomy: Essays in Political Philosophy.* Oxford: Oxford University Press, 1991.

Chiba, Shin. "Hannah Arendt on Love and the Political: Love, Friendship, and Citizenship." *Review of Politics* (Summer 1994): 505–35.

Cobb, William. *The Symposium and the Phaedrus: Plato's Erotic Dialogues.* Albany: SUNY Press, 1986.

Coles, Romand. *Self/Power/Other: Political Theory and Dialogical Ethics.* Ithaca: Cornell University Press, 1992.

Connolly, William. *The Augustinian Imperative: A Reflection on the Politics of Morality.* London: Sage Press, 1991.

Ehrenreich, Barbara. *Blood Rites: Origins and History of the Passions of War.* New York: Holt, 1997.

Elshtain, Jean Bethke. *Democracy on Trial.* New York: Basic Books, 1995.

Euben, J. Peter. *Corrupting Youth: Political Education, Democratic Culture, and Political Theory*. Princeton: Princeton University Press, 1997.

Euben, J. Peter, John R. Wallach, and Josiah Ober, eds. *Athenian Political Thought and the Reconstruction of American Democracy*. Ithaca: Cornell University Press, 1994.

Farley, Wendy. *Eros for the Other: Retaining Truth in a Pluralistic World.* University Park: Pennsylvania State University Press, 1996.

Felman, Shoshona. "Psychoanalysis and Education: Teaching Terminable and Interminable." In *Jacques Lacan and the Adventure of Insight* (Cambridge: Harvard University Press, 1987), 69–98.

Ferguson, Kathy. *The Man Question: Visions of Subjectivity in Feminist Theory*. Berkeley: University of California Press, 1994.

Finkel, Donald, and William Ray Arney. *Educating For Freedom: The Paradox of Pedagogy*. New Brunswick: Rutgers University Press, 1995.

Fisher, Berenice. "The Heart Has Its Reasons: Feeling, Thinking, and Community-Building in Feminist Education." *Woman's Studies Quarterly* (Fall/Winter 1987): 47–57.

FitzGerald, Frances. *America Revised: History Textbooks in the Twentieth Century*. New York: Random House, 1979.

Freire, Paulo. *Pedagogy of the Oppressed*. New York: Seabury, 1992.

————. *A Pedagogy for Liberation: Dialogues on Transforming Education.* New York: Bergin and Garvey, 1987.

————. *Teachers as Cultural Workers: Letters to Those Who Dare Teach.* Boulder: Westview Press, 1998.

Freud, Sigmund. *Civilization and Its Discontents.* London: Hogarth Press, 1961.

Garrison, James. *Dewey and Eros: Wisdom and Desire in the Art of Teaching.* New York: Teachers College Press, 1997.

————. "A Deweyan Theory of Democratic Listening." *Educational Theory* 46 (1996): 429–51.

Gibson, James William. *Warrior Dreams: Paramilitary Culture in Post-Vietnam America.* New York: Hill and Wang, 1994.

Giddens, Anthony. "Intimacy as Democracy." In *The Transformation of Intimacy* (Palo Alto: Stanford University Press, 1992), 184–203.

Giroux, Henry. *The Mouse That Roared: Disney and the End of Innocence.* Lanham, Md: Rowman and Littlefield, 1999.

————. *Disturbing Pleasures: Learning Popular Culture.* New York: Routledge, 1994.

Greene, Maxine. "In Search of a Critical Pedagogy." *Harvard Educational Review* 4 (November 1986): 427–41.

———. "The Passion of the Possible: Choice, Multiplicity, and Commitment." *Journal of Moral Education* 19, no. 2 (May 1990): 67–76.

———. "What Counts as Philosophy of Education?" In *Critical Conversations in Philosophy of Education*, edited by Wendy Kohli, 3–23. New York: Routledge, 1996.

Griffin, Susan. *The Eros of Everyday Life: Essays on Ecology, Gender, and Society.* New York: Doubleday, 1995.

Hall, Cheryl. "Uses of the Erotic: Contemporary Feminists and Plato on Eros, Power, and Reason." Ph.D. diss., Princeton University, 1993.

Halperin, David M., John J. Winkler, and Froma I. Zeitlin, eds. *Before Sexuality: The Construction of Erotic Experience in the Ancient Greek World.* Princeton: Princeton University Press, 1990.

Hartsock, Nancy. *Money, Sex, and Power: Toward a Feminist Historical Materialism.* New York: Longman Press, 1983.

Hawthorne, Susan. "Diotima Speaks Through the Body." In *Engendering Origins: Critical Feminist Readings in Plato and Aristotle* (Albany: SUNY Press, 1994), 85–89.

Heyward, Carter. *Touching Our Strength: The Erotic as Power and the Love of God.* San Francisco: Harper and Row, 1989.

hooks, bell. *Teaching to Transgress: Education as the Practice of Freedom.* New York: Routledge, 1994.

———. *Resisting Representations.* New York: Routledge, 1995.

Jaeger, Werner. *Paideia: The Ideals of Greek Culture*. Vol. 2. New York: Oxford University Press, 1943.

Jaspers, Karl. *Plato and Augustine*. New York: Harcourt Brace, 1957.

Jay, Martin. *The Dialectical Imagination: A History of the Frankfurt School and the Institute of Social Research, 1923–1950*. Boston: Brown, Little, 1973.

Keen, Sam. *Faces of the Enemy: Reflections of the Hostile Imagination*. San Francisco: HarperCollins, 1986.

———. *The Passionate Life*. San Francisco: Harper and Row, 1983.

Kelly, Ursula. *Schooling Desire*. New York: Routledge, 1997.

Kline, Stephen. "Limits to the Imagination: Marketing and Children's Culture." In *Cultural Politics in Contemporary America* (New York: Routledge, 1989), 299–316.

Kozol, Jonathan. *Savage Inequalities: Children in America's Schools*. New York: HarperCollins, 1991.

———. *On Being a Teacher*. New York: Seabury, 1981.

Kuhn, Thomas. *The Structure of Scientific Revolutions*. Chicago: University of Chicago Press, 1962.

Lasch, Christopher. "The Common Schools: Horace Mann and the Assault on Imagination." In *The Revolt of the Elites and the Betrayal of American Democracy* (New York: Norton, 1995), 141–60.

Lear, Jonathan. *Open Minded: Working Out the Logic of the Soul*. Cambridge: Harvard University Press, 1998.

Leistyna, Pepi, Arlie Woodrum, and Stephen A. Sherblom, eds. *Breaking Free: The Transformative Power of Critical Pedagogy*, no. 27. Cambridge: Harvard Educational Review, 1996.

Levine, Lawrence. *The Opening of the American Mind: Canons, Culture, and History*. Boston: Beacon Press, 1996.

Loewen, James. *Lies My Teacher Told Me*. New York: New Press, 1995.

Lorde, Audre. *Sister/Outsider*. Freedom, Calif.: The Crossing Press, 1984.

Lummis, Douglas. *Radical Democracy*. Ithaca: Cornell University Press, 1997.

Lusted, David. "Why Pedagogy?" *Screen* (1986): 2–16.

Lutz, Mark. *Socrates' Education to Virtue*. Albany: SUNY Press, 1998.

Marcuse, Herbert. *Eros and Civilization*. Boston: Beacon Press, 1955.

———. *One Dimensional Man*. Boston: Beacon Press, 1964.

Martin, Jane. "Sophie and Emile: A Case Study in Sex Bias in the History of Educational Thought." *Harvard Educational Review* (August 1991): 357–72.

May, Rollo. *Love and Will*. New York: Norton, 1969.

Monoson, Sara. "Frank Speech, Democracy, and Philosophy: Plato's Debt to a Democratic Strategy of Civic Discourse." In *Athenian Political Thought and the Reconstruction of American Democracy* (Ithaca: Cornell University Press, 1994), 172–97.

Needleman, Jacob. *The Heart of Philosophy*. New York: Knopf, 1982.

Neill, A. S. *Summerhill School: A New View of Childhood*. New York: St. Martin's Press, 1992.

Nussbaum, Martha. "The Speech of Alcibiades: A Reading of Plato's Symposium." *Philosophy and Literature* (Spring 1986): 131–72.

———. *Cultivating Humanity*. Cambridge: Harvard University Press, 1997.

Nygren, Anders. *Eros and Agape*. Chicago: University of Chicago Press, 1932.

Oldenski, Thomas. "Critical Discourses of Liberation Theology and Critical Pedagogy." In *Liberation Theology and Critical Pedagogy in Today's Catholic Schools* (New York: Garland Publishing, 1997), 61–93.

Osborne, Catherine. *Eros Unveiled: Plato and the God of Love*. Oxford: Clarendon, 1996.

Pagels, Elaine. *Adam, Eve, and the Serpent*. New York: Vintage, 1988.

———. *The Gnostic Gospels*. New York: Vintage, 1979.

Palmer, Parker. *To Know as We Are Known*. San Francisco: Harper College, 1983.

Parker, Walter, ed. *Educating The Democratic Mind*. Albany: SUNY Press, 1996.

Pateman, Carole. *The Disorder of Women*. Stanford: Stanford University Press, 1989.

Patterson, Thomas C. *Inventing Western Civilization*. New York: Monthly Review Press, 1997.

Plato. *Phaedrus*. Vol. 3, *The Dialogues of Plato*. 4th ed. Translated by Benjamin Jowett. Oxford: Clarendon Press, 1954.

———. *Symposium*. Vol. 1, *The Dialogues of Plato*. 4th ed. Translated by Benjamin Jowett. Oxford: Clarendon Press, 1953.

———. *Republic*. Translated by A. D. Lindsay. New York: E. P. Dutton, 1957.

———. *Meno*. Translated by W. K. C. Guthrie. New York: Penguin Books, 1974.

———. *Theatetus*. Translated by Benjamin Jowett. Chicago: Regnery Company, 1951.

Rabinow, Paul, ed. *The Foucault Reader*. New York: Pantheon, 1984.

Rappaport, Elizabeth. "On the Future of Love: Rousseau and the Radical Feminists." In *Woman and Philosophy*, ed. Carol Gould and Max Wartofsky. New York: Putnam, 1976.

Rorty, Richard. *Achieving Our Country: Leftist Thought in Twentieth-Century America.* Cambridge: Harvard University Press, 1998.

Rousseau, Jean-Jacques. *Emile.* Translated by Allan Bloom. New York: Basic Books, 1979.

———. *The Confessions.* London: Penguin, 1954.

———. *The Social Contract.* Translated by M. Cranston. London: Penguin, 1968.

Rud, Anthony, and James Garrison, eds. *The Educational Conversation: Closing the Gap.* Albany: SUNY Press, 1995.

Santas, Gerasimos. *Plato and Freud: Two Theories of Love.* Oxford: Basil Blackwell, 1988.

Schor, Juliet. *The Overspent American.* New York: Basic Books, 1998.

Schott, Robin. *Cognition and Eros: A Critique of the Kantian Paradigm.* Boston: Beacon Press, 1988.

Scolnicov, Samuel. *Plato's Metaphysics of Education.* London: Routledge, 1988.

Spring, Joel. *Wheels in the Head.* New York: McGraw-Hill, 1994.

Taylor, Charles. *Sources of the Self: The Making of Modern Identity.* Cambridge: Harvard University Press, 1989.

Theweleit, Klaus. *Male Fantasies, 1. Women, Floods, Bodies, History.* Minneapolis: University of Minnesota Press, 1987.

Torres, Carlos Alberto. "Education and the Archeology of Consciousness: Freire and Hegel." *Educational Theory* (Fall 1994): 429–45.

Trask, Haunani-Kay. *Eros and Power: The Promise of Feminist Theory.* Philadelphia: University of Pennslyvania Press, 1988.

Tuana, Nancy, ed. *Feminist Interpretations of Plato.* University Park: Pennsylvania State University Press, 1994.

Vlastos, Gregory. "The Individual as Object of Love in Plato." In *Platonic Studies* (Princeton: Princeton University Press, 1973), 31.

———. *Socrates, Ironist and Moral Philosopher.* Ithaca: Cornell University Press, 1991.

Voegelin, Eric. *Plato.* Baton Rouge: Louisiana State University Press, 1966.

Weiler, Kathleen. "Freire and a Feminist Pedagogy of Difference." *Harvard Educational Review* 4 (November 1991): 449–74.

———. "Myths of Paulo Freire," *Educational Theory* (Summer 1996): 353–71.

Weiss, Penny. *Gendered Community: Rousseau, Sex, and Politics.* New York: New York University Press, 1993.

West, Cornel. *Race Matters.* New York: Vintage Books, 1994.

———. "Prophetic Pragmatism: Cultural Criticism and Political Engagement." In *The American Evasion of Philosophy* (Madison: University of Wisconsin Press, 1989), 211–39.

Index

Studies in the Postmodern Theory of Education

General Editors
Joe L. Kincheloe & Shirley R. Steinberg

Counterpoints publishes the most compelling and imaginative books being written in education today. Grounded on the theoretical advances in criticalism, feminism, and postmodernism in the last two decades of the twentieth century, Counterpoints engages the meaning of these innovations in various forms of educational expression. Committed to the proposition that theoretical literature should be accessible to a variety of audiences, the series insists that its authors avoid esoteric and jargonistic languages that transform educational scholarship into an elite discourse for the initiated. Scholarly work matters only to the degree it affects consciousness and practice at multiple sites. Counterpoints' editorial policy is based on these principles and the ability of scholars to break new ground, to open new conversations, to go where educators have never gone before.

For additional information about this series or for the submission of manuscripts, please contact:

Joe L. Kincheloe & Shirley R. Steinberg
637 West Foster Avenue
State College, PA 16801

To order other books in this series, please contact our Customer Service Department:

(800) 770-LANG (within the U.S.)
(212) 647-7706 (outside the U.S.)
(212) 647-7707 FAX

Or browse online by series:
www.peterlang.com